## Africa Now

Africa Now is published by Zed Books in association w~~~~ D1765018 respected Nordic Africa Institute. Featuring high-quality, cutting-edge research from leading academics, the series addresses the big issues confronting Africa today. Accessible but in-depth, and wide-ranging in its scope, Africa Now engages with the critical political, economic, sociological and development debates affecting the continent, shedding new light on pressing concerns.

## Nordic Africa Institute

The Nordic Africa Institute (Nordiska Afrikainstitutet) is a centre for research, documentation and information on modern Africa. Based in Uppsala, Sweden, the Institute is dedicated to providing timely, critical and alternative research and analysis of Africa and to co-operation with African researchers. As a hub and a meeting place for a growing field of research and analysis, the Institute strives to put knowledge of African issues within reach of scholars, policy makers, politicians, media, students and the general public. The Institute is financed jointly by the Nordic countries (Denmark, Finland, Iceland, Norway and Sweden).

www.nai.uu.se

## Forthcoming titles

Thiven Reddy, *South Africa: Settler Colonialism and the Failures of Liberal Democracy*
Anders Themner (ed.), *Warlord Democrats in Africa*
Tobias Hagmann and Filip Reyntjens, *Aid and Authoritarianism in Africa*

## Titles already published

Fantu Cheru and Cyril Obi (eds), *The Rise of China and India in Africa*
Ilda Lindell (ed.), *Africa's Informal Workers*
Iman Hashim and Dorte Thorsen, *Child Migration in Africa*
Prosper B. Matondi, Kjell Havnevik and Atakilte Beyene (eds), *Biofuels, Land Grabbing and Food Security in Africa*
Cyril Obi and Siri Aas Rustad (eds), *Oil and Insurgency in the Niger Delta*
Mats Utas (ed.), *African Conflicts and Informal Power*
Prosper B. Matondi, *Zimbabwe's Fast Track Land Reform*
Maria Eriksson Baaz and Maria Stern, *Sexual Violence as a Weapon of War?*
Fantu Cheru and Renu Modi (eds), *Agricultural Development and Food Security in Africa*
Amanda Hammar (ed.), *Displacement Economies in Africa*
Mary Njeri Kinyanjui, *Women and the Informal Economy in Urban Africa*
Liisa Laakso and Petri Hautaniemi (eds), *Diasporas, Development and Peacemaking in the Horn of Africa*
Margaret C. Lee, *Africa's World Trade*
Godwin Murunga, Duncan Okello and Anders Sjögren (eds), *Kenya: The Struggle for a New Constitutional Order*

## About the editors

*Lisa Åkesson* is Associate Professor in Social Anthropology at the School of Global Studies, the University of Gothenburg, and Senior Researcher at the Nordic Africa Institute.

*Maria Eriksson Baaz* is Associate Professor at the School of Global Studies, the University of Gothenburg, and Senior Researcher at the Nordic Africa Institute. She is the co-author (with Maria Stern) of *Sexual Violence as a Weapon of War?* (Zed Books, 2013) and the author of *The Paternalism of Partnership* (Zed Books, 2005).

# Africa's return migrants

The new developers?

edited by Lisa Åkesson and
Maria Eriksson Baaz

Nordiska Afrikainstitutet
The Nordic Africa Institute

Zed Books
LONDON

*Africa's Return Migrants: The New Developers?* was first published in 2015 in association with the Nordic Africa Institute, PO Box 1703, SE-751 47 Uppsala, Sweden by Zed Books Ltd, The Foundry, 17 Oval Way, London SE11 5RR, UK.

www.zedbooks.co.uk
www.nai.uu.se

Set in OurType Arnhem, Monotype Gill Sans Heavy by Ewan Smith
Index: ed.emery@thefreeuniversity.net
Cover designed by www.roguefour.co.uk

A catalogue record for this book is available from the British Library

ISBN 978-1-78360-234-6 hb
ISBN 978-1-78360-233-9 pb
ISBN 978-1-78360-235-3 pdf
ISBN 978-1-78360-236-0 epub
ISBN 978-1-78360-237-7 mobi

MIX
Paper from
responsible sources
FSC
www.fsc.org     FSC® C013604

Printed and bound in Great Britain by
CPI Group (UK) Ltd, Croydon, CR0 4YY

# Contents

# 1 | Introduction

Lisa Åkesson and Maria Eriksson Baaz

Many African migrants who reside in Europe nurture a hope to one day return, either permanently or on a more temporary basis. Increasingly restrictive
migration policies make many migrants hesitant to 'return', as that might imply
closing the door to Europe (de Haas 2006; Schoumaker et al. 2013). Yet, in the
wake of developments in Africa and in Europe, it is possible that the impetus
to return might increase in the coming years. The economic crisis in parts
of Europe has made the lives of migrants particularly difficult, as manifested
in their further marginalisation in labour markets but also in the upsurge of
xenophobic, anti-migrant discourses and practices. At the same time, many
African economies are growing at a fast rate[1] and have an increased demand
for skilled labour.

Contemporary policy discourse has come to attach great expectations to
African returnees, portraying them as 'agents of development'. Return migration
– particularly to sub-Saharan Africa – occupies a central position in current
policy debates on migration and development. In recent years, governments in
the global North, international agencies and non-governmental organisations
(NGOs) have come to expect returnees to play an important role in the development of their 'home countries' (see, for example, European Commission 2011;
Global Forum on Migration and Development 2012). As Sinatti and Horst (2015:
144) note, return is emerging as a key issue in the most recent policy documents
on development in the European Union (EU) as well as in various member
countries – representing 'a new chapter within the migration–development
debate'. Also, some African migrant sending countries, such as Senegal, Cape
Verde and Ghana, are promoting return migration, at least of highly skilled
migrants. Hence, in the contemporary policy discourse, returnees are often
portrayed as agents of development who will bring back economic capital,
knowledge and skills as well as social connections, values and attitudes gained
in 'a developed North'.

Yet little attention so far has been directed to the experiences of return
migrants themselves or to the structural factors shaping returnees' possibility
of assuming the role of 'the new developers'. While there is an extensive literature on how African migrants contribute to 'development at home' through

---

1 See the Africa section on the World Bank website: www.worldbank.org/en/country.

remittances (for example, Bardouille et al. 2008; Mohapatra and Ratha 2011; Pérouse de Montclos 2005), the experiences of African return migrants have received only scanty attention (for an exception, see Grabska 2014). This silence is even more problematic given the often great – and individualised – expectations put on these migrants in policy debates.

Based on original qualitative ethnographic and interview material with return migrants in Ghana, the Democratic Republic of Congo (DRC), Senegal, Somaliland, Burundi, South Sudan and Cape Verde, this book fills a gap in current knowledge on African return migration. It aims to further our understanding of the constraints and opportunities attached to migrants' efforts to return and to reintegrate within 'their society of origin'. What kind of capital (social, economic and cultural) have migrants acquired abroad and how useful is that capital for their capabilities when settling in their place of return? How can returnees' stories shed light on their ability (and willingness) to occupy this role as 'new developers'? In short, this book aims to provide an in-depth understanding of the structural factors that shape this willingness and ability, highlighting the interplay between return migrants' experiences and the political, social and economic circumstances in the societies to which they return.

The book problematises the common tendency in Northern policy to locate the 'useful' social, economic and cultural capital firmly in the migration experience. According to this dominant perspective, it is the various forms of capital that migrants obtain in Europe that are valuable and will somehow automatically provide the skills required for a 'successful return' – not only for the migrants themselves but for society at large. By contrast, this book highlights the fact that 'successful return' is a manifestation of a multi-directional transfer of different forms of capital, also acquired 'at home' before migration and upon return. Moreover, the contributions show that the capital obtained in Europe is not always advantageous and can sometimes even hamper successful entrepreneurship and other forms of economic, political and social engagement. While the structural context in the destination country (the prospects provided in terms of education, skilled job opportunities and savings) plays a crucial role, so too do the migrants' own capacity to transform this capital, and acquire new capital, upon their return.

Hence, the book highlights mismatches between policy assumptions and migrants' actual practices, opportunities and willingness to act as 'new developers'. This mismatch is reflected in, on the one hand, the tendency to conceptualise the migration experience as something that is inherently useful, and, on the other hand, the propensity to ignore the challenges posed by the circumstances encountered upon return. As the contributions reveal, there are numerous challenges attached to transforming the migration experience into something useful, both for the migrants themselves and for the society of origin. Successful return migration is not primarily dependent on the various forms of social, cultural and economic capital obtained abroad, but on the various obstacles posed by the structures encountered upon return and the returnees' ability to transform the 'migration capital' they have attained.

A qualification is needed. While the book casts doubt on the celebratory story of return migration and development, its intention is not to refute the development contributions of returnees. Clearly, many individual returnees play a significant part in economic and political development. Rather than discarding such contributions, the book highlights the importance of critically evaluating the expectations placed on returnees in migration and development policies, and demonstrates the various challenges migrants face upon their return.

In the following parts of this introductory chapter, we first elaborate further on current tendencies in policies relating to returnees' contributions to development, highlighting driving forces and limitations. We then present the conceptual and analytical framework guiding the contributions to the book, further elucidating the concepts of 'development contribution', 'return' and 'returnees', as well as the theoretical framework that views return as being contingent on economic, social and cultural capital.

## The celebratory story of returnees' contribution to development

Migrants' skills and knowledge transfers also constitute assets for development. These could translate into remittances, technology transfers, links to professional networks, investment and – arguably – a better integration of origin countries into the global markets.

This statement by the European Commission (2011: 7) sums up some key assumptions in current policies on migration, return and development. A major supposition is that migration to Northern countries is an enriching experience that leads to the accumulation of different forms of capital that are valuable to the developing countries in the South. The main idea is that the capital obtained is used for investment and business activities, which in turn promote jobs and economic growth. As Black and Castaldo (2009) argue, returnees' development of small-scale businesses is often construed as being part of the solution to reducing poverty in Africa. In line with this, European donors are funding new programmes to help returnee entrepreneurs set up businesses in their country of origin (Sinatti and Horst 2015: 145). In addition to business activities, returnees are exhorted to also take up political office, work for different types of international organisation and engage in reconstruction processes after armed conflict (Hammond et al. 2011; Kleist and Vammen 2012).

This celebratory story of return has been manifested in a number of new programmes. As Kleist and Vammen (2012) point out, return programmes – both forced and more voluntary versions – date back to the 1970s. Rejected asylum seekers and irregular migrants have mostly been sent back against their will and have been prohibited from returning to the country of immigration. Other return programmes have targeted regular migrants but have imposed conditions on their return, such as the loss of legal status in the European country of residence. Overall, these approaches have failed, since migrants have been unwilling to participate (de Haas 2006; Kleist and Vammen 2012). However, while return programmes are not a novel phenomenon, there has been an increase in new examples in recent years, and these have taken slightly new forms. Influenced by the policy discourse on circular migration, and acknowledging migrants' transnational involvement and mobility, contemporary programmes focus more on temporary return for short- or long-term qualified work assignments and, unlike before, they often include the right to maintain legal status in the country of immigration. These programmes seem to have had some success in engaging highly skilled migrants in home country development (Kleist and Vammen 2012: 59). However, in general, the impact of such programmes is rather disappointing. Research demonstrates that the majority of returns are spontaneous, and that returnees often have little knowledge of state-led initiatives (Boccagni 2011; Kleist and Vammen 2012). This is also reflected in the research presented in this book, where an overwhelming majority of the returnees have returned on their own, without any assistance from, and often little knowledge of, existing return programmes.

*Understanding the increased policy attention to return migration*  In European migrant receiving countries, the promotion of returnees as 'the new developers' can partly be understood as a reflection of more general discourses on the limitations and failures of state-centred development programmes (Turner and Kleist 2013). Conceptualisations of returnees as the new developers gain purchase through representations of the African state as weak and failed, characterised by corruption, and with inefficient bureaucracies and 'bad governance' more generally (Abrahamsen 2000; Hansson 2013; Harrison 2004). Along with their other efforts to go beyond the state by supporting business initiatives and various forms of NGO activity, development organisations have increasingly come to see returnees as part of the solution. Hence, the increased attention to return migration in development policy fits well with the contemporary neoliberal understanding (Åkesson 2011; Turner and Kleist 2013) in which the responsibility for development is moved from politics and the state to individuals. While the focus of much development intervention is still on state building to ensure good governance, the neoliberal approach entails partly new techniques of government, by a multitude of different actors, and through the production of self-governing responsible subjects (Abrahamsen and Williams 2011; Duffield 2010; Hansson 2013). Transferred to the field of migration, neoliberal policies present migrants as being responsible for positive social and economic changes in their countries of origin. Migrants are encouraged not only to send remittances, but also to return with money, new ideas and entrepreneurial skills as well as access to influential transnational social networks.

Moreover, returnees – who supposedly are both rooted in African contexts and in tune with European development thinking – are cast in the role of brokers who can mediate between donors' ideas about development on the one hand and institutions, cultural norms and practices in recipient countries on the other. As Turner and Kleist (2013) argue, the category of the broker is by no means a novelty in European–African relations. Colonial administrations, missionary societies and development organisations have all used brokers as go-betweens and role models. The returnee as represented in migration and development policy has an affinity with the *assimilado* in the Portuguese African empire and the *évolué* in the French colonies. The returnee – like the *assimilado* and the *évolué* – is often portrayed as somebody who has accepted European values while simultaneously maintaining a rootedness in the African context. The brokers' exposure to European values has been represented as a guarantee that they will transmit 'civilisation' during colonial times and 'development' in the postcolonial era.

In addition to being assigned a dubious task, this broker position entails vulnerability, reflecting its liminal location between the European and the African sphere (ibid.). Returnees often experience exclusion in multiple places. In Europe they are often defined as 'African' and 'immigrant' outsiders, while people in their country of origin may criticise them for having lost their culture and their understanding of local realities. Also, people who return after having escaped conflicts or deep economic insecurity are often condemned by those who have stayed behind – named as disloyal opportunists who escaped the hardships only to take advantage of the new opportunities when they arise (Grabska 2014; Stefansson 2004).

However, while reflecting trends in development discourse and practice, the celebratory story of return migration also takes place against the background of the 'fight against illegal immigration' and the elaboration of restrictive and security-oriented control instruments. As Sinatti and Horst (2015: 145) remark, there is a significant overlap between the latest surge of interest in return and efforts to remove unwanted immigrants from destination countries. The wish to control the entrance and exit of migrants to the European territory, and to keep out unwanted migrants, implies that 'return is coupled with the terms "removal" and "readmission", and is a means for the turning back of undesired immigrants such as irregular stayers, rejected asylum seekers and people living in marginal conditions' (Sinatti 2014: 279). Thus, in the discourse of European policy makers, the issue of return also reflects the management and control of migration (Cassarino 2004).

This restrictive understanding is also reflected in the policy debates on

**5**

circular migration that emerged around 2005. In 2008, the Global Forum on Migration and Development praised circular migration as a win–win solution, combining the interests 'of highly industrialized countries in meeting labour needs ... with [those] of developing countries in accessing richer labour markets, fostering skills transfer and mitigating risks of brain drain' (2008: 75). This was followed by similar statements and policy documents from a range of institutions, such as the EU and various member states (see, for example, European Commission 2011). In these texts, migration is portrayed as a 'triple win' solution: in receiving countries, circular migrants are expected to meet temporary labour shortages while countries of origin will gain access not only to remittances but to the skills and experiences of the migrants, while the migrants themselves benefit too. Yet, as argued by Hansen and Jonsson (2011), this policy is shaped by demographic projections and efforts by the EU to channel migration to its own benefit – in a similar way to previous European labour migration policies.

However, the celebratory story, which describes migration as part of the solution to 'development problems', is articulated and reproduced not only by European governments. Attracting highly skilled migrants to return is also the explicit objective of some migrant-sending African states. This tendency is especially strong in countries with a long history of migration and a substantial diaspora. Governments in these states in particular are reaching out to migrants they assume can contribute with major investments and sought-after knowledge. From the perspective of the sending country, these are the 'policy ideal returnees'. Senegal, for instance, encourages 'the return of a small portion of migrants with sought-after skills' (Sinatti 2014: 281), Ghana courts 'especially highly skilled migrants to return' (Kleist, in Chapter 4), and Cape Verde 'promotes and attracts returnees with qualifications that are essential for the development of the country' (Ministério das Comunidades 2014: 89, our translation). When it comes to the majority of migrants – that is, those who do not belong to the category of highly qualified professionals – countries of origin are generally less interested in their return. A massive return of large numbers of migrants is not a desirable option as it would bring about a decrease in the inflow of remittances, and at the same time increased competition for employment in already strained labour markets.

*Problematic assumptions in the celebratory story of return and development* There are a number of problematic assumptions in this celebratory story of the development potential of return migration. Firstly, there is a lack of attention to structural constraints in the country of return and the subsequent challenges in transforming the migration experience into something 'useful' – the silence on this issue resonates with neoliberal notions of development more generally. The transfer of skills and capital is portrayed as an easy task; returnee entrepreneurs bring needed capital that is simply absorbed by the country of origin. However, and as concluded by de Haas (2010), the development potential of migration is fundamentally contingent on more general conditions in the country of origin or return. The extent to which migration can contribute to local, regional and national development depends on the more general context, in terms of public infrastructure, social facilities, legislation and market access, among other things. Reforming these elements requires structural reforms and state intervention and cannot be achieved by individual migrants. As de Haas points out, policy discourses celebrating migrants as providers of 'self-help development "from below" shift the attention away from structural constraints and the real but limited ability of individuals to overcome these' (ibid.: 258). The crucial importance of the various challenges posed by the political, cultural and social structures encountered upon return is highlighted throughout this book. As the contributions demonstrate, there are numerous problems attached to transforming the migration experience into something 'useful', both for the migrants themselves and for the society of origin.

A second omission in the celebratory story relates to the tendency to conceptualise the migration experience as something that is inherently useful. The assumption seems to be that migrants returning from Europe inevitably have acquired useful skills, experiences and social connections. One obvious aberration is the fact that this narrative neglects the workings of racism and discrimination in the host societies. Whereas the public debate on the integration of non-European migrants points to a number of serious failings, such as housing segregation, marginalisation and exploitative working conditions, the return and development discourse represents the migrants' sojourn in Europe as highly rewarding. While the educational levels and qualifications of African migrants are usually higher than those of non-migrants, they are often over-represented in low-skill occupations (de Haas 2006; Schoumaker et al. 2013). This means that African migrants in Europe are often subjected to high levels of discrimination in the labour market and are overworked and underpaid in monotonous, unskilled jobs that provide limited access to influential social networks or 'new knowledge'. Moreover, many migrants are often primarily concerned with the economic and social reproduction of family members living in different places (Åkesson et al. 2012). This situation is not conducive for gaining new skills and knowledge, and it stands in stark contrast to the 'spin' created by policy makers in the field of migration and development who celebrate migrants as the innovative new heroes of development (Glick Schiller 2012).

A further, related, shortcoming in this storyline of migration to Europe being inherently useful is located in the familiar echo of Eurocentric colonial imageries. Just as in the colonial library that has continued to shape mainstream development discourse (Eriksson Baaz 2005; Escobar 1995; McEwan 2009;

**7**

Nederveen 2001), Africa is portrayed in terms of 'lack' and 'void' – as a site where people who have lived in Europe can simply come and transfer skills and technology. One problem with this imagery – and one that is connected to the argument above about the need to recognise structural constraints in the countries of origin – is the idea that social and cultural capital acquired in Europe is universally applicable. Yet, as several contributions in this book demonstrate, the capital obtained abroad is not always helpful for returnees, but can even be debilitating. While the structural context in the country of immigration (for example, the opportunities provided in terms of education, skilled job opportunities and savings) plays a crucial role, so do the migrants' capacity and ability to transform this capital, and acquire new capital, upon their return. In Nauja Kleist's chapter on Ghanaian elite returnees, she shows that even the most privileged return migrants meet serious challenges when trying to transform and use capital acquired abroad. Moreover, and as argued by Maria Eriksson Baaz (forthcoming), the view that migration to Europe is inherently useful can be seen to feed 'return failures'. Migrants often embrace the dominant discourse – imagining the country of origin or return as an underdeveloped space and themselves as 'more developed and advanced'. Consequently, successful entrepreneurship is often (initially) assumed to require little in the way of preparation – in turn making returnees less inclined to engage in in-depth preparation and market analysis. According to Cassarino (2004), this is fatal, as returnees' preparation for their return is absolutely fundamental to their ability to become actors of change and development.

An additional problem with the tendency to conceptualise migration to Europe as inherently useful is that it implies a claim to proprietorship, with Europe portrayed as the 'owner of development' and the provider of 'development-useful capital'. In many European policy texts, the benefits of migration are located in migration to, and return from, Europe, thereby neglecting useful capital acquired through South–South migration. Migration experiences from other African countries – which, in this familiar cataloguing of societies into developed and underdeveloped, traditional and modern, tend to be situated in the same category of tradition, lack and void – are rarely assumed to be accompanied by capital associated with modernity and development. Such categorisations of societies as modern versus traditional obscure the ways in which modernity is (unevenly) global beyond North–South distinctions and how modernity is experienced differently over space and time (Appadurai 1998; Tomlison 1999). An example of this is provided in the contribution of Katarzyna Grabska to this book, which demonstrates how adolescent girls returning to South Sudan from other African countries are seen as agents of change – bringing 'development' that is both attractive and threatening.

A third problem with the celebratory story of return and development is the assumption that all returnees nurture a desire to contribute to their country of origin. This idea seems to be particularly salient in European policy texts, compared with policies in the sending countries. Whereas sending countries underline the necessity to court and promote themselves to their expatriates in order to gain their loyalty, European policy makers in the field of migration and development tend to simply assume that all migrants harbour an inherent desire to assist their 'homeland'. This assumption rests ultimately on methodological nationalism (cf. Wimmer and Glick Schiller 2002) and the idea that an individual is rooted in a specific country and has special responsibilities towards this homeland. Turner and Kleist (2013: 202) argue that the idea that migrants have a particular desire to support development 'at home' has been propelled by the dominance of the transnational perspective in migration studies, as this perspective has the tendency only to see – and emphasise – migrants' continuous re-creation of ties to their country of origin. However, such assumptions also clearly and simply reflect familiar and more long-standing essentialist discourses, defining cultural and national identity in terms of 'one, shared culture, a sort of collective "one true self", hiding inside the many other, more superficial or artificially imposed "selves", which people with a shared history and ancestry hold in common' (Hall 1990: 223).

In this storyline, 'return' is the 'natural ending' of migrant trajectories and a wish to 'assist the homeland' is construed as a natural desire – and indeed a duty in relation to 'the people of shared history and ancestry'. As is reflected in the contributions to this book, some migrants certainly do feel an urge to support development in their 'homeland', but it is the implied inevitability and duty within this notion that is problematic (Sinatti and Horst 2015: 25). It renders other motivations – which often play a crucial role in decisions to return – improper and disloyal. Research shows that the main reason behind both out-migration and return is that people want to improve their own and their families' lives in different ways (cf. Castles and Miller 1993; Nyberg Sørensen and Fog Olwig 2002). While some returnees (see Chapter 3 by Laura Hammond) articulate a wish to contribute to development, mobility – including return – is often not primarily about people's desires to support national development. Rather, such aspirations sometimes arise as a secondary effect of leaving one's country behind.

After this overview of the increased policy attention paid to return migration and its shortcomings, let us focus on the conceptual and analytical framework of this book – elucidating how we conceptualise 'development contribution', 'return' and 'returnees', and how return is shaped by access to economic, social and cultural capital.

### Conceptual and analytical framework

*Return, returnees and stayers* As indicated above, dominant conceptualisations of 'return' and 'returnees' tend to reinforce sedentary and essentialised understandings of migration, identity and belonging. Moreover, they also reflect a mismatch between policy makers' objectives and the realities of ongoing transnational movements of people. As this book demonstrates, transnational returns or circular migration (Skeldon 2012) are often the preferred strategy for many migrants in European countries, especially for those who return to insecure and unstable conditions. Transnational returns extend over a long period of time and involve much movement back and forth between the country of origin and the country of immigration; a prerequisite for this kind of return is often citizenship in the country of immigration (Eastmond 2006; Hansen 2007).

The somewhat problematic concepts of 'return' and 'returnee' used in this book should be read with this in mind. In contrast to dominant conceptualisations, we do not understand 'return' as being the 'natural ending' but rather as a partial return to a place where the migrants once lived. Hence, and as we will see, most of the returnees in the cases analysed should be seen as transnational returnees or circular migrants. Nor do we view returnees as being people with an inherent identification with and duty to assist an assumed 'homeland'. Rather, this book describes the experiences of people engaged in a partial return to a place where they once lived. While many display a strong identification with this place and call it their homeland, they also often articulate strong feelings of estrangement towards this homeland, describing themselves as 'outsiders', as 'different' and 'not really fitting in'. Moreover, they also often identify themselves with the country they partially left, describing themselves as also – and sometimes even mainly – Europeans.

As many of the chapters in this book show, relationships with 'stayers' are of key importance for returnees' reintegration. Yet, like the notion of returnees, the concept of stayers is inherently problematic. In mainstream research, stayers are understood to have been resident in a place migrants left behind. Yet many 'stayers' have moved, either internally – for instance between rural and urban areas – or across borders without having assumed an identity as migrants. This is frequent in Africa, where cross-border movements continue to be a part of many people's livelihoods (Bjarnesen 2013). Accordingly, people described as 'stayers' by returnees (or researchers) may have a history of movement between places.

*Development?* The meanings attached to development in this book also differ from those in the dominant celebratory stories of development and return. As highlighted above, the general notions of development in such discourses often reflect familiar Eurocentric assumptions about where 'development' and 'development-useful capital' are located. This book takes a critical stance towards such representations, and the contributions question the assumption that capital obtained in Europe is inherently useful. In order to further problematise such conjectures, the book also includes a chapter on adolescent girls returning from Kenya to South Sudan. This chapter clearly demonstrates that the resistance and struggles around meanings of 'tradition' and 'modernity', and about what constitutes desirable development, that are typically associated with North–South migration dynamics are not unique to this particular form of migration and return.

This book also goes beyond the more narrow and economistic notions of development in policy texts on migration and discusses development contributions in terms of their contribution to social change more generally. Many studies on the migration–development nexus are quantitative and take the form of measuring remittances, diaspora contributions to community development organisations and investments in the country of origin (cf. Maimbo and Ratha 2005; World Bank 2011). Moreover, some studies on return migration are preoccupied with determinants of return (and a new departure after return); levels of education and skills before, during and after migration; and levels of (re)integration in the host country and country of origin or return, measured mainly through employment rates or levels of self-employment (cf. Kilic et al. 2009; Lianos and Pseiridis 2009; Schoumaker et al. 2013). Such data is undoubtedly crucial in providing a better understanding of general patterns of migration and return. In addition, it provides some general clues about the benefits and limitations of migration and possible development contributions by returnees, for instance by measuring the levels of education of returnees and their levels of employment upon return.

However, such studies tend to offer limited insights into crucial circumstances in the countries of origin or return and the various challenges shaping returnees' opportunities. They often fail to provide a better understanding of the crucial 'why' questions. For example, why do returnees tend to choose one business over another? Why do so many seem to fail in their attempts? As emphasised above, studies on migration and development tend to lack any in-depth understanding of the structural conditions in the countries of origin or return and how these shape migrants' ability to assume their role as 'the new developers'. In contrast, it is the interplay between the capital acquired by migrants and the political, social and economic circumstances in the societies to which they return that is the focus of this book.

While the contributions in this book go beyond narrow definitions of 'development contributions' as signifying levels of economic investment, contributions to development organisations and education before migration and upon return, some chapters address the more classical issues of entrepreneurship and investments. However, rather than merely measuring levels of monetary flows, they examine the qualitative aspects of these engagements. In the chapter on Congolese returnees (Chapter 2), Maria Eriksson Baaz explores how returnee businesses differ from stayee businesses, demonstrating both similarities and differences. In her discussion of Cape Verde (Chapter 8), Lisa Åkesson explores the contribution that Cape Verdean returnees make to everyday economic life by probing into the types of business in which they are engaged and how such choices can be understood given the challenges posed by the specific economic conditions in the country. Similarly, in her contribution (Chapter 5), Giulia Sinatti describes the gap between the optimistic policy view in Senegal and the challenges of return migration by focusing on the types of business engagement undertaken by returnees and by showing how a return that is financially sustainable for a migrant and his or her family may not necessarily be in line with the government's goal of national economic growth. Moreover, the chapters on Ghana by Nauja Kleist (Chapter 4) and Somaliland by Laura Hammond (Chapter 3) both centre on returnee contributions through engagement in local and national associations and various development initiatives. But also here the focus is on the dynamics of such engagement, the constraints and the local and national readings of, and responses to, such initiatives, rather than simply measuring financial contributions.

*Return as shaped by various forms of capital* This book analyses the conditions of return by drawing on theorisations of various forms of capital. One of the main assumptions is that returnees' opportunities to accumulate different forms of capital are fundamental for their ability to engage in activities that may be positive for development. As explained earlier, the book seeks to address questions around what kind of capital (social, economic or cultural) migrants have acquired abroad and how useful that capital is for reintegration. The notion of capital also occupies a central role in the policy discourses elaborated above. However, in contrast to such policy discourses (and, to a certain extent, research on return migration), which tend to focus on economic and human capital, our understanding and use of the notion of capital are wider and draw upon a critical reading of Bourdieu (1986; 2005).

In broad terms, capital can be defined as 'anything that can be used to influence the behaviours of others or to aid in achieving desired goals' (Smart 1993: 390).[2] Hence, from this perspective, cultural and social capital produce 'returns that in some way benefit its holders in a similar way as financial capital' (Field 2003: 70). Moreover, like financial capital, cultural and social capital can be accumulated, invested, spent and lost over time (Wilk and Cliggett 2007: 187). This approach, which recognises history, process and change and the fact that capital 'takes time to accumulate' (Bourdieu 1986: 241), is particularly relevant to an analysis of return, since the capital acquired by returnees has often been gathered over a long period of time and in different places.

---

2 However, Bourdieu (1986) underlines the fact that there is a difference between capital and other kinds of resources, as only capital is convertible into other forms of capital.

One of Bourdieu's fundamental ideas is that capital is unequally distributed among individuals, and that this determines their possibilities of success. For Bourdieu, the unequal distribution of different forms of capital is absolutely vital for social hierarchies, and he maintains that this distribution 'represents the immanent structure of the social world' (ibid.: 242). Thus, he underlines the importance of power relations. Yet the unequal distribution is not totally determinant for social hierarchies, but is mediated by the way in which individuals strategise when employing their capital in order to pursue their goals, a situation that leaves some room for individual agency. The distribution is also influenced by the valuation of certain forms of capital, which is determined by the context – or, in Bourdieu's vocabulary, 'the field'.

While some contributions concentrate on economic capital, the main focus of this book is on cultural and social capital. Transdisciplinary migration studies tend to use the term 'human capital' to refer to returnees' transfer of knowledge, ideas and skills. However, we have chosen to refer to this as 'cultural capital'. Researchers using the concept of human capital sometimes, in line with the celebratory policy narrative, lean towards a reifying approach and represent returnees' skills and knowledge as a ready-made 'package' picked up abroad and simply applied in undifferentiated homeland conditions (Åkesson forthcoming). In order to distance ourselves from this approach, we have chosen the term 'cultural capital'.

The role and dynamics of social capital occupy a particularly central position in this book. As the contributions show, returnees often face challenges when they try to (re)create social relationships and networks that may be useful for their economic, social or political activities in the country of return. According to Bourdieu (1986), the value of individuals' social capital depends on how many connections they can mobilise and on the social, cultural and economic capital possessed by each of these connections. However, and in contrast to this view, this book underlines the importance of confining the notion of social capital to 'useful' connections, and not to include *all* kinds of networks and social connections (see Anthias 2007; Whitehouse 2011). As Field (2003) points out, Bourdieu – in common with other leading theoreticians on social capital, such as Coleman (1994) and Putnam (2000) – tends to see social capital as benign for those who possess it. This is a tendency that is also prominent among developmentalist policy makers, who in the neoliberal era, often see social capital as a mechanism for promoting economic growth and bypassing the state (Whitehouse 2011). However, social relationships are not always beneficial for the individuals embedded within them. As is demonstrated in several contributions to this book, the 'dark side of social capital' (Field 2003) is a burden to many migrants who feel that obligations towards their families and communities stifle their individual initiatives and opportunities (Whitehouse 2011). This is especially true for returnees who are perceived to be successful and 'rich', and thereby obliged to share their resources with relatives, neighbours and friends. These returnees' experiences are captured by the anthropologist Keith Hart, who argues that 'those who manage to enrich themselves [are] a widespread target for the aspirations, hopes, fears and antipathies of their less fortunate fellows' (1975: 16). However, returnee entrepreneurs often have to strike a balance between investing in their businesses and meeting the demands of kin.

In analyses of social capital, a distinction is often made between, on the one hand, networks of kin, friends, neighbours and other homogeneous groups of people, and, on the other, networks of socially heterogeneous people. Putnam (2000) refers to the first kind of ties as 'bonding ties' and the second as 'bridging ties'. As some of the chapters in this book show, returnees who have been abroad for many years often lack access to bridging ties outside the family and a small group of friends, which can hamper their efforts to start a business or engage in the social and political development of their homeland. Putnam defines 'bridging social capital' as a connection between different strata of a society; a social hierarchy is therefore implicitly embedded in the concept. As we will see in the chapters by Åkesson, Eriksson Baaz and Heggli Sagmo, access to influential politicians and other 'big men' is often a prerequisite for a 'successful return'.

*The positionality of returnees* As stated earlier, this book is based on original qualitative ethnographic material and interviews with return migrants. While the contributions of Grabska and Hammond also rely on interviews and ethnographic data collected from members of the communities to which the migrants return, the book is mainly based on fieldwork among and interviews with returnees, with the aim of highlighting the experiences of returnees themselves. This focus raises pertinent questions about knowledge claims: what do such experiences represent? What can returnee stories actually tell us?

While this book takes the narratives of the returnees seriously in that it assumes that the stories they tell about their experiences have something important to convey to us about the challenges involved in return – as well as the political and economic context to which they return – it has to be recognised that such stories are necessarily partial. Importantly – and in contrast to significations often attached to notions of the diaspora experience, as well as portrayals of returnees as 'brokers' – we do not assume that returnees occupy a privileged knowledge position compared with stayers or others. Listening closely to returnees' experiences can contribute to a better understanding of the conditions of return, but their stories certainly do not reflect an 'objective' reality beyond the workings of dominant discourses. As mentioned earlier, returnees' images of themselves sometimes mirror the imagery promoted in policy documents.

In Chapter 2, focusing on returnees to the DRC, Maria Eriksson Baaz (see also Eriksson Baaz forthcoming) demonstrates that returnees tend to embrace the dominant imagery that portrays the country of origin or return as an underdeveloped space and themselves as 'more developed and advanced' by virtue of having resided in a developed Europe. Those who remained in the country of origin are sometimes depicted as inferior, echoing classic colonial representations of Africans as underdeveloped, unreliable and lazy (McEwan 2009; Eriksson Baaz 2005). Such images of self and of stayee others – reflecting the complex and contradictory ways in which colonial discourses continue to shape contemporary identities (cf. Hall 1996; Appiah 1992) – are just one reflection of the particular positionality of returnees, making any claim to a privileged knowledge position inherently problematic. Hence, while returnee stories are useful in shedding further light on the conditions of return, their accounts cannot be read as conveying objective and impartial information about return or the countries of return.

Lastly, it should be emphasised that returnees constitute a vastly hetero-geneous group – differentiated in terms of age, social class, access to various forms of capital and (in relation to this) gender. Yet, while returnees constitute a differentiated group, current research suggests that return – to a greater extent than migration – is primarily dominated by groups already privileged before migration (Schoumaker et al. 2013). Moreover, while return is gendered in different ways in different countries, in some of the cases presented in this book, return is mainly a male experience. This gendering reflects gender norms in combination with efforts to ensure a safe return, in terms of both security and economy. Return is often a risky endeavour in a number of ways. Some of the countries discussed here, such as South Sudan, Somaliland and DRC, are marked by a history of widespread violence and are still often described as unsafe for women and children. In particular, return entails a number of risks for the household economy. Reflecting gendered norms – associating men/masculinity with the provider role and risk taking, and femininity with nurturing and child rearing – returnees' businesses are often managed by men at first, with the family staying on in Europe. Initial incomes upon return are also often insufficient for paying school fees, health costs and other expenses for the whole family. Thus return is often a male experience – and this is also reflected in the contributions to this book, except in the cases of South Sudan and Cape Verde. In South Sudan, both males and females of all ages have returned (and re-migrated) after displacement caused by the civil war. In the Cape Verdean case, a long period of independent female migration is being reflected in an increase in the number of women return migrants.

**The chapters**

In Chapter 2, Maria Eriksson Baaz analyses Congolese (DRC) returnee narratives from the perspective of their potential development contribution and the challenges they encounter upon return. The chapter highlights how returnee investment and livelihood strategies often mirror those of stayers; this is reflected both in efforts to 'multiply possibilities' (Trefon 2004) and in areas of investment. However, while the chapter points to a tendency among returnees to follow general investment trends, it also shows how migration has facilitated the creation of a (potentially) profitable niche for returnees as brokers for foreign investors – a role that is clearly also potentially profitable for the Congolese economy on a larger scale. Yet, the chapter demonstrates the immense challenges attached to these – and other – investment efforts in which returnees engage. Many returnees fail and, in addition, have long histories of various botched investments. Navigating and connecting to powerful social networks and 'big men' emerges as one of the main challenges in returnee narratives, as well as the most time-consuming. While such networks (as well as their useful nodes or 'big men') cut across state and non-state boundaries, politicians and state agents who can use their positions within the state to enable and regulate business emerge as particularly vital for returnees. Yet accessing and maintaining such connections is demanding in the DRC context, which is typified by frequent rotations of office and social networks in flux, and social capital is easily lost.

In Chapter 3, Laura Hammond analyses the large numbers of returnees who have gone back to Somaliland as peace and security have returned. Many have become involved in government or development work as volunteers, consultants and full-time staff. However, as this chapter demonstrates, their contributions are not universally welcomed by local residents. Some feel resentment at what they see as diaspora returnees taking jobs that locals could have filled. Others see returnees as introducing new class hierarchies into a socio-economic environment where they had not previously been a major feature. Still others complain that returnees do not really know what local priorities and realities are, so their efforts are at best wasted and at worst causing damage because of their unrealistic views and expectations. This chapter addresses the experiences of returnees and the attitudes of local people towards them. Based on interviews with returnees and locals, it argues that, while some returnee contributions are valued, local communities are increasingly critical of their own kin who seek to 'develop' them. The chapter argues that development planners in the Somaliland government and the aid business must strike a balance between reaping the benefits that returnees offer and becoming over-reliant on this group of people, who may have limited support from their communities.

In Chapter 4, Nauja Kleist presents a case study of highly skilled male return migrants, or 'policy ideal returnees', from Europe to Ghana. Since the beginning of the 2000s, changing Ghanaian governments have promoted re-turn migration to Ghana, especially of highly skilled migrants who are seen as having the potential – and responsibility – for contributing to national development. This perception is shared by the male elite returnees who see themselves as having obtained important knowledge and resources through their experiences abroad. In relation to this positioning, the chapter develops two arguments. First, the possession of local social and cultural capital, as well as a thorough mastering of the local 'rules of the field', is a precondition for these returnees to manage the many challenges relating to return, and, in particular, to contribute to development processes. Thus, the chapter demonstrates that the idea of simply transferring capital to development processes in the country of origin is fundamentally flawed, even in the case of the 'ideal' returnees studied here. Second, the chapter argues that the highly skilled male return migrants articulate their position in Ghana as 'big men': successful, wealthy and powerful men who take responsibility for and are engaged in their local communities. Their positioning as development agents mirrors popular policy notions of return migration, but it is also intertwined with understandings of 'bigmanity' (Utas 2012) and the mastering of different registers of legitimacy and power. In addition, the chapter points out that the trans-local elite with experiences of internal Ghanaian migration may sometimes constitute a more promising group for resource mobilisation than international migrants.

In Senegal, return migration has also been the focus of policy interest, with authorities advocating the repatriation of financial resources, emphasising the potential of migrant investment to promote economic growth. In Senegal's diaspora policies, return migration and returnees' business investments are viewed as having the potential to help in the country's development. In Chapter 5, Giulia Sinatti identifies three underlying myths on which this policy thinking is based. First, migrants are seen as preferring consumption to economic investment. Second, migrants are assumed to automatically acquire useful capital while abroad. Third, migrants have a natural commitment to homeland development. The chapter compares these policy myths with ethnographic insight into the efforts of Senegalese returnees to establish independent economic activities in their home country. Contrary to policy assumptions, Sinatti's case study shows that the state and migrants converge on the importance attributed to investment. However, policy underestimates both the significance of home-held capital in shaping business outcomes and the importance of social capital accumulated at home before and after migration. Moreover, the chapter demonstrates that there are strong mismatches in the underlying logics and (development) expectations of policy makers and migrants. Senegalese policy aspires to control the returnees' economic initiatives and direct them towards state-identified target sectors. However, the return migrants' savings and investments are private resources and they tend to invest in activities that are not subordinated to the government's own goals of national economic growth. As a result, policy makers downplay migrant businesses and often dismiss them as 'conspicuous consumption'.

In Chapter 6, Tove Heggli Sagmo explores returnee experiences and strategies in Burundi, a country that has suffered a long period of violence and instability that has created substantial changes in the political, social and economic landscape. Understanding these changes, which are often referred to as the 'new rules of the game', and their implications for individuals is a challenging task for those who return or consider returning. Based on fieldwork and taking its point of departure from Bourdieu's notion of *field* as an arena of struggle over the valuation of different kinds of capital and behaviour, this chapter analyses returnee experiences of the 'rules of the game' in the economic field in Burundi. It demonstrates that the economic field in Burundi is structured around trust as an important symbolic capital. Finding people to trust and being trusted by centrally positioned individuals are key to becoming a successful entrepreneur. The chapter demonstrates that trust building is a lengthy and time-consuming task that requires physical presence in Burundi and that return visits are therefore a crucial preparatory activity. Citizenship abroad, access to economic capital and relevant skills are some of the main forms of capital that facilitate this process. Far from all returnees have the necessary capital to be successfully established in the economic field, or even to be in a position to influence the 'game' itself.

Chapter 7, 'Threatening miniskirts', by Katarzyna Grabska, can partly be read as an antidote to many of the other chapters in the book, where the majority of the returnees are relatively privileged men. In Grabska's chapter we meet young females returning from forced displacement. The chapter explores the experience and consequences of the return of displaced South Sudanese Nuer adolescent girls following Sudan's civil wars (1983–2005). Based on ethnographic research in Kenyan refugee camps and South Sudan, it analyses the perceived and actual contributions to social change of returning displaced adolescent girls. At times, returning young women and girls are perceived as agents of change, bringing education, valued foreign experiences and new knowledge, but their attempts at greater autonomy, freedoms and gender equality are often judged as threatening. This chapter demonstrates that displacement might not only result in a loss but also create an opportunity to construct new social norms in the context of interactions between returnees and those who stayed behind. In this case, the adolescent returnee girls contributed to (re)negotiations of gender orders, gender identities, aspirations and norms. Thus, the chapter shows that social and cultural capital accumulated by migrants and refugees needs to be deconstructed in its gendered and generational dimensions and in its place- and context-specific meaning. The chapter emphasises the double meaning of the capital accumulated by these young female migrants: a source of social change as well as of stigma and marginalisation. Furthermore, it challenges the policy assumption that only migrant capital accumulated in Europe is associated with modernity and development.

The final chapter, by Lisa Åkesson, focuses on the constraints and opportunities Cape Verdean returnees encounter when trying to set up a business. In recent years, the government in the island state of Cape Verde has come to see returnees' businesses as a solution to the high rates of unemployment and to the country's economic dependency on the outside world. Both the government and various development organisations hope that return migrants will play a key role in investment and entrepreneurship. In light of this, the chapter explores the contribution that Cape Verdean returnees actually make to everyday economic life. This exploration builds on 15 years of intermittent fieldwork in Cape Verde in combination with recent interviews with returnees. In these interviews, the returnee business owners underline the fact that the specific economic conditions in Cape Verde are absolutely crucial in determining their room for manoeuvre. The chapter discusses the multi-layered economic challenges the return migrants have to confront, and, in addition, analyses 'bridging' social ties, which the returnees describe as vital for succeeding with a business. In particular, it looks into ties to politicians and to custom officers, the latter being a category of officials who are particularly important in their role as gatekeepers to the outside world. This case study concludes that, in terms of cultural and social capital, it is uncertain whether returnee business owners in general are more resourceful than their colleagues who have stayed behind. Due to discrimination and segregation in countries of immigration, most migrants do not accumulate skills or knowledge that is useful for entrepreneurship. Moreover, they often lack insights into the workings of the local market and they possess a limited social capital, especially in terms of bridging ties. Yet despite this, there are a few returnees with extremely varying backgrounds who develop an entrepreneurial spirit and become good at recognising and exploiting the limited openings in the local market.

## Bibliography

Abrahamsen, R. (2000) *Disciplining Democracy: Development discourse and good governance in Africa*. London: Zed Books.

— and M. C. Williams (2011) *Security Beyond the State: Private security in international politics*. Cambridge: Cambridge University Press.

Åkesson, L. (2011) 'Making migrants responsible for development: Cape Verdean returnees and northern migration policies'. *Africa Spectrum* 41(1): 61–83.

— (forthcoming) 'Multi-sited accumulation of capital: Cape Verdean returnees and small-scale business'. *Global Networks*.

— J. Carling and H. Drotbohm (2012) 'Mobility, morality and motherhood: navigating the contingencies of Cape Verdean lives'. *Journal of Ethnic and Migration Studies* 38: 237–60.

Anthias, F. (2007) 'Ethnic ties: social capital and the question of mobilisability'. *Sociological Review* 55: 788–805.

Appadurai, A. (1998) *Modernity at Large: Cultural dimensions of globalization*.

Minneapolis MN: University of Minnesota Press.

Appiah, K. A. (1992) *In My Father's House: Africa in the philosophy of culture*. New York NY: Oxford University Press.

Bardouille, R., M. Ndulo and M. Grieco (eds) (2008) *Africa's Finances: The contribution of remittances*. Newcastle upon Tyne: Cambridge Scholars Publishing.

Bjarnesen, J. (2013) 'Diaspora at home? Wartime mobilities in the Burkina Faso – Côte d'Ivoire Transnational Space'. PhD thesis, Uppsala University.

Black, R. and A. Castaldo (2009) 'Return migration and entrepreneurship in Ghana and Côte d'Ivoire: the role of capital transfers'. *Tijdschrift voor economische en sociale geografie* 100(1): 44–58.

Boccagni, P. (2011) 'The framing of return from above and below in Ecuadorian migration. A project, a myth or a political device?' *Global Networks* 11(4): 461–80.

Bourdieu, P. (1986) 'The forms of capital'. In J. Richardson (ed.) *Handbook of Theory and Research for the Sociology of Education*. Westport CT: Greenwood Press.

— (2005) *The Social Structures of the Economy*. Cambridge: Polity Press.

Cassarino, J.-P. (2004) 'Theorising return migration: the conceptual approach to return migrants revisited'. *International Journal on Multicultural Societies* 6(2): 253–79.

Castles, S. and M. Miller (1993) *The Age of Migration: International population movements in the modern world*. Basingstoke: Macmillan.

Coleman, J. S. (1994) *Foundations of Social Theory*. Cambridge MA: Belknap Press.

de Haas, H. (2006) *Engaging Diasporas: How governments and development agencies can support diaspora involvement in the development of origin countries*. Oxford: International Migration Institute, University of Oxford.

— (2010) 'Migration and development: a theoretical perspective'. *International Migration Review* 44(1): 227–64.

Duffield, M. (2010) 'The liberal way of development and the development–security impasse: exploring the global life-chance divide'. *Security Dialogue* 41(1): 53–76.

Eastmond, M. (2006) 'Transnational returns and reconstruction in post-war Bosnia and Herzegovina'. *International Migration* 44(3): 141–66.

Eriksson Baaz, M. (2005) *The Paternalism of Partnership: A postcolonial reading of identity in development aid*. London and New York: Zed Books.

— (forthcoming) 'Relational Deficits and Debilitating Expectations: An exploration of the disadvantages of migration among Congolese return migrants'. *Journal of Development Research*.

Escobar, A. (1995) *Encountering Development: The making and unmaking of the third world*. Princeton NJ: Princeton University Press.

European Commission (2011) *Commission Staff Working Paper: Migration and development*. Brussels: European Commission. Available at http://ec.europa.eu/home-affairs/news/intro/docs/2_EN_autre_document_travail_service_part1_v3.pdf.

Field, J. (2003) *Social Capital*. London: Routledge.

Glick Schiller, N. (2012) 'Unravelling the migration and development web: research and policy implications'. *International Migration* 50: 92–7.

Global Forum on Migration and Development (2008) *Report of the First Meeting of the Global Forum on Migration and Development 2007*. Brussels: Bruylant.

— (2012) *Enhancing the Human Development of Migrants and Their Contribution to the Development of Communities and States*. Sixth meeting of the Global Forum on Migration and Development, Port Louis, Mauritius, 19–22 November.

Grabska, K. (2014) *Gender, Identity and Home: Nuer repatriation to Southern Sudan*. Woodbridge: James Currey.

Hall, S. (1990) 'Cultural identity and diaspora'. In J. Rutherford (ed.) *Identity, Culture, Difference*. London: Lawrence and Wishart.

— (1996) 'When was "the post-colonial"? Thinking at the limit'. In I. Chambers and L. Curti (eds) *The Post-Colonial Question: Common skies, divided horizons*. London and New York NY: Routledge.

Hammond, L., M. Awad, A. I. Dagane, P. Hansen, C. Horst, K. Menkhaus and L. Obare (2011) *Cash and Compassion: The role of the Somali diaspora in relief, development, and peace-building*. Nairobi: UNDP Somalia.

Hansen, P. (2007) 'Revolving returnees: meanings and practices of transnational return among Somalilanders'. PhD thesis, Department of Anthropology, University of Copenhagen.

— and S. Jonsson (2011) 'Demographic colonialism: EU–African migration management and the legacy of Eurafrica'. *Globalizations* 8(3): 261–76.

Hansson, S. (2013) 'Who brings water? Negotiating state responsibility in water sector reform in Niger'. PhD thesis, School of Global Studies, Gothenburg University.

Harrison, G. (2004) 'The World Bank and Africa: the construction of governance states'. *British Journal of Politics and International Relations* 7: 240–60.

Hart, K. (1975) 'Swindler or public benefactor? The entrepreneur in his community'. In J. Goody (ed.) *Changing Social Structure in Ghana: Essays in comparative sociology of a new state and on old tradition*. London: International African Institute.

Kilic, T., C. Carletto, B. David and A. Zezza (2009) 'Investing back home: return migration and business ownership in Albania'. *Economics of Transition* 17: 587–623.

Kleist, N. and I. Vammen (2012) *Diaspora Groups and Development in Fragile Situations*. DIIS Report 2012:09. Copenhagen: Danish Institute for International Studies (DIIS).

Lianos, T. and A. Pseiridis (2009) 'On the occupational choices of return migrants'. *Entrepreneurship & Regional Development* 21(2): 155–81.

Maimbo, S. M. and D. Ratha (2005) *Remittances: Development impacts and future prospects*. Washington DC: World Bank.

McEwan, C. (2009) *Postcolonialism and Development*. London and New York NY: Routledge.

Ministério das Comunidades (2014) *Estratégia nacional de emigração e desenvolvimento: Linhas de orientação para acção*. Praia: Ministério das Comunidades.

Mohapatra, S. and D. Ratha (eds) (2011) *Remittance Markets in Africa*. Washington DC: World Bank.

Nederveen, P. J. (2001) *Development Theory: Deconstructions/reconstructions*. London and Thousand Oaks CA: Sage Publications.

Nyberg Sørensen, N. and K. Fog Olwig (2002) *Work and Migration: Life and livelihoods in a globalizing world*. New York NY: Routledge.

Pérouse de Montclos, M.-A. (2005) *Diasporas, Remittances and Africa South of the Sahara: A strategic assessment*. Pretoria: Institute for Security Studies.

Putnam, R. D. (2000) *Bowling Alone: The collapse and revival of American community*. New York NY: Simon and Schuster.

Schoumaker, B., M.-L. Flahaux, M. Mangalu and J. Agbada (2013) *Changing Patterns of Congolese Migration*. MAFE Working Paper 19. Paris: Institut National d'Études Démographiques (INED).

Sinatti, G. (2014) 'Return migration as a win–win–win scenario? Visions of return among Senegalese migrants, the state of origin and receiving countries'. *Ethnic and Racial Studies* 38(2): 275–91. doi: 10.1080/01419870.2013.868016.

— and C. Horst (2015) 'Migrants as agents of development: Diaspora engagement discourse and practice in Europe'. *Ethnicities* 15(1): 134–52.

Skeldon, R. (2012) 'Going round in circles: circular migration, poverty alleviation and marginality'. *International Migration* 50(3): 43–60.

Smart, A. (1993) 'Gifts, bribes and guanxi:

a reconsideration of Bourdieu's social capital'. *Cultural Anthropology* 8: 388–408.

Stefansson, A. (2004) 'Sarajevo suffering: homecoming and the hierarchy of homeland hardship'. In F. Markowits and A. Stefansson (eds) *Homecoming: Unsettling paths of return*. Oxford: Lexington Books.

Tomlison, J. (1999) *Globalisation and Culture*. Cambridge: Polity Press.

Trefon, T. (ed.) (2004) *Reinventing Order in the Congo: How people respond to state failure in Kinshasa*. London: Zed Books.

Turner, S. and N. Kleist (2013) 'Introduction: agents of change? Staging and governing diasporas and the African state'. *African Studies* 72(2): 192–206.

Utas, M. (ed.) (2012) *African Conflicts and Informal Power: Big men and networks*. London: Zed Books.

Whitehouse, B. (2011) 'Enterprising strangers: social capital and social liability among African migrant traders'. *International Journal of Social Inquiry* 4(1): 93–111.

Wilk, R. and L. Cliggett (2007) *Economies and Cultures: Foundations of economic anthropology*. Boulder, CO: Westview Press.

Wimmer, A. and N. Glick Schiller (2002) 'Methodological nationalism and beyond: nation-state building, migration and the social sciences'. *Global Networks* 2(4): 301–34.

World Bank (2011) *Migration and Remittances Factbook 2011*. Washington DC: World Bank.

## 2 | Successive flops and occasional feats: development contributions and thorny social navigation among Congolese return migrants

Maria Eriksson Baaz

As a returnee you have to adapt yourself. There is an expression that says 'When in Rome, do like the Romans do' (Congolese return migrant).

Many Congolese migrants in the large Congolese diaspora dream of returning to their country of origin. While the Democratic Republic of the Congo (DRC) is still afflicted by protracted armed conflicts in the eastern parts and while large parts of the increasingly politicised diaspora population are engaged in (sometimes violent) opposition against the current regime (Demart and Bodeux 2013), some Congolese migrants voluntarily leave Europe (partially) to try their luck in their country of origin (Lardeux 2012; Schoumaker et al. 2013a). Some migrants always lived with a wish to return; for many others, the dream of a good life in Europe was dashed by experiences marked by discrimination and unemployment (Schoumaker et al. 2013b; Vause 2011; Schoonvaere 2010). Such difficult experiences seem to have become more common in recent years due to the economic crises and rising unemployment levels in large parts of Europe. In this context, investing in the (supposedly) booming economy of the DRC appears increasingly attractive – not only for foreign investors, but for Congolese migrants too.

In addition to individual ambitions and aims, return is also often construed as a way to 'give back': to use the knowledge acquired in Europe to contribute to the development of 'the homeland'. Informed by familiar assumptions of where 'capacity' and 'knowledge' reside in a world of developed and underdeveloped countries and of representations of the DRC as 'a land of opportunities', the task at hand is often portrayed as a rather simple one (Eriksson Baaz forthcoming). Being Congolese by origin, not only do you have a right to claim the land, you supposedly also know the country. Moreover, the time spent in Europe is assumed to have endowed the migrant with capacities that will profit the country of origin and further development. In this way, the image of many migrants tends to echo the policy discourses presented in the introductory chapter. Hence – as in the policy discourses – aspiring returnees often present themselves as 'agents of development' who will bring back economic, social and cultural capital gained in Europe (ibid.).

However, little is known about the challenges associated with return or about the contributions returnees are able to make. Based on interviews with Congolese migrant entrepreneurs who are engaged in efforts to return to the DRC either permanently or temporarily, this chapter analyses returnee narratives from the perspective of their potential development contribution. How can their stories shed light on the possible 'novelties' with which they contribute? To what extent do returnees appear to invest in innovative areas? And in which ways (if any) do they appear to conduct business 'in a different way'? Moreover, what can returnee stories tell us about the challenges they encounter upon return and the 'worth' of capital acquired abroad?

A caveat is needed. This chapter is based on qualitative research involving 49 returnees. Clearly, it cannot claim to provide a generalised account of the development contribution of Congolese returnees from Europe. Yet, the stories collected hint at important gaps and omissions in the celebratory story of return migration. In particular, they shed light on the importance of returnees' 'social navigation' (Vigh 2009). In doing so, the chapter highlights the importance of social and political networks in the DRC, which tend to be forgotten in the rosy story of return migration (see Chapter 1). It seeks to demonstrate the agency of the returnees and the complex interplay between their agency and the 'big man' networks (Utas 2012) they navigate. The chapter therefore also underlines the importance of social capital; however, the term 'social capital' is used here with some reservations. As highlighted in Chapter 1, Bourdieu's (and others') notion of social capital comes with certain limitations – limitations that will be discussed further in this chapter.

First, I provide a brief background to Congolese return migration and the context of return in terms of conditions for business. I then detail the methodology adopted and what the narratives can (and cannot) tell us. The next part of the chapter addresses the question of the types of business returnees are engaged in and to what extent they appear to invest in new areas. This is followed by an analysis of the ways in which business is conducted – do returnees appear to conduct business in different ways to those adopted by 'stayers'? As will become clear in these sections, social networks occupy a particularly important role in returnee narratives. While the limited access to economic capital (i.e. credit facilities) was often mentioned, connecting to powerful social and political networks emerged as the main challenge. The final section discusses these challenges, illustrating returnees' thorny social navigation.

## A brief background to Congolese return migration and the context of return

*Congolese migration* While some Congolese migrated to Europe, in particular Belgium, during colonial times, emigration to Europe became more substantial after independence. In the 1960s, most migrants came from the elite, moving to Belgium in order to study (Schoonvaere 2010) and then returning to the Congo after completing their studies. In the wake of the repressive rule of Mobutu and the economic crises in the DRC (then Zaire) that started during the mid-1970s and intensified in the 1980 and 1990s, migration to Europe increased and destinations also began to include countries other than Belgium, in particular France, the UK and Germany. Reflecting the deteriorating living conditions and efforts to search for income opportunities elsewhere, an increasing number of migrants came from less privileged backgrounds from the 1980s onwards. The attempt to send a family member abroad became an integral and important part of livelihood strategies, especially in Kinshasa (Sumata et al. 2004; Sumata 2002). Hence, from the 1970s, Congolese migration to Europe – and increasingly also to the US and Canada – increased substantially, while levels of return decreased.

Studies of Congolese return migration are as yet quite limited. Most of the available data takes the form of returnee profiles produced by the (quantitative) MAFE (Programme sur les migrateans entre l'Afrique et l'Europe) project.[1] According to recent data from this project, only 10 per cent of migrants return to the DRC within ten years, leading the authors to conclude that 'the Congolese practically do not return from Europe anymore' (Schoumaker et al. 2013a: 10). Yet, while the average return rate certainly has decreased over time, such conclusions appear to be a bit hasty. It is, for instance, possible that many return after more than ten years in Europe – as is the case with many of the returnees included in this study.[2] At any rate, in light of the challenges of making a living in the DRC, a return rate of 10 per cent within ten years could be considered rather high.

According to data from the MAFE project – based on a small sample due to low levels of return – those returning are mainly male (65 per cent) and

---

[1] See http://mafeproject.site.ined.fr/en/.

[2] Moreover, citing figures showing that fewer than 5 per cent of Congolese migrants living in the UK have visited the DRC within five years of their first arrival, they conclude that visits have decreased over time, and have not replaced return. This means that the authors also refute what Lututala (2006) in the Congolese case termed 'residential ubiquity' – pointing to a transnational way of living in which visits and circulation have become a substitute for definitive return. While this study is based on qualitative data and by no means provides any useful data on average levels of return and circulation, it indicates that such conclusions might be misleading. For instance, a majority of the (partial) returnees interviewed spent more than five years in Europe before they first visited the DRC. Importantly, a majority of them would probably not qualify as returnees in statistical analysis since they maintain their European citizenship (Congolese law does not permit double citizenship) and residence permits and travel to Europe frequently. In addition, given the stigma attached to a failed return and fears that spending time outside Europe might have unforeseen consequences for migrants' legal residence status in Europe, it is likely that circulation is slightly underreported in surveys.

relatively old (73 per cent aged 45 and over). Moreover, the majority have a higher level of education (66 per cent) and almost all of them were documented migrants upon return. As the authors conclude: 'return migrants from DRC are essentially privileged people', resulting from 'a double selection: better-off people are more likely to migrate to Europe, and once in Europe, they are (or at least until very recently) more likely to return' (ibid.: 24). As we will see, this profile is reflected in the 'sample' of this study and also accounts for the challenges we faced in ensuring that it was varied in terms of gender and levels of privilege before migration.

Let me now provide a brief snapshot of the context to which the migrants return, focusing on what in policy terms is often termed the 'business climate'.

*A brief snapshot of the context of return* The DRC, ranked 178 out of 183 in the 2012 World Bank's *Doing Business* report, is generally portrayed as an extraordinarily unfriendly place for business. Some of the reasons for this negative ranking derive from political instability and the protracted armed conflict in the eastern parts of the country, the crippled infrastructure and (allegedly) high formal taxes.[3] However, a large part is attributed to the informal workings of the state and what is often described as a 'dysfunctional public administration' (ibid.), which create unpredictability and weak protection of property rights.

The current workings of the state apparatus have deep historical roots, dating back to the 1980s and the Mobutu era's ('formal') economic collapse, with state agents playing an increasingly active part in the informalisation of the economy. The strategies and manifestations of Mobutu's rule – including how he tolerated and indeed encouraged this process through various infamous dictums – have been well documented, often epitomised in expressions such as 'kleptocracy', '*le mal Zaïrois*' and '*débrouillez-vous*', and will not be repeated here (Callaghy 1984; MacGaffey 1986; 1991; Willame 1992; Schatzberg 1988). Importantly, the drying up of state resources following formal economic decay was not accompanied by a disintegration or collapse of state functions (Englebert 2003; Trefon 2009). Rather, state agents, deprived of formal salaries, became increasingly involved in the 'real economy' (MacGaffey 1991) through the opportunities and advantages that state office provided. Hence, state agents increasingly resorted to rent-seeking activities by using their bureaucratic power – and also their military power, given the involvement of the armed forces.[4] They were therefore able to control commercial networks

---

3 PricewaterhouseCoopers (PwC) concludes: 'The DRC's high taxes are a further discouragement for investors, with a corporate income tax rate of 35% and additional types of taxes that can increase the total tax payable significantly.' See www.pwc.com/gx/en/transportation-logistics/publications/africa-infrastructure-investment/assets/drc.pdf.

4 In his efforts to keep the army loyal and to avoid engaging it in political affairs, Mobutu tolerated and even encouraged military entrepreneurship (see Schatzberg 1988).

using a range of different means: coercion and intimidation, granting market access and permission and protection through shares in businesses (or other forms of economic compensation) and by imposing a range of informal taxes (MacGaffey 1991; Young and Turner 1985; Schatzberg 1988).

While the government embarked on a series of reforms supported by the World Bank (and others) after the elections in 2006, many observers argue that the results have been meagre and superficial and that '*le mal Zaïrois*' has simply mutated into '*le mal Congolais*' (Robinson 2013). While such conclusions are overly pessimistic, reflecting a general tendency among external actors caught in Congo-pessimism not to recognise achievements (Stearns et al. 2013; Koddenbrock 2014), the DRC remains a challenging place in which to conduct business. As we will see, accounts of strained navigation in an unpredictable environment, with complex webs of overlapping state functions and 'big men' networks, were abundant in the returnees' narratives.

Following Utas (2012: 1), 'big men' are understood here as 'nodes in [fluid] networks, combining efforts in projects of joint action'. As such, the term highlights 'a position within social relations' rather than being a fixed label (ibid.: 8–9). While such nodes and networks in the DRC – as elsewhere – can be seen to a certain extent as a response to fragile 'formal' structures, they are not situated outside the state.[5] The social networks cross across state/non-state boundaries, and nodes in the form of politicians and state agents who can use their positions within the state to enable and regulate business take on a particularly important role for returnees (and for many others).

### Some notes on methodology

This chapter is based mainly on qualitative in-depth interviews with 49 Congolese voluntary returnees or circular migrants in Kinshasa. Starting from returnees identified through contacts with the diaspora in Europe (mainly Sweden), other returnees were selected through snowball sampling once in Kinshasa. The migrants interviewed had returned from various countries in Europe – Belgium, France, the UK and the Nordic countries. Several of them had stayed in more than one European country, reflecting the ways in which migrants' itineraries have become more diverse (Schoumaker et al. 2013a), as they move around in their search for better opportunities. The aim of the research project was to collect a diversity of stories, particularly in terms of gender, socio-economic background before migration, areas of investment or

---

5 Hence, the concept of 'big men' networks used here differs from the ways in which this model often appears in the literature on African neo-patrimonialism (for example, as a root cause, produced by tradition). Rather, such networks are present in all societies, but are more pronounced in those like the DRC, which is marked by the long-standing weakening of formal state governance, further aggravated by the protracted conflict.

occupation, and levels of 'return success or realisation'. As noted above, this was not an easy task given the gendered, and particularly the 'class-based', patterns of return migration (ibid.). While we managed to interview a number of women returnees, very few of the returnees interviewed came from markedly non-privileged backgrounds.[6] Moreover, some of the returnees coming from less privileged circumstances before migration whom we identified were reluctant to share their experiences since their efforts had not been very successful – reflecting the strong shame and stigma around 'failed migration and return' in the DRC, as in many other contexts (see Åkesson forthcoming).

Almost all of the migrants interviewed in the DRC could be defined as partial returnees or circular migrants in that they maintained European citizenship and legal residence permits and travelled to Europe frequently. A majority of male returnees still had their wives and children in Europe and regularly visited them for longer or shorter periods. The DRC was described by many returnees as still unsafe and therefore unfit for children and women. Also, the incomes generated in the DRC were often simply not enough to pay school fees, health costs and other expenses for the whole family. In other cases, the wife and children did not share the wish to return. Moreover – and importantly, since there are many risks associated with return – retaining a base in the host country was presented as a safety measure in case businesses failed. Resonating with other research on circular migration, the transnational lifestyle or circulation adapted by the returnees interviewed 'improves the welfare of the members of the households and reduces their risk of external shock' (Skeldon 2012: 45). While in the following sections the migrants are referred to as 'returnees', it should be remembered that most of them are partial returnees, or circular migrants, with one foot still in Europe.

While the aim of having a varied sample in terms of gender and levels of privilege before migration met with some difficulties, attempts to include a mixed sample in terms of areas of investment or occupation upon return were straightforward. While (as will be elaborated further below) there is a tendency among returnees to follow investment trends, the returnees were engaged in a wide repertoire of business: transport; the importing and exporting of cars, clothes, appliances and other commodities; politics, either as political advisers or as (aspiring or real) holders of political office; agricultural businesses; the hotel and leisure industry; religious work (as priests or pastors); journalism; artistic work; human rights and non-governmental organisation (NGO) development activities; health and medical service provision; the minerals trade; and consultancy work to facilitate foreign investors. Moreover, while a large majority of the participants were self-employed (in any of the above sectors),

---

6 Most had at least one parent with a university degree and formal (private or public) sector employment.

some were employees in private companies, often family-owned businesses, but also with international NGOs.

Referring to diverse activities such as NGO development work, the minerals trade and politics under the rubrics of 'business' and 'investment' might be considered incongruous in that these occupations tend to be linked to different motives – commercial activities being associated with private profit generation and NGOs with non-profit activities for the common good. However, while such distinctions are always tenuous, they tend to become particularly elusive in the DRC context, where engaging in NGO development work, politics or religious organisations constitutes an important source of income generation more generally (Trefon 2004). In addition, in order to minimise levels of administrative harassment and taxes, many Congolese (including returnees) register what is in reality a private company as an NGO. I do not intend to suggest that income-earning prospects are the only, or even the main, motive for returnees to engage in NGO, religious and other activities that in dominant lexicons are associated with the non-profit sector; rather, these activities are informed by a range of complex motives – of which resource generation is often central, and indeed necessary, in order to sustain oneself in a context in which state-provided social security is absent. Finally, it should be noted that many of the returnees are 'polyvalent' in terms of both their history of activities and the activities in which they were engaged when we met them. Most of them were involved in several activities simultaneously – reflecting more general livelihood strategies in the volatile political and economic context of the DRC, which are characterised by efforts aimed at 'multiplying possibilities in the hope of achieving results' (ibid.: 2). Hence, in this respect (as in many others), the livelihood strategies of returnees tend to mirror those of stayers.

*Co-written narratives* The interviews were conducted by the author and Karin Elfving in Kinshasa in May and September 2012 and in July 2013 in a variety of languages: French, Lingala and sometimes Swedish and English. Some of the migrants were interviewed only once, while we met others on several occasions. If we were invited, we visited the returnee at their work and/or home to get a better sense of their activities and situation. In the discussions we pursued lines of questioning on the subjects of background and history before migrating, activities and experiences in Europe, motivations to return, activities engaged in upon returning, perceptions of their own contribution, the main challenges encountered, how they addressed those challenges, and the reasons for any family arrangements made.

Clearly, the interview data must be understood as co-constructed narratives (Stern 2006), reflecting the stories the returnees wanted us to hear.[7] As

7 In most cases, we naturally had no opportunity to 'verify' their accounts regarding, for instance, the extent of and incomes from current activities. In terms of what

such, their narratives were informed by our positionality as Swedish/European researchers (although the author has lived in the DRC for a long time) and the subject positions that this activated. It appears that the interviews often triggered a sense of common identification as Europeans, a common 'us' – as people who have lived elsewhere, who 'do and see things differently' and 'are more evolved' (*sic*), compared with a homogenised Congolese (stayee) Other. As we will see, accounts of difficulties encountered sometimes echoed familiar representations often articulated by outside interveners in the development industry and diplomatic circles, portraying Congolese as backward, unreliable and lazy. Importantly, such representations must be read as contextual, partly activated by our positionality as white European researchers. They must also be understood as reflecting the ways in which colonial discourses continue to shape contemporary identities – often in contradictory ways (Hall 1996; Appiah 1992; Mudimbe 1994). While the returnees strongly condemned European racism, sometimes citing experiences of discrimination in Europe as what 'drove them to return' (Eriksson Baaz forthcoming), their representations of Congolese stayers were sometimes curiously similar to the racist discourses they disavowed.

Let me now explain how the material collected can shed light on what possible 'novelties' returnees bring in terms of areas of investment and ways of conducting business.

### Engaging in new 'innovative' business?

As mentioned above, the returnees interviewed were engaged in a vast range of businesses. Certainly, many of them can be assumed to bring valuable skills and new perspectives to their respective areas of activity, particularly as many of them had a high level of education. In addition, while many had been exposed to discrimination in the labour markets of Europe (Schoumaker et al. 2013b), which had forced them into employment below their education level, some had occupied highly skilled positions. Hence, such returnees (and presumably many others) undoubtedly contribute skills to their various activities and employments in the DRC. However, assessing that contribution is beyond the scope of this chapter; it would require an in-depth technical knowledge of valued skills and expertise in the respective areas in which migrants engage, which is clearly not possible given the diversity of their occupations. Instead, I will focus on areas of investment on a more general level among self-employed returnees.

---

kind of stories they chose to tell, our reading is that they differed considerably between the returnees, but also between discursive contexts where we met the returnee several times. Some seemed to have a tendency to highlight their achievements, while others instead emphasised difficulties, miscalculations and failures. Moreover, sometimes some of them appeared to talk about failures and insolvencies experienced by themselves by instead referring to others.

*A varied picture: innovative and imitative businesses* A handful of the returnees interviewed had visibly invested in innovative areas. One of them was Pierre, who left for Europe in 2001 after he finished his studies in Kinshasa as an electrical engineer. Once in Europe, he was unable to get his qualifications validated and instead decided to retrain in computing and economics. He returned to visit the DRC for the first time in 2007, for a short visit. After that – like many others – he maintained a circulating lifestyle and still retained a part-time position with a small company in France. When we met him in 2011, he had started a company in Kinshasa selling software programs for cash registers. He explains:

> Within my area I have no competition. I am alone. No one sells software for cash registers as I do. I did a market survey and studied economy over there [in Europe] and learned how to analyse things. I found that the computing sector here was unexploited so I decided to invest in that.

Pierre's story is a positive one in which the time spent in Europe – despite the initial disappointment of not having his qualifications validated – turned out to be useful, enabling him to invest in a new area with no (or few) competitors. Like many others, however, Pierre has a long history of investing and his is by no means a straightforward success story. As he explained, he had several failures behind him. Like many other returnees, he first started importing and selling cars (see below), but given the high custom fees, fierce competition and other problems, this was not profitable. After this he came into contact with a multinational pharmaceutical company and tried to facilitate their access to the Congolese market for surgical equipment. However, this failed since the equipment – while allegedly being of a better quality – was not able to compete with cheaper versions imported from China. Pierre tells us that it was only after these failures (and a few others) that he realised that he needed to analyse the market and find something new. It was after such analysis that he came up with the idea of software programs for cash registers – an investment which, when we met him, appeared to be rather successful.

The need to study the market was something that was emphasised by many returnees, who furthermore argued that the main problem with returnee business was a tendency to act on hearsay and invest in similar sectors. Charles, who was involved in a range of business activities (importing cars and used tyres and constructing houses) argued as follows:

> There is a mentality here: if someone starts building hotels, everybody starts to build hotels! If someone starts doing transport to the interior, everyone wants to do it. There is no innovation! It is the same for Congolese here [in the DRC] and the diaspora. When they hear that something works, they throw themselves into the business! But you need to search for something new, something not already exploited.

Similar conclusions were made by several other returnees – particularly those who had a longer history of engagement, and of failures. Moreover, their conclusions are reflected in the data we collected on returnee business trajectories. One popular area of investment, in which many returnees had invested at some point, is the importation of vehicles and spare parts, either to sell or to use in public transport. While some of the returnees were still involved in such businesses, it appears to have been particularly popular during the 1990s. Another common area of investment is the construction of hotels and motels. Willy, who had been involved in previous investments and currently put most of his energy into 'work[ing] on his address book' (see below), put it as follows:

> Everything is from hearsay [*bouche-à-oreille*]. When I came here, for example, they said that 'more recently hotels are really good business' ... And I could really see a lot of hotels being built. But when I studied all the investment costs, personnel costs and advertising ... and the sensitivity to seasonal changes with the diaspora coming in the summer – the diaspora leaves and the rooms are almost empty. For Congolese they think that you have built a hotel with five floors and that means success. But as an economist I know that just because it is beautiful it does not mean that it works.

Ignoring the advice he received, Willy instead decided to invest in an area which at that time was rather new – solar panels – and tried to negotiate a contract with the state energy company. However, this project failed. Like many others, he attributed the failure to his limited connections to social networks, a factor that is discussed further below.

The interview material indicates that the current investment in vogue is agriculture. This was mentioned as a lucrative form of investment by many returnees and several of them were engaged in agriculture, either as a main or a secondary activity. Stayee Kinois encountered during the fieldwork also presented agriculture as being very profitable, and many with the means to do so invested in various agricultural projects. Hence, rather than being restricted to the diaspora, it seems that the shifting trends in investment among returnees reflect popular investment patterns in Kinshasa more generally.

Yet while there appears to be a tendency among returnees to invest in popular business areas, the migration experience has created a (potentially) profitable niche for returnees as brokers for foreign investment.

*Foreign investment brokers* Like Pierre, whom we encountered earlier, quite a few returnees acted as brokers for foreign companies seeking to invest in the DRC. Around a quarter of the returnees were or had been engaged in facilitating foreign investors in different ways, either as their primary or a secondary activity. As in Pierre's case, this engagement was often project-based and involved particular companies, but two migrants had started up a consultancy business specialising in facilitating foreign investment; for example, they offered to negotiate contracts, make feasibility and due diligence studies and provide legal support.

Clearly, this is an example of an area where returnees appear to engage in activities that stayers find difficult to access. Many of the returnees had established contacts with the companies in question when they lived in or circulated back to Europe. Moreover, many emphasised the importance of their language (often English) and 'cultural' skills in establishing such relations. In their experience, their exposure to Europe made the foreign company representatives trust them more. Teddy, for instance, who among other things had worked as a facilitator for a petroleum company searching for drilling rights, concluded that her knowledge of English was important for the company representatives (due to their limited French) and that the experience she had gained in Europe made them feel that 'we were more similar' and 'closer to each other (compared with other Congolese)'.

However, while these facilitator returnees occupy a new niche in relation to foreign investment – one that is clearly facilitated by their migration experience – it should be borne in mind that the role of fixer or broker is by no means a novel phenomenon in the DRC. In the wake of the deterioration of state functions and the formal economy during the Mobutu era, middlemen or fixers came to inhabit an increasingly important position. They are called upon to provide their services in relation to a range of needs: facilitating access to government officials in order to receive documents and permits, getting access to housing, electricity or water, and so on (Trefon 2004; Piermay 1997). There are fixers available for most of the needs and problems that may arise. While local and national fixers live by solving people's everyday problems, returnees try to earn a living by solving the problems faced by foreign investors. A common denominator that allows both positions to exist is a negotiated state apparatus infused by competition between different networks.

Moreover, while such roles potentially facilitate foreign investment in important ways, the interview material highlighted the difficulties experienced by these internationalised returnee brokers. Like Pierre, most of the returnees had not been very successful in their efforts. Willy, for instance, went back to Europe after his solar panel investment failed. There, he came into contact with a big pharmaceutical company that was interested in starting up production in the DRC. However, that project also failed; according to Willy, this was because well-connected Indian businessmen who dominated the market had bribed politicians in order to prevent competition. Two other circular migrants who were interviewed were acting as facilitators for a smaller European building company without much success. When we met them, after two years of negotiations they had still not managed to arrange a contract, allegedly due to the 'envelopes' or 'encouragement' that the minister in question demanded in order to provide a permit and the reluctance of the company to satisfy such requests.

Let me now turn to the ways in which businesses are conducted. Do returnees appear to conduct business in a different way to stayers?

## Conducting business differently?

As indicated in the section on methodology, many returnees distanced themselves from stayee Congolese in certain discursive contexts. A common theme in such representations of difference was work ethics. Some returnees argued that the migration experience had provided them with a different work ethic. They described themselves as being more focused, industrious and honest compared with stayee Congolese, and some maintained that they made a contribution by instilling this work ethic in stayers. One returnee summarised the difference between her work ethic and that of stayers as follows:

> People are offhand here. They postpone until tomorrow what they can do today.
> They're not used to work pace here, real work pace ... If I had not migrated
> I would probably have had some laxity too, a laxity I can't tolerate any more.
> There [in Europe] I learned the value of work. I learned the value of money too.
> Here they spend easily.

Two other returnees put it in a similar way, emphasising that the years spent in Europe had taught them the value of hard work:

> I understand that the white man is laborious. To evolve you have to work and
> think a lot. One must not give up. But here people spend all their time praying
> to God when they have problems. He [the Congolese] believes that when he
> sleeps, the good fortune will rain from the sky.
>
> We have learned to be strict and honest. It's not because people around
> us [in the DRC] are a bit lazy that we also should become like that. So that is
> also something I think we can contribute with, to show and be an example to
> others.

Reflecting their identity as being 'more honest and diligent' (often referred to as *logique* or *reglo*), most returnees (though not all) strongly condemned what they often termed 'corruption' – describing it as shocking and abhorrent. Stories involving bizarre and expensive taxes imposed by greedy and unpredictable state agents were common in the interviews. Such accounts of state agents often featured a strong sense of repugnance. Rose, who spent six years in Europe before she returned in 2009 to work in a family-owned medical clinic, described her experiences in the following way:

> It's difficult ... because it is always these institutions that manage to swindle

you. I call them swindlers/crooks [*raquetteurs*]. In official institutions you always have an inspector who comes to ask you for something. It is tiring ... Every day. Every day. It becomes downright cranky ... yes really cranky. Because you put [in] lighting equipment you must pay $800. You know what it is $800? So if you meet a guy like that you talk and you pay him $100. Frankly, it is a bit disgusting ... Or the hygiene tax. They give you a figure with a large sum. Eventually you will pay a small amount because you will ... how do you call it? ... it's a kind of corruption ... You do not pay the amount, because it is always exaggerated even if they come with documents of the law ... You discuss and you pay the invisible ... Well, that's what's annoying with the Congolese. And when he has the money he goes to drink his beer.

Many returnees tended to portray themselves as morally superior – as somehow situated outside such corruption – to stayee Congolese (or simply Congolese in general in Rose's case, where the returnee describes herself as non-Congolese). As argued in the methodology section, such representations of the returnee 'self' and the stayee 'other' are curiously similar to the racist representations of the Congolese as backward, unreliable and lazy that recur in discourses by outsiders in the development industry and diplomatic circles (Eriksson Baaz 2005; Eriksson Baaz and Stern 2013). Importantly, such representations must be read as a reflection of the stories returnees like to tell about themselves – which were surely activated in part by our position as Swedish/European researchers – rather than as informed accounts of the difference between returnees and stayers (or between Europe and the DRC). Moreover, it should be noted that returnees are far from alone in their critique of the workings of state institutions and 'corruption'. Stayers (even those with very limited formal education) are often critical of 'corruption', describing it as illicit, damaging and generally not 'how things should be', as do returnees in their accounts (Eriksson Baaz and Verweijen 2014).

Yet, and most importantly, the narratives of the returnees were marked by a strong ambivalence, or rather by a contradiction between the sometimes quite self-congratulatory depictions of the returnee 'self' and accounts of how they actually conduct their business. Their portrayals of the attributes they had acquired through migration in the form of superior work ethics often contrasted quite sharply with their accounts of everyday navigation – particularly in terms of 'managing corruption'. Oscar, who had spent over ten years in Europe and was now engaged in a range of activities in the DRC, from importing salted fish to political engagement in an opposition party and chairing a human rights NGO, concluded as follows:

If you come with your Swedish principles to the Congo, the business here is not like that ... Here there are no rules. If you are not the son of ... or have contacts with someone in the presidency, or the agents from local government or the environment ministry, you'll have the agents from the hygiene tax ... you'll have all the different agents of the state visit you and each comes for receiving an envelope. You really have to accept this mafia to invest. If you are someone in order [*reglo*], do not come to the Congo ... You must learn to adapt. If you want to invest in Congo, you should ... it's like politics: I'm in politics, I know what to expect, and I am committed. It's the same thing for the business or other economic activities, everyone who comes here must expect corruption. This is the field and you have to learn how to navigate in it. You have to adjust to the corruption, otherwise you will not do good business ... If you refuse, they will ask you for 10,000 instead of 1,000 and your business can no longer work. Or you must officially give them a share of the business ... No, in order to invest in the Congo you have to adapt to the system, otherwise it is a waste of money.

Another returnee, Charles, whom we encountered above and who was engaged in a range of business activities, put it in a similar way with regards to customs, the state institution that tended to be described as being particularly complicated (as is the case in Cape Verde; see Chapter 8):

You have no choice. If you do not corrupt the customs you have no chance to pass. You have to accept the system. If you do not pay they can keep your stuff ten months instead of one week. There is no choice. It is a system that exists. I was not prepared for it but I have accepted it. I handle the situation – you have to adapt. You cannot have too many principles but you have to be flexible. Otherwise, you will do nothing here.

Similar accounts – describing how returnees, and anyone else interested in investing in the DRC, have to 'adapt to the system' – are repeated in the interview material. Hence, and not surprisingly, it appears that returnees conduct their businesses in a similar way to stayers, despite their self-congratulatory presentations of themselves as embodying a more superior, honest and strict work ethic. In short, returnees' narratives of their strategies of navigation therefore underscore continuity rather than discontinuity in relation to stayee businesses in terms of managing 'corruption'.

As indicated in the stories above, social networks occupy a central position in returnee narratives. In the following, I will elaborate further on how the returnees seek to navigate various 'big man' networks in order to succeed in their businesses.

## The main challenges: social capital and networks

*Navigating shifting 'big man' networks* While limited availability of economic capital due to a lack of credit was raised as a major problem by many returnees, access to 'big man' networks was presented as the main challenge. As noted earlier, 'big men' should be understood as 'nodes in [fluid] networks'

(Utas 2012: 8) rather than as a fixed label or as an inherited patron–client structure rooted in tradition. While such networks cut across state and non-state boundaries, the nodes or 'big men' who are important for returnees (and for many others) are politicians and state agents who can use their positions within the state to enable and regulate business. Being able to connect to such nodes in social networks was described as a prerequisite for a 'successful return'. As one returnee put it:

> A very important factor is the network. The contacts, the umbrellas. When you have that your chances to succeed are much better. Because then you are protected. When you personally know a minister in the government and you get a problem you call him and then he calls his colleagues who stop bothering you.

While, like the individual quoted above, some returnees (in particular foreign investment brokers) emphasised the need to connect to high-level political 'big men' such as government ministers, others recounted how they attempted to establish contacts with senior state agents in state agencies regulating and taxing their businesses. However, social navigation is not restricted to those state agents whose formal responsibilities have a bearing on an individual's activities. It is also crucial to connect to 'big men' and fixers who are not immediately useful to the business, given the multiplicity of relations, nodes and spheres of influence. For instance, it can turn out that a high-level military official, who can activate his connections to intervene in support of a returnee, is more useful to an import business entrepreneur than relationships with mid-level customs officials. In short, relationships were described as being essential in order to access required papers and permits, as well as (as expressed in the quote above) to shield people from harassment by state authorities. A majority of the returnees interviewed maintained that, without such relationships, businesses are bound to fail. As Emmanuel, who was currently employed by a private company while at the same time struggling to establish a newspaper, explained:

> One is forced to have contacts with almost all authorities, all of which are likely to come and bother you. When people come with an 'ordre de mission' to check a document for the fourteen thousandth time, though in reality it is only to try to get some money from you, you have to have someone to call who can say 'do not touch him' or 'It's already done'. You can have all the paperwork but they [the state agents] will always find something that does not work. Everywhere: the tax authorities, municipality, city hall, Ministry of Economic Affairs, Ministry of Environment ... My advantage is that almost all my friends are here and today I have friends who are advisers to various ministers, bankers, and various state agencies ... I'm trying to restore my address book to always have an umbrella and have someone who can guide me so I avoid being scammed.

Many more successful returnees attributed the relative ease with which they conducted their business to their networks. One returnee, who at the time of the interview was employed in a family-owned company but previously had tried other ventures, described the reasons for his economically stable situation in the following way, in comparison with returnees from less privileged backgrounds:

There are different groups in society. One could use the term class because it's still a kind of class distinction. If you come from a family and a social class that is quite well off then it's easier to return because even if you come back on your own you can use your parents' contacts in order to get started. Because much is about contacts. And they remember you: 'Yes, you are the son of Jean; yes, I have worked with him.' And then it will be easier to get in or get started. 'Sure, I can help you! You need a bank loan? Yes, but then we lower interest rates ...' If you come from a lower class or level of society ... you do not have the same connections, even though you would need them very much ... Those who move out and come from higher social classes know they have good opportunities to come back. They have left behind a network of contacts.

This account, which also demonstrates the important links or convertibility (Bourdieu 1986) between social and economic capital, reflects the data collected in the course of our study. As concluded initially, it is mainly migrants from privileged backgrounds who return, as they know that they have better chances of succeeding; a majority of the successful returnees we interviewed came from privileged backgrounds, with developed access to influential networks. Hence, most returnees constitute a group that could be defined as being richly bestowed with social capital.

Yet the DRC context also highlights the limitations of dominant notions of social capital. While Bourdieu's concept of social capital acknowledges that it can be lost over time (as can other forms of capital), his definition of social capital as 'the aggregate of the actual or potential resources which are linked to possession of a durable network of more or less institutionalized relationships of mutual acquaintance' (ibid.: 248) implies a sense of continuity and durability that is not well adapted to the DRC context, which is characterised by constant power struggles between different power networks and political manoeuvring through frequent rotations of office. In such a shifting context in which power networks rise, fluctuate and disintegrate and where the 'big man' of today might be without influence tomorrow, social capital is easily lost. As a consequence, it is crucial to be linked to and maintain relations with a multiplicity of 'big men' and networks, and not merely rely on one. Social navigation therefore tends to be quite demanding and time consuming, in particular for returnees who have spent much of their time abroad. As described elsewhere (see Eriksson Baaz forthcoming), some returnees argued that their diaspora status did not provide them with any privileged access to powerful networks, and they talked about their time in Europe as wasted in that it had created a relational deficit [*deficit relationnel*]. One of them was Willy, whom we encountered above (and who had engaged in a range of unsuccessful investments). When we met him, he told us that he had learned from his previous mistakes and currently spent most of his time in Kinshasa 'work[ing] on his address book':

> This week I met with the Minister of Media ... The first day I waited four hours without being received. I also scheduled a meeting with the Minister of Interior. I went there yesterday and waited from 8am to 5pm without being received. And yet I had a scheduled meeting. Today I went back to his office. There were many who were not received. On Monday, I have a scheduled meeting with the Minister of Culture since I have a project relating to that. If they do not receive me the first time I will do the same, I will continue regardless. Each day costs me about $10 for transport into town and the soda you may drink while you wait. The money I brought [this time to Kinshasa] starts to dry out. Sometimes I walk on foot from here to town. It takes two hours. But when I do not have money for transport it is not a problem. I go anyway. The problem is that when you go to visit a minister you must have a jacket and tie. It is not convenient to walk with that on. I have a determination that even makes myself surprised. Before I encountered these problems I did not know what I was capable of. Sure, I sometimes think that I should leave everything and go back to Europe permanently, but Europe is not a solution for me. I do not have much pension savings in France. If I want to have a nice and quiet old age I have to fight now. I prefer to fight now while I'm still young.

While the strategies adopted and narrated by this returnee stand out as being particularly arduous and persistent through their strong focus on ministerial levels, most returnees described their efforts to 'work on their address books' as time and energy consuming. Moreover, the narratives clearly reveal that the social capital acquired in Europe is not easily transferable to the DRC (ibid.).

*The 'dark side' of social capital* As highlighted in Chapter 1, one limitation of dominant notions of social capital is that they tend to portray social capital as benign for those who possess it. But social capital also has a 'dark side', as argued by Field (2003); this is reflected in the high levels of demands placed on migrants and returnees by their families and close, or 'bonding', networks or ties (Whitehouse 2011). One main reason for the frequent appearance of failed businesses and budgets in the interview material relates to the needs of the family. The challenge to successful businesses posed by family members' needs and requests was a recurrent theme in the interviews – particularly among those less privileged, whose conditions of return stand in stark contrast to those of returnees from privileged backgrounds. While the more privileged returnees came back to a family that could offer them contacts, business opportunities, a place to stay and funds to cover a range of expenses, others returned to families who requested assistance from them and employment opportunities in their businesses. Responding to such requests was highlighted as a major reason for failure by many returnees. As Pablo, who was setting up an agricultural project and also managed an NGO focusing on human rights, concluded:

> It is really difficult. The family always thinks that our brother is back and he has lots of money. He can help us, with this and that. That person is ill. That one cannot pay his school fees. But you need to be disciplined. You need to be a bit tight-fisted [*maboko makasi*]. Because the money you came with is not for the family but for the business. If you start helping people out, you will go bankrupt.

In addition, involving the family in the business – and letting relatives manage the business while the returnee was away – was presented as a guaranteed recipe for bankruptcy in almost all interviews. It was constantly repeated that if you want businesses to work, you have to be present in the country yourself – otherwise the money will be eaten by hungry and greedy relatives whom you (due to your family relationship) cannot discipline. For that reason, many concluded that they refrain from involving family members in their business altogether – or, if they do, they find ways to avoid letting the money pass through the hands of the family.

## Conclusions

This chapter has analysed Congolese returnee narratives from the perspective of their potential development contribution, especially with regards to the 'novelty' of their engagement. As such, it has presented a varied picture. While there seems to be a tendency to follow investment trends, some returnees have undoubtedly invested in unexploited (or underexploited) areas. In particular, migration has facilitated the creation of a (potentially) profitable niche for returnees as brokers for foreign investors. Clearly, this role also has the potential to be profitable for the Congolese economy on a larger scale. However, while these broker returnees occupy a 'new niche' in relation to foreign investment that can potentially bolster economic development, the position of the facilitator or broker is by no means a novel phenomenon in the DRC, as we have seen. Moreover, it is not obvious that such positions are disposed towards change, since they are dependent on a continuation of 'complications to fix';[8] nor can it be assumed that all foreign investment is

---

8 As argued by Piermay (1997) in the context of stayee fixers, it could be assumed that fixers/facilitators may have limited interest in change, feeding the temptation to bolster problems and obstacles in order to secure their positions.

positive to development. But, above all, the interview material demonstrates the immense challenges attached to these investment efforts (and others) and the fact that few returnees seem successful in facilitating access and deals for foreign companies.

The chapter also casts doubt on assumptions that returnees conduct their businesses in a different way when it comes to work ethics and 'managing corruption'. While many returnees in the DRC, as in many other contexts (see Chapters 4 and 6 on Ghana and Burundi respectively), often portrayed themselves as embodying a different, more superior, honest and industrious work ethic compared with that of stayers, such representations must be read as reflecting the stories returnees like to tell about themselves rather than as informed accounts of the difference between returnees and stayers. Importantly, their narratives were marked by a strong contradiction between such self-congratulatory representations of themselves and their accounts of their everyday navigation – particularly in terms of 'managing corruption'. Such accounts underscored continuity rather than discontinuity in relation to stayee businesses.

In conclusion, returnees' attempts to successfully re-establish themselves in the DRC are fraught with difficulties. As demonstrated, many fail and, in addition, have long histories of various failed investments. Accessing and navigating powerful social networks were identified as major challenges and prerequisites for a 'successful return'. Yet accessing and maintaining relationships with 'big man' networks that facilitate business are particularly demanding in the DRC context, which is characterised by frequent rotations of office and social networks in flux. In such contexts, social capital is easily lost; this in turn reveals some of the limitations in dominant notions of social capital, which tend to emphasise continuity and durability. Moreover, the chapter has also demonstrated the 'dark side' of social capital, highlighting that social capital cannot be conceptualised as inherently beneficial.

Most importantly, rather than simply *bringing* the social capital obtained in Europe *to* the DRC, the narratives demonstrate that successful return depends on the capacity and determination needed in order to *transform* social capital, and particularly to acquire *new* social capital upon return.

## Bibliography

Åkesson, L. (forthcoming) 'Multi-sited accumulation of capital: Cape Verdean returnees and small-scale business'. *Global Networks*.

Appiah, K. A (1992) *In My Father's House: Africa in the philosophy of culture*. New York NY: Oxford University Press.

Bourdieu, P. (1986) 'The forms of capital'. In J. Richardson (ed.) *Handbook of Theory and Research for the Sociology of Education*. Westport CT: Greenwood Press, pp. 15–29.

Callaghy, T. (1984) *The State-Society Struggle: Zaire in comparative perspective*. New York NY: Columbia University Press.

Demart, S. and L. Bodeux (2013) 'Postcolonial stakes of Congolese (DRC) political space: 50 years after independence'. *African Diaspora* 6: 72–96.

Englebert, P. (2003) 'Why Congo persists: sovereignty, globalization and the violent reproduction of a weak state'. Queen Elizabeth House Working Paper 95. Oxford: Oxford University.

Eriksson Baaz, M. (2005) *The Paternalism of Partnership: A postcolonial reading of identity in development aid*. London and New York NY: Zed Books.

— (forthcoming) 'Relational deficits and debilitating expectations: an exploration of the disadvantages of migration among Congolese return migrants' (article under review).

— and M. Stern (2013) 'Willing reform? An analysis of defence reform initiatives in the DRC'. In A. Bigsten (ed.) *Globalization and Development: Rethinking interventions and governance*. Abingdon and New York NY: Routledge.

— and J. Verweijen (2014) 'Arbiters with guns: the ambiguity of military involvement in civilian disputes in the DR Congo'. *Third World Quarterly* 35(5): 803–20.

Field, J. (2003) *Social Capital*. London: Routledge.

Hall, S. (1996) 'When was "the postcolonial"? Thinking at the limit'. In I. Chambers and L. Curti (eds) *The Post-colonial Question: Common skies, divided horizons*. London and New York NY: Routledge.

Koddenbrock, K. (2014) 'Malevolent politics: ICG reporting on government action and the dilemmas of rule in the Democratic Republic of Congo'. *Third World Quarterly* 35(4): 669–85.

Lardeux, L. (2012) 'De l'exil au retour: dispositifs de rapatriement et carrières migratoires des retournes congolais (RDC)'. PhD thesis, Lumière University Lyon 2, Mondes et Dynamiques des Sociétés (MODYS).

Lututala, B. (2006) 'L'ubiquité résidentielle des migrants congolais. Une enquête auprès des migrants à Paris'. *Civilisations* 54: 117–24.

MacGaffey, J. (1986) 'Fending-for-yourself:

economic organization in Zaire'. In Nzongola-Ntalaja (ed.) *The Crisis in Zaïre: Myths and realities*. Trenton NJ: Africa World Press, pp. 141–56.

— (1991) *The Real Economy of Zaire: The contribution of smuggling and other unofficial activities to national wealth*. London and Philadelphia PA: James Currey and University of Pennsylvania Press.

Mudimbe, V. Y. (1994) *The Idea of Africa*. Bloomington IN: Indiana University Press.

Piermay, J.-L. (1997) 'Kinshasa: a reprieved mega-city'. In C. Rakodi (ed.) *The Urban Challenge in Africa: Growth and management of its large cities*. Tokyo: United Nations University Press. Available at http://archive.unu.edu/unupress/ unupbooks/uu26ue/uu26ueok.htm.

Robinson, J. A. (2013) *Prosperity in Depth: Democratic Republic of Congo: Curing the mal Zaïrois: The Democratic Republic of Congo edges toward statehood*. London: Legatum Institute.

Schatzberg, M. (1988) *The Dialectics of Oppression in Zaire*. Bloomington IN: Indiana University Press.

Schoonvaere, Q. (2010) 'Etude de la migration congolaise et de son impact sur la présence congolaise en Belgique: analyse des principales données démographiques'. Brussels: Groupe d'Étude de Démographique Appliquée (GEDAP) and Centre pour l'Égalité des Chances et la Lutte contre le Racisme (CECLR).

Schoumaker, B., M.-L. Flahaux, M. Mangalu and J. Agbada (2013a) 'Changing patterns of Congolese migration'. MAFE Working Paper 19. Paris: Institut National d'Études Démographiques (INED).

Schoumaker, B., E. Castagnone, A. Phongi Kingiala, N. Rakotonarivo and T. Nazio (2013b) 'Integration of Congolese migrants in the European labour market and re-integration in DR Congo'. MAFE Working Paper 27. Paris, Institut National d'Études Démographiques (INED).

Skeldon, R. (2012) 'Going round in circles:

circular migration, poverty alleviation and marginality'. *International Migration* 50(3): 43–60.

Stearns, J., J. Verweijen and M. Eriksson Baaz (2013) *The National Army and Armed Groups in the Eastern Congo: Untangling the Gordian knot of insecurity, Usalama project*. London: Rift Valley Institute.

Stern, M. (2006) 'Racism, sexism, classism and much more: reading security-identity in marginalized sites'. In B. Ackerly, M. Stern and J. True (eds) *Feminist Methodologies for International Relations*. Cambridge: Cambridge University Press, pp. 174–99.

Sumata, C. (2002) 'Migration and poverty alleviation strategy issues in Congo'. *Review of African Political Economy* 39(93–4): 619–28.

— T. Trefon and S. Cogels (2004) 'Images et usages de l'argent de la diaspora congolaise: les transferts comme vecteur d'entretien du quotidien à Kinshasa'. In T. Trefon (ed.) *Ordre et Désordre à Kinshasa: Réponses populaires à la faillite de l'Etat*. Tervuren and Paris: Institut Africain and L'Harmattan, pp. 135–54.

Trefon, T. (ed.) (2004) *Reinventing Order in the Congo: How people respond to state failure in Kinshasa*. London: Zed Books.

— (2009) 'Public service provision in a failed state: looking beyond predation in the Democratic Republic of Congo'. *Review of African Political Economy* 36(119): 9–21.

Utas, M. (2012) 'Introduction: bigmanity and network governance in Africa'. In M. Utas (ed.) *African Conflicts and Informal Power: Big men and networks*. London: Zed Books, pp. 1–34.

Vause, S. (2011) 'Différences de genre en matière e mobilité professionnelle des migrants congolais (RDC) en Belgique'. *Espace, Population, Sociétés* 2011/2: 195–213.

Vigh, H. E. (2009) 'Motion squared: a second look at the concept of social navigation'. *Anthropological Theory* 9(4): 419–38.

Whitehouse, B. (2011) 'Enterprising strangers: social capital and social liability among African migrant traders'. *International Journal of Social Inquiry* 4(1): 93–111.

Willame, J.-C. (1992) *L'Automne d'un Despotisme: Pouvoir, argent et obéissance dans le Zaïre des années quatre-vingt*. Paris: Karthala.

Young, C. and T. Turner (1985) *The Rise and Decline of the Zairian State*. Madison WI: University of Wisconsin Press, pp. 248–75.

# 3 | Diaspora returnees to Somaliland: heroes of development or job-stealing scoundrels?

Laura Hammond

One evening in June 2012, I was asked to give a talk to a group of development studies students at the University of Hargeisa on the role of the diaspora in relief, development and politics in Somaliland. The topic was one on which I had recently concluded research. I began by asking those gathered – a roomful of mostly men in their early to mid-twenties, but also a sizeable minority of women – what they thought were the benefits and disadvantages to diaspora involvement in Somaliland. The room became emotionally charged, and dozens of hands went into the air. 'They take our jobs.' 'They drive house rent prices up.' 'They come looking for wives that they can bring back with them to their homes in America or Europe.' 'Sometimes they send their children who have gotten into trouble while living outside to live here, and they are a bad influence on our society.' These were a few of the objections people raised.

I asked how many people were receiving support from people abroad for their studies. Nearly every hand in the room went up. I then asked if there were any positive aspects to people returning. 'They bring skills and investment with them when they return.' 'They have experience working in democratic countries and can help us build our political system.' What followed was a fascinating discussion on the contentious subject of diaspora involvement and the influence of returnees on life in Somaliland, as seen from the perspective of people who had, with few exceptions, remained in the state all of their lives. This exchange was both nuanced and heated. Everyone, it seemed, had an opinion about the large number of returnees coming back to Somaliland. And everyone could see that this was not a clear-cut issue, but that the returns had both positive and negative implications.

In this chapter I explore some of the perceptions of return, from the perspective of both those returning and those in the local society. The arguments draw on a research project that I led in 2010 which considered the role of the diaspora in relief, development and peace building in Somali areas. This project, funded by the United Nations Development Programme in Somalia (UNDP-Somalia), included research in six diaspora hubs – Dubai, London, Nairobi, Minneapolis, Oslo and Toronto – as well as in Somaliland, Puntland and South Central Somalia. The research team, made up of seven researchers with long experience working in Somali areas, focused on the impact of the diaspora on local non-governmental organisations (NGOs), social service providers (SSPs) and private investment in the areas being studied (see Hammond et al. 2011). The chapter considers a subsection of the data collected during that project, particularly quantitative and qualitative data that we collected concerning those who had returned to Somaliland. A total of 159 individuals were interviewed from these sectors, including 72 representatives of local NGOs, 47 SSPs and 40 private investors. The sample included significant numbers of returnees (although respondents were selected at random) (ibid.). The chapter also includes data concerning the interaction between diaspora and local populations gathered during visits to Somaliland in 2012 and 2013 (Hammond 2013b; 2013c) and from my long-term research with Somalilanders and the Somali diaspora (from 1998 to the present).

To set the context, I begin by providing a brief history of migration out of Somaliland. This process began during the British colonial period but accelerated as the area descended into conflict during the late 1980s. Returns began with the end of the conflict in the early 1990s; they have increased as the peace has been strengthened and the capacity of the government has improved. I describe the ways in which returnees to Somaliland have become involved socially, economically and politically in their country of origin. I first examine their returns through a largely positive lens, considering the ways in which they have tried, and in many ways succeeded, to contribute to the post-war reconstruction of Somaliland. I then consider the main challenges that they have encountered, both individually and in the face of tensions that have been wrought by their interactions with wider society. I argue that return should be seen not as the end result of a migratory life story, but as the further development of the transnationally connected post-war society that Somaliland has become.

The returnees to Somaliland whom I discuss here are global citizens with a high level of mobility, strong social networks that span the globe, and very often with considerable resources to commit both to their personal return and to the development of their homeland. They are, to borrow from Horst's aptly titled book, 'transnational nomads' (Horst 2006). Having lived outside Somaliland for several years, they face significant challenges on return. Most take considerable time to feel their way, exploring an environment that has been radically changed in the years since they went into exile. Not only is the physical environment different, the social networks are also transformed. Indeed, their own return contributes to that transformation in significant ways, as I describe below. Returnees are subjects who are often carving out a new relationship to their country of origin, and towards Somaliland society, even as they maintain active ties to one or more of the countries in which they have been living since their emigration from Somaliland. My analysis challenges the notion that migration is necessarily a linear process of movement from one point to another, of adaptation or integration into a single new place. It calls into question the idea that a returnee or migrant need necessarily have a single place to which he or she feels primarily attached, and considers returnee participation in post-war reconstruction as a creative use of resources borrowed from multiple locales, often for both individual and collective benefit. I also consider the Somaliland government's attempts to adapt its development strategies to take into account diaspora and returnee engagement, seeking to harness the positive potential of both financial and human capital.

Taken together, the different sources of data considered here paint a complex picture of interaction between people living outside Somaliland and those inside it. However, rather than being a binary relationship between insiders and outsiders, the reality is much more fluid, and is closely tied to the shifting presence of returnees – people who left the country and gained permanent residence or citizenship in another country, only to return several years later to Somaliland. Returnees are not a discrete category, however. They include people who come and go, spending significant portions of the year in one or more other countries while simultaneously maintaining a home, family ties, a business and often community involvement within Somaliland. Such returnees, whom I refer to as 'part-time diaspora' (Hammond et al. 2011) and whom Hansen calls 'revolving returnees' (2007), have had an enormous impact on social, economic and political life in Somaliland.

### Who is a returnee?

During our research, which considered the role of the diaspora in relief, development and peace building, we had difficulty trying to determine to whom exactly we should apply the term 'returnee'. Reflecting on the mobility and livelihood practices of those with transnational ties, we opted to define as members of the diaspora anyone who spent three months or longer per year outside Somaliland on a regular basis. Our reasoning was that people who left Somaliland for shorter periods were likely to be embarking on family visits or holidays, whereas someone who was abroad for three months or longer was probably engaged in business, study or other activities as a resident of another country. Using the same logic, the term 'returnee' was used to refer to diaspora members who spent three months or more per year in Somaliland – they might have residence and maintain lives and immediate family members outside Somaliland, but they are also involved in the social, economic or political life inside the territory in a way that holidaymakers or others on shorter visits would not be.

As discussed below, returnees tend to settle in Somaliland's cities. They bring with them professional training and expertise, new ideas about what government should prioritise and how it should relate to its citizens, and what their own place in society should be. At the same time, many who return find it difficult to adjust to being back, not only because of the more limited infrastructure and services available, the more conservative society, and the often slow and complicated process of establishing themselves and their businesses, but also because they are met with resentment, hostility or just plain bewilderment by local residents who often see them as outsiders and as a source of competition for jobs and other resources.

## Background to migration out of Somaliland

Migration out of Somaliland began during the British colonial period, which started in the 1880s and continued until 1960. The first international migrants from Somaliland were traders and merchant seamen who established themselves in cities such as Aden and Sanaa, across the Red Sea and Gulf of Oman. Many later travelled further afield to the United Kingdom, Dubai, and other places. The next wave of Somali migrants to travel to Europe were students, selected for further education after having attended British schools in Somaliland. In the UK, where Europe's largest population of Somalilanders is settled, there are large and well-established Somali communities in the seaports of Cardiff and Liverpool and in Manchester that were founded by these first-comers (Change Institute 2009: 24). The post-World War Two economic boom brought more migrants from Somaliland to the UK; the large Somali community in east London was established during this time (Bradbury 2008: 175).

Refugees began fleeing Somaliland en masse during the late 1980s as civil war between the Somali National Movement – a liberation movement formed by the Somali diaspora in London – and the government's military engulfed the territory. Somalia President Mohamed Siad Barre ordered the national air force to bombard the capital city of Hargeisa, its planes taking off from the city's airport in repeated sorties until most of the city had been destroyed. The siege drove more than 600,000 people westward into Ethiopia, with smaller numbers seeking refuge in Djibouti, Kenya and Yemen. A small proportion of those with the greatest financial resources or with relatives who had already migrated out of the region eventually made their way further afield, most settling in Europe, North America and the Middle East. Today, in addition to the UK, there are large Somali communities throughout Europe – including large numbers of Somalilanders – in the Netherlands, Norway, Sweden, Denmark and Italy.

The collapse of the government of Somalia in Mogadishu in 1991 brought an end to the worst of the fighting in Somaliland, and paved the way for the establishment of a de facto independent state that year in the former British protectorate, even as the fighting continued throughout much of the rest of the country. The peace was temporarily shattered in 1994–95 with the outbreak of the 'Airport War', a clan-based dispute in Hargeisa, but since that time peace has prevailed, for the most part. Despite operating without international recognition for 23 years, the government of Somaliland has established a bicameral parliament with a clan-nominated house of elders, or *guurti*, and an elected council of representatives. It has successfully held two presidential elections, the more recent of which in 2010 involved the smooth transition of power from the incumbent, Dahir Riyale Kahin, to his opponent, Ahmed Mohamed Mohamoud, better known by his nickname 'Silanyo'. The government has developed the ability to provide rudimentary basic services in most parts of Somaliland, including free primary education and healthcare for all.[1]

As the conflict ended and peace returned to Somaliland, refugee outflows to the camps and cities in neighbouring countries were gradually reversed. Large-scale assisted return from Ethiopia during the late 1990s saw approximately 200,000 refugees returning (Ambroso 2002). Many of these returnees have been settled in camps on the outskirts of the city of Hargeisa and two decades later continue to live in precarious and hazardous conditions. They lack access to clean water, adequate housing and basic services such as education and healthcare. In 2014, the government of Somaliland, with support from the Danish and Norwegian governments as well as the United Nations High Commissioner for Refugees (UNHCR), UN-Habitat and the United Nations Office for the Coordination of Humanitarian Affairs (UNOCHA), sought to relocate some of the returnees in more permanent housing (Sabahi Online 2013). This is a process that is long overdue, but at the time of writing it is too soon to know how successful the scheme will be.

The refugees who had moved further from Somaliland – to Europe, North America, Australia and Asia – have been slower to return and are fewer in number, but it can be argued that they have had more of an impact on Somaliland society than their poorer compatriots. It is these returnees who are the subject of this chapter.

The Somali diaspora – including those from Somaliland as well as from the rest of the territory now recognised as Somalia – is estimated at roughly 1 million to 1.5 million people. Exact numbers are difficult to come by given that many destination countries keep records only of people of African origin, or, if population figures on Somalis are available, they include those from Somaliland, Puntland and South Central Somalia as a single category. Figures also typically include only those born within Somalia, and do not include children born to refugees and migrants outside the country. Over time, this makes any attempt at determining the real number of Somalis living in the

---

1 Despite the fact that primary education is free, a lack of schools, poor infrastructure and the extreme poverty of communities has resulted in a net enrolment level of only 49 per cent in 2010, the most recent year for which statistics are available (Republic of Somaliland 2011: 262).

diaspora extremely difficult. Does one count the children of someone who came to the UK as a refugee or a student if those children were born abroad? Does one count those who were born in the refugee camps of Kenya or Ethiopia and then later resettled in Europe and are now young adults? In the United Kingdom, current estimates of the number of Somali residents range from 95,000 to 250,000. The Office for National Statistics gives a total for the number of people living in the UK but born in Somalia as 115,000 (APS 2011), but this figure does not include those who were born outside the country. Nor, of course, does it count those who lack legal status and are therefore likely to have opted not to be counted. According to UK Census figures from 2001, 89 per cent of all UK Somalis were living in London. This percentage is almost certainly lower now as a result of a dispersal policy introduced in 1999 as well as considerable secondary migration of Somalis from other EU countries, in particular the Netherlands (there is a large Somali-Dutch community in the city of Leicester; see van Liempt 2011). Large Somali communities have subsequently formed in Bristol, Birmingham and other cities. People tend to settle mostly, though not exclusively, among their clan relatives, upon whom they can depend for social and economic support.

Evidence from multiple countries in Europe and North America suggests that a sizeable proportion of Somali migrants plan to eventually return to Somalia or Somaliland. Data from a survey of living conditions in Norway indicates that 30 per cent of Somalis in Oslo 'expect to return to the country of origin' (Government of Norway 2007). People move between the UK and Somaliland easily. There is a Somaliland consulate in London, while regular flights to Hargeisa via Addis Ababa (Ethiopia), Dubai or Nairobi (Kenya) make such travel easy, if expensive. A 2013 survey of remittance senders found that 25 per cent of relatives who sent funds were located in the United Kingdom; this was the largest representation of any country, and many of these relatives not only send money to their relatives, they come back regularly for extended periods as well (Hammond 2013b).

While people are attracted by the idea of returning to Somaliland now that the environment is safer, many are reluctant to act on that impulse until they have regularised their immigration status. Only once they have secured permanent residence, and in some cases full citizenship, in their country of resettlement or immigration do they feel willing and able to return to Somaliland. This may be partly explained by the fact that Somaliland passports are not recognised internationally; it is also difficult to travel on Somalia passports if they are still valid, since they are easy to forge. People prefer, therefore, to travel once they have a European or North American passport. Having a European passport also enables them to leave Somaliland if their planned re-entry does not go as well as they hope it will. The documentation also entitles them to establish a mobile livelihood, moving to and fro between two (or more) places, maintaining homes and business activities in those places. They usually keep their children in schools in the diaspora country while one or other parent spends time in Somaliland.

The protracted nature of the asylum and settlement process in most countries where Somalis emigrate means that it usually takes many years before an individual or family receives permanent residence. Legally recognised refugees are prohibited from returning to the country from which they have fled, although in practice people with multiple passports may be able to circumvent this restriction by travelling on a passport other than the one associated with their refugee status. I have argued elsewhere that, whereas opponents of migration may claim that quick and/or easy settlement processes can act as a pull factor and encourage more people to seek to settle in a destination country, facilitating faster regularisation could have the counterintuitive effect of enabling people to return to their country of origin sooner (Hammond 2013a). I have interviewed many individuals who have said that they are merely waiting in Britain for their citizenship papers to come through, and then they plan to return to Somalia or Somaliland for at least part of the year. Some say that they intend to return permanently.

### Return to Somaliland

Beginning in the late 1990s, the number of returns from Europe and North America to Somaliland began to increase. Some came first for short visits to test the waters, to check on the condition of their property, and to look for business opportunities. The two largest cities, Hargeisa and Burco,[2] had been almost completely destroyed, so those who wanted to return either had to find new housing or renovate or rebuild their damaged homes. I spent a year living in Hargeisa in 1998; at that time there was no public electricity or water supply – these resources were available only for a fee from private suppliers. Most houses lacked roofs, and people who had returned were just beginning to rebuild.

Fifteen years later, the city has undergone a dramatic transformation. Gone are the rubble-lined streets and people living in temporary shelters outside the ruins of their stone houses. Freshly painted homes of all sizes spread across the city, including into new areas that were previously scrubland at the edges of the city. Some of these houses are like small palaces – very large structures with enormous walls surrounding a compound. One neighbourhood, on the southern side of the city, is referred to as 'Half London' in recognition of the many returnees who have come back to the city from the UK. Several new hotels advertising themselves as being of 'international standard' have opened, one of the largest being owned by a returnee from the UK. The political elites gather at the Maan-Soor and Ambassador hotels (the only two places certified

---

2 Pronounced Burao.

as having the necessary security protection to enable international aid workers to stay, but also attractive to the Somali elites of the city) – the choice still largely depends on which clans they belong to – but diaspora returnees also fill the likes of the smaller and slightly more modest Safari and Oriental hotels.

Hargeisa in particular is being transformed by the short- and long-term return of people from the diaspora. During the summer months the city is booming with weddings, conferences and cultural events. Restaurants compete for the business of returnees – the young, hip *'dayuusboro'* or *'qurba-joog'* (diaspora returnees) gather at the Summertime restaurant, or at Fish and Steak (which specialises in fresh fish from Berbera – fish having become more popular among returnees than with local residents – as well as pizza), while those with young families head to the swings and slides at Gulaid Park or one of the playground centres on the edge of the city. In the summer, diaspora returnees host house parties for their friends who have also returned from the same countries – the Danish Somalis, Dutch Somalis, or 'Fish and Chips' (as British Somalis are known) seeking out others like them to compare notes on their return visits and talk about life in their other home.

While some people return only for their summer holidays to visit their relatives, others have returned for longer periods, and increasing numbers are making the move permanently. Suldan, who worked for an international organisation for many years, decided to return to Somaliland after his retirement; he now works as a part-time adviser to one of the key ministries and lives close to other members of his family who have also returned from abroad in houses they have built recently. He says that he is happy to be back in Somaliland. He is reunited with his old friends and relatives, and has been able to contribute to the development of his homeland.

Many older Somalilanders say that, after years away, they were eager to return to the place that they came from, where people *know* them – to know someone is to have been a child with them, to know their family members and their history – and where they are respected and valued.

### Dhaqan ceelis and changing cultural norms

While older people are returning to Somaliland to retire, or to work for a few more years before they retire, another group of younger Somalilanders is also returning, though not always voluntarily. Some diaspora parents are sending their teenage children to go to school in Somaliland in order, they say, to learn about their heritage and to instil in them a stronger respect for cultural and religious ideals. Many of these young people have run into trouble with gangs, substance abuse or poor performance at school in their diaspora homes. They are referred to as *dhaqan ceelis*, or young people who have lost their culture and are sent back to Somaliland to live with their extended family or to attend boarding school. Abaarso Tech, a secondary boarding school founded in 2008, reportedly has several children in attendance who have returned from the UK. While some of the youth have embraced being sent back, many see it as a punishment and are eager to leave.

Despite the influences from the returning diaspora, Somaliland society has in some ways become more conservative than it was when I first lived there. Women's dress and behaviour are more conservative. Whereas previously more women wore brightly coloured *dirac* – long, gauzy dresses with short sleeves – more women now wear black *abayas* that cover them completely, and they are more likely to wear full *hijab* – a covering over their hair, neck and shoulders, and often even covering their faces as well when out in public. This trend towards conservative behaviour may be seen as the result of the increased impact of religious practice in daily life due to imported influences (from outside the Horn of Africa as well as from other Somali territories) and a greater embrace of religion as a way of providing order and security in an environment in which the relatively weak state has not been able to provide these basic functions.

Somali families in the diaspora face some of the same challenges: youth often lack effective male role models because their fathers are permanently or periodically absent, while girls are considered to be at risk of abandoning honourable Islamic practice. Returning their children to Somaliland is seen as a way of reinforcing positive cultural influences.

## Support to civil society organisations

Many people return during the summer holidays, not only to immerse themselves in Somali culture and visit relatives but also to volunteer their services at hospitals, in government offices, and with local NGOs. The Hargeisa International Book Fair, a cultural extravaganza of free poetry readings, appearances by Somali and international authors and musical performances, has been held every year since 2008 and draws hundreds of people each day for a week. The book fair is the product of Ayan Mohamoud, based in London with Dutch citizenship, and Italian Somalilander Jama Musse Jama. Each year, dozens of diaspora returnees volunteer their time to host the event. International diplomats time their visits to coincide with the book fair, and for a week the city is transformed into a place of culture and fun. So successful have the organisers been that they have recently secured funding to open a cultural centre in Hargeisa, with a library and performance space, to be able to work on an ongoing basis.

Many who return from the diaspora seek to become involved in the development of Somaliland, often through involvement with civil society organisations. These organisations provide paid and voluntary work opportunities, entry points for entrepreneurial activities, and outlets for political participation that are attractive to diaspora returnees. The Edna Adan University Hospital, a private hospital opened by Somaliland's first trained midwife in 1998, hosts several Somali volunteer and trainee health professionals at any given time. Many Somalis, including those youth who left the country when they were small children, have chosen to study fields that prepare them for practical work in healthcare, education, business administration or development. They say that they have done so at least in part so that they can have a skill to bring back to Somaliland. Indeed, this appears to be one of the reasons why people return – to find more fulfilling work and to escape the marginalisation and exclusion that many Somali migrant communities are exposed to in societies where they have resettled.

Our 2011 survey considered three kinds of civil society actors: local NGOs, SSPs, and private investors who run medium- to large-scale businesses. In our study of diaspora-supported organisations, we found that all three kinds of institutions were benefiting from in-kind support given by people who have returned either temporarily or permanently. Forty-three per cent of local NGOs reported that they received in-kind support from people in the diaspora, mostly through people returning to work with them. Thirty-three per cent said that they had staff from the diaspora. In the private sector, just over half of the respondents said that they had spent time living abroad. Civil society institutions reported that returnees provide advice, leadership, training and other human assets in their organisations.

The motivations of those who return to provide such technical support appear to be mixed. One businessman who had returned from the USA commented:

I think we teach people values that are perhaps lacking here at this particular time. It's all there in our tradition, but much has been lost in the transition from rural to peri-urban to urban living. Values like hard work, commitment, and good and consistent work ethics are inherent in our tradition. I find it rather ironic that I'm importing these values from the USA. Without these values, pastoralism would never have seen the light of day and we all know what pastoralism means to this country and its people.

When asked what challenges he had faced in returning to Somaliland and beginning his business, he said:

this place is full of challenges. Aside from the bigger things like the lack of the many conveniences that have made my life abroad so much easier, most challenges are very personal. I returned to a place that is completely different from the way I left it. The land is different, the social and political landscape is different, and even the environment is different. The days of enjoying listening to the *galool* (*Acacia bussel*) whistle in the wind are long gone. I too am not safe from the perils of metamorphosis; returning with a new perspective and personal identity is part of the challenge. Naturally, the result of all this is a clash of ideals and nostalgia and a new reality spawned by the legacy of war. Trust and understanding are two very difficult things to achieve when engaging with the locals. This could only mean that I too am benefiting from all of this, learning from the locals.

This reference to the process of learning from locals is an important one. In multiple conversations with local and returnee Somalilanders, we were told that the tensions that exist between returnees and locals – which will be further discussed below – can be minimised if returnees take the time to listen to locals and to try to understand their perspectives and priorities rather than imposing their own judgements on them.

*Returnees starting up or working for local NGOs* Many local NGOs in Somaliland, including the biggest and most successful, have been started or managed by those returning from North America and Europe. Typically, returnees receive some form of financial support from relatives and friends living abroad when they set up the NGO, and they then try to find support in the long run through grants for particular projects by other donors, including international aid agencies. For many years people have returned to Somaliland and have engaged with local NGOs that are involved in the development of the region. Previously, returnees tended to stay in Somaliland for – at most – only a couple of years and then would leave again to return to their homes in the diaspora. Respondents said that increasingly people are settling in Somaliland more permanently. As the infrastructure improves, they are also bringing their spouses and children with them. Several private primary schools offering English-language education have opened, with teachers brought from Kenya and Ethiopia as well as Somali returnees. Although these schools charge fees that are prohibitive for most locals, they are easily affordable for returnees with access to foreign currency.

Returnees engaged in local NGOs typically have educational, language, IT and management skills from the West that are important assets when applying for funds, communicating with donors and setting up and running a development or relief organisation. Moreover, besides having formal skills, they often have an inside understanding of how the development field works and what kinds of projects are likely to get funding, as many of them also have work experience with international development organisations. In this sense, diaspora returnees have an advantage vis-à-vis the local population, which typically lacks these kinds of skills. Besides being able to work within their field of expertise, bring back skills to Somaliland and participate in the development of their homeland, many also seek employment with local and international NGOs in order to be able to earn a comfortable salary. Locals somewhat cynically refer to these self-made development professionals as 'laptop cowboys'.

The many temporary volunteers from the diaspora also bring important human skills to local NGOs. These include expertise in communication, language teaching, workshop and conference organising with non-Somalis, reporting to donors, and so on. They typically have up-to-date IT competencies that are used, for example, to set up homepages targeting the diaspora. Many have studied development or social science at a Western university and use a visit to Somaliland as a means of gaining some practical research or development experience. In addition, diaspora volunteers reportedly help create a bridge between local NGOs and potential supporters living abroad by advocating for the work of the NGO in terms that funders recognise and value.

Several sponsored voluntary return programmes have sought to place Somali professionals in temporary employment for periods ranging from a few months to more than a year (see Horst et al. 2010 for examples of programmes supported by European governments). Perhaps the longest running of these is the Qualified Expatriate Somali Technical Support–Migration for Development in Africa (QUESTS–MIDA) programme, administered by the International Organization for Migration and UNDP-Somalia. This project places people for periods ranging from a few to 18 months in positions in the government administration. Participants are paid a salary and it is hoped that they will train national staff to take over from them by the time their placement ends. Some participants in the project have stayed on in Somaliland once their placements are over, working in the private sector. However, many say that they are not able to stay because they do not feel they can resettle their family back in Somaliland or because they do not think that the infrastructure is adequate.

*Political participation* Diaspora returnees engaged with local NGOs say that they believe they are contributing to the development of Somaliland. They also believe that, by engaging with and strengthening civil society, they can play an important role in challenging the political establishment. Many speak out in public forums or, through their connections with diaspora communities, provide an independent monitoring function that helps further the causes of democratisation and human rights. Women heads of organisations also stressed that they are able to challenge traditional gender roles in Somaliland by becoming leaders within civil society. They lobby the political establishment and international development community to promote the rights and opportunities of women in Somaliland society. However, despite women's involvement in civil society, they have not yet been a significant presence in formal politics. Only a few women have served as cabinet ministers and very few have served in parliament or on local councils.

During political campaign seasons, many people have returned to Somaliland to work for their preferred candidates and parties. With links to fundraisers in the diaspora, they are able to help set up campaign offices and prepare publicity materials, but they also influence the formation of political platforms and campaign strategies (see Hammond 2012). In the 2010 election, the Kulmiye party of Somali British candidate Silanyo won the presidency; Kulmiye was widely considered to have the strongest diaspora support base. President Silanyo's cabinet included several prominent returnees, including the Minister of Foreign Affairs and the Minister of Planning, both of whom relocated from London to take up their posts. One-third to a half of the presidential cabinet is typically composed of returnees from the diaspora, some of whom are selected even before they have returned. During 2011 fieldwork in Somaliland, informants estimated that between 20 and 30 per cent of members of parliament were from the diaspora, and fully one-half of President Silanyo's first cabinet were returnees.

*Settling in the cities* Thus far, most returnee diaspora activity in Somaliland has been focused on Hargeisa, and to a lesser extent Burco. Even those returnees who are originally from other areas have come to these cities when they return. This is due to the more developed infrastructure and more vibrant business climate. One returnee from the Sanaag region of eastern Somaliland explained why so few people were returning to those areas:

> I don't think Sanaag has a diaspora at all. I mean, it does and there are many people from this region who have migrated to all corners of this globe ... but where are its diaspora? You look at the diaspora of Hargeisa and Awdal and you wonder has no one left this place [Sanaag] to return, to help, to even look back? Many of the region's returning diaspora are based in Hargeisa and other regions. Many of the diaspora who are active in the development and reconstruction of this country as a whole are actually originally from this region. Government officials, prominent development workers, and private investors are all from this region originally. But what have they done for this region specifically? You look at many of the institutions, civil society and private and public clinics and you are bound to find individuals from this region who are either leading these initiatives or making significant contributions. It is very sad, however, that their home region continues to fall further behind as a result of their efforts. All in all, the diaspora of this region are not involved ... Don't get me wrong, though, they do help out. Many families live on the remittances sent by their sons, daughters, brothers, sisters and relatives.

He explained, however, that very often even those who receive remittances from relatives living abroad use the money they receive to relocate closer to the urban centres:

> It's somewhat ironic that while at the family level remittances were sustaining the lives of many households, remittances encourage recipients to move to other regions looking for better education and health services. That's the difference they are making, inadvertently further depopulating this region.

*Short-term returns: a resource for development* Return visits are important catalysts for support. One such example is an orphanage in Hargeisa that has received support from diaspora returnees who came to Somaliland to visit. Having seen the needs of the orphanage, these visitors felt they should do something to support it. Previously, the diaspora had supported the orphanage by sending funds to buy food and equipment, but according to one woman who had returned on a part-time basis from Canada and who was involved in supporting the orphanage, once in Somaliland they realised that there was more they could do by working with the local community to also provide support. They started to inform the local population about the needs of the orphanage and initiated a discussion about how local people could help rather than waiting for assistance from abroad. They collected funds from local business people and secured support from the local government in Hargeisa to engage professionals (such as doctors and accountants) to bring their expertise to the orphanage. They also set up a 'sponsor a child' scheme for local benefactors, and recruited local women to wash clothes and clean the orphanage for free. More than simply bringing funds, goods and services to the orphanage, the diaspora returnees said that they feel they have helped bring a new mentality to the local population of Somaliland – that they can do something themselves, that they should not sit back simply waiting for remittances or support from the international community, but that they should take responsibility themselves. In the opinion of one supporter, the transfer of values and practices from the diaspora to Somaliland (i.e. the transfer of social remittances) is even more important than the transfer of financial remittances or the sending of charity, as it directly affects local cultural values such as gender roles, ownership over development, patriotism and entrepreneurship.

### Private investment: a partnership between local, diaspora and returnee investors

In our survey of private investors in Somaliland, a little more than half (53 per cent) said that they were returnees from abroad. Returnees own most of the larger hotels and restaurants. They are major shareholders in the money transfer and telecommunications companies. In addition, they have opened franchises of large businesses such as Coca-Cola (begun by a returnee who attended university in the United Kingdom). These businessmen and -women are part of a significant trend that is bringing increasing investment into the area. Their actions, however, may have multiple motivations, including personal ambition or a desire for profit, the aspiration to help promote recovery and development in Somaliland, or a combination of both. An investor who had returned from the UK to Sanaag explained:

> I often hear people raving about the level of investment that's happening here from abroad. Well, it is most often a favourable conscious decision that the

diaspora make for themselves first and foremost: this is the easiest place we could do this. It would take twice, thrice even, the effort, time and financial prowess to do the same in Virginia [USA]. If it's making a difference, that's an unintended positive outcome. But I don't think the two are that interrelated.

Another man who had returned to Erigavo from the USA was more positive about his motivations, although he agreed that there were advantages to working in Somaliland over the US:

You have to keep things in perspective: I employ 13 people; I provide monthly assistance to a dozen households or more; I'm squeezed for money almost every day by relatives, friends, and complete strangers alike. That's big. I'm needed here and I'm making a difference in the lives of so many people. In the USA, I would be just another number. I try to keep that reality at the forefront of my overall outlook on this place and my people.

Private investment in Somali areas has traditionally operated on a share company basis, with individuals contributing a share of the overall start-up costs for a business and then collecting a share of the profits once they start to accrue. Many companies and businesses in Somaliland, like some of the NGOs, involve shareholders from both inside and outside the region. Some are based predominantly or exclusively in the diaspora; others are returnees; still others are local business people who have never migrated. These kinds of partnerships can also involve a sharing of technical skills – diaspora and returnee partners contribute their skills and fresh ideas, but they find that businesses must also rely on the skills, social networks and cultural capital of local business people. Effective partnerships are those that successfully manage to tap into the different skills of all the different kinds of shareholders.

*The Somaliland government's efforts to attract returnees* As noted above, the Somaliland administration is no stranger to courting the diaspora and encouraging the return of both people and capital. The government has increasingly become involved in trying to influence investment and remittance flows in order to fulfil its development goals. In 2012, Somaliland established the Somaliland Development Corporation (SDC) with assistance from the UK government and several prominent members of the Somaliland diaspora to attract investment from Somali and non-Somali sources. The Somaliland government has also established a Somaliland Diaspora Liaison Office (SDLO), which provides advice to would-be investors, hosts trade fairs, and lobbies on behalf of the business interests of those who have returned as well as those who want to invest while remaining abroad. The Somaliland *National Development Plan* for 2012–16 (Republic of Somaliland 2011) includes a section dedicated to diaspora engagement. The plan commits:

To further facilitate the flow of Diaspora capital and know-how, the government will encourage Diaspora engagement by: (i) Establishing [a] National Diaspora development trust fund, (ii) Developing private investment funds that target the Diaspora, (iii) offering special tax exempt savings accounts for the Diaspora, (iv) Supporting Diaspora community development organisations, (v) Initiating Diaspora youth and professionals volunteers exchange and placement schemes, and (vi) Promoting Diaspora cultural tourism.

In a further attempt to capitalise on the large flows of remittance money being sent to Somaliland and to direct them towards the government's development priorities, the *National Development Plan* includes a scheme to ask Somalilanders living abroad for a US$1 voluntary contribution for every remittance transaction sent to Somaliland. According to the plan:

> The Diaspora will be asked to contribute just US$1 for every send transaction to a special trust fund. Annual remittance from the Diaspora is estimated to be in the order of US$500 to US$600 million. Average remittance is about US$300, which implies 1.8 million transactions per year on average. Assuming that only 25% of the remitters comply in the first year and that an annual 10% increase thereafter is realized, achieving 65% compliance by 2016, contributions in the first year will amount to US$0.45 million and are expected to rise to US$1.17 [million] by 2016. The trust fund will be managed by a trust board with members representing the government, the private sector and civic societies. The fund will be used exclusively to finance capital projects within the five-year National Development Plan. The government will also encourage the Diaspora to invest in the country and will provide the necessary incentives to entice them (ibid.: 320–1).

In 2012, the Minister of Planning, Sa'ad Shire, presented the *National Development Plan* to a mixed group of Somali diaspora, UK law makers, other government staff and members of the public at a briefing held in the House of Commons in London. Members of the diaspora welcomed the Minister of Planning's announcement about the voluntary contribution but asked him why the government did not make the payment obligatory. 'We do not want to force people to pay,' he replied. 'We are confident that if we ask people to make the contribution, they will do so freely.'

These vehicles for channelling investment are experiments that have yet to be proven to be effective. If the Somaliland diaspora and part-time returnees can be persuaded to invest through the SDC or the SDLO, then the government may be able to harness more of the economic benefit of the diaspora. However, while some returnee investors may seek to take advantage of these services, it is likely that most returnee investors will look first to their own family and clan networks to identify business opportunities.

So far, the picture painted here of returnee involvement in Somaliland shows it as having many positive aspects. One local business leader remarked: 'People from the diaspora have prestige – people here see them as competent. Those from the diaspora can make a difference. They have experience in other countries. They are [also] less ruled by clannism.' While such positive perspectives are widespread, they are not held by everyone, and even some of those who are positive about some aspects of returnee contributions to development are critical in other ways, as will be discussed below.

## Diaspora as scoundrels

I began this chapter by suggesting that the return of people from the diaspora constitutes not only an opportunity but also a challenge for Somaliland society. I turn now to consider this more problematic nature of returns.

In recent years, as the number and rate of returns has increased, the impact on urban life in Hargeisa has become more pronounced. While new businesses catering to the consumer needs of the diaspora have opened and have created new jobs for many local residents, there is still a widespread public perception that too many jobs, particularly those requiring high-skilled workers, have been taken up by returnees. Local graduates of the many universities in the city complain that they have to compete with returnees for jobs and often lose out to them, even if the returnees do not have as strong a skill set or understand the local context as well as they do. They see that those who have left Somaliland, even if they have not done well or have returned without money, are accorded greater social status than those who have remained behind. This encourages young people to aspire to leave the country. Yet without travel documents, and very often without much money, the journey out of Somaliland is perilous. Many people travel to one of the port towns and try to buy a place on a dhow travelling to Yemen. These overcrowded and often unseaworthy vessels, as well as unscrupulous smugglers, have been responsible for the deaths of thousands of refugees and migrants. Others try to travel northwards to the north coast of Africa to travel across the Mediterranean Sea, another extremely hazardous journey. Despite hearing about the dangers of these routes, many young people still seek to try their luck with one of them.

Many returnees have prepared for their return by having houses built for themselves and/or their families in Somaliland before they actually arrive back to take up residence. Some of these buildings, as noted, are extremely large, and the families rent them out to international organisations or to commercial users, using the rent as an income source. Some local residents complain that the rent of even basic one-room dwellings has gone up due to the demand from diaspora returnees.

There is a perception among some local Somalilanders that returnee politicians are in fact not as skilled or as knowledgeable as they would like others to believe. Some informants said that they think that many returnee politicians are only in Somaliland because they are unable to make a living in the diaspora, and as such have returned because of their lack of qualifications and personal capacities. Moreover, some returnee politicians are said to be ignorant of local values and political practices. Like their younger compatriots, they are often referred to as *dhaqan ceelis*, and accused of having 'lost their culture'. Thirdly, returnee politicians are often thought to be arrogant towards locals in that they do not take time to learn from them about their problems, or to learn from local politicians about how to go about their political work. Also, they are often not physically in Somaliland very much, spending a great part of the year abroad with their families. This gives the impression, whether justified or not, that they are not really committed to Somaliland. Fourthly, and related to the above, some returnee politicians are said to be less pragmatic and opportunistic and less open to local political support through the clan system.

Some returnee politicians are said to openly use and inflame clan antagonism and loyalties to secure their own political careers. However, in the eyes of many local Somalilanders, the idea that a politician would defer to his clan's interests in all matters is in reality out of sync with how the clan influences politics. Clans regularly make compromises and alliances between each other, and these shifting dynamics are the stuff of which daily political practices are made. In fact, some argue that because local politicians have been through war and mediation together, and have worked together to forge a new state in the aftermath of the conflict, they are accustomed to finding compromises with one another and therefore display a more open political culture than returnee politicians who are often more idealistic and 'radical' in their political stance. Returnees are said to often take the clan as a more rigid structure than necessary, and not to engage in clan matters as flexibly as those who understand how clan structures work in contemporary Somaliland. Finally, the fact that political parties are largely funded by the diaspora means that returnee politicians (as well as some locals) are not primarily accountable to the local population in Somaliland, but instead see other members of the diaspora as their main constituency.

*Returnees as threats to society* Not only do parents of misguided young people worry about the influence of diaspora countries, many local residents complain that diaspora returnees – not just the *dhaqan ceelis* but more broadly – bring with them harmful influences. Returnees are accused of bringing alcohol, drugs and promiscuity into the community and posing a threat to the religious fabric of society. Women's roles are said to have been affected in inappropriate ways by women who have spent time living abroad and then return to Somaliland expecting to be able to live in the same way or to influence other women to also defy social mores. While it may be true that many women living abroad have been influenced by their experiences, it has also been my observation over the past 15 years, and as noted above, that gender roles have become much more conservative in recent years. This is therefore not so much a clash between tradition and modernity, but between competing influences on gender norms.

## Conclusion

In this chapter I have argued that diaspora return constitutes both an opportunity and a challenge for the returnees themselves as well as for wider Somaliland society. Whereas government and some international actors have tried to guide the influence of the diaspora and of returnees' financial and human contributions in order to maximise their impact on development, these efforts do not appear to have had much success. Where returnees have made a huge difference has been in their own interactions with local residents. This impact has been largely positive, but not entirely so. Their engagement with locals in Somaliland society is sometimes welcomed, but also sometimes resented, particularly where diaspora returnees are seen to be taking away the chances of others, whether in employment, marriage, the securing of affordable housing, or accessing political power.

Those returnees who have been most successful in their return process have achieved this by moving slowly, learning from local people, and coming to understand people's interests, priorities and worries. By gaining the trust of local residents, they have come to be accepted and are seen as having integrated back into Somaliland society. Development investments that have worked best have been partnerships that exploit the resources of both returnees and locals most effectively. Returnees have brought about an accelerated emergence of a wealthy class, and this is not universally welcomed.

Whether, and in which direction, returnees from Somaliland's diaspora will continue to influence their society of origin will depend on their ability to garner this trust and be welcomed and accepted. This will also depend on returnees treading a careful line between cosmopolitanism and loyalty to the social and political identity of Somaliland. Somaliland as a territory has a great deal to gain from harnessing the potential benefits of diaspora and returnee engagement, but such a positive outcome should not be taken for granted.

## Acknowledgements

The author would like to thank her collaborators on this research: Mustafa Awad, Ali Ibrahim Dagane, Peter Hansen, Cindy Horst, Ken Menkhaus and Lynette Obare. Much of the research that forms the basis of this chapter was part of a project commissioned by UNDP-Somalia on diaspora involvement in relief, development and peacebuilding. The views expressed here are entirely those of the author, and should not be taken as the positions of either UNDP-Somalia or the other collaborators in the research.

## Bibliography

Ambroso, G. (2002) 'Pastoral society and transnational refugees: population movements in Somaliland and eastern Ethiopia 1988–2000'. New Issues in Refugee Research Working Paper 65. Geneva: Evaluation and Policy Analysis Unit, United Nations High Commissioner for Refugees (UNHCR).

APS (2011) *Population by Country of Birth and Nationality, April 2010 to March 2011.* Newport: Office for National Statistics, Annual Population Survey (APS).

Bradbury, M. (2008) *Becoming Somaliland: Understanding Somaliland and Somalia.* Bloomington IN: Indiana University Press.

Change Institute (2009) *The Somali Muslim Community in England.* London: Change Institute, Communities and Local Government.

Government of Norway (2007) *LKI (Living Conditions of Immigrants) Survey.* Oslo: Government of Norway.

Hammond, L. (2004) *This Place Will Become Home: Refugee repatriation to Ethiopia.* Ithaca NY: Cornell University Press.

— (2012) 'The absent but active constituency: the role of the Somaliland UK community in election politics'. In P. Mandaville and T. Lyons (eds) *Politics from Afar: Transnational diasporas and networks.* London: C. Hurst and Co., pp. 157–80.

— (2013a) 'Somali transnational activism and integration in the UK: mutually supporting strategies'. *Journal of Ethnic and Migration Studies* 39(6): 1001–17.

— (2013b) *Family Ties: Remittances and support in Puntland and Somaliland.* Nairobi: Food and Nutrition Security Analysis Unit, Food and Agriculture Organization.

— (2013c) *Safety, Security and Socio-Economic Wellbeing in Somaliland.* Hargeisa: Danish Demining Group.

— M. Awad, A. I. Dagane, P. Hansen, C. Horst, K. Menkhaus and L. Obare (2011) *Cash and Compassion: The Somali diaspora's contribution to relief, development and peacebuilding.* Nairobi: United Nations Development Programme (UNDP).

Hansen, P. (2007) 'Revolving returnees: meanings and practices of transnational return among Somalilanders'. PhD thesis, University of Copenhagen.

Horst, C. (2006) *Transnational Nomads: How Somali refugees cope with life in the Dadaab camps of Kenya.* Oxford: Berghahn Books.

— P. Pirkkalainen, R. Ezzati, V. Saggiomo, M. Guglielmo, G. Sinatti, P. Mezzetti and A. Warnecke (2010) *Participation of Diasporas in Peacebuilding and Development. A Handbook for Practitioners and Policymakers.* PRIO Report 2. Oslo: Peace Research Institute of Oslo (PRIO).

Republic of Somaliland (2011) *National Development Plan* (2012–2016). Hargeisa: Republic of Somaliland, Ministry of National Planning and Development. Available at http://slministryof planning.org/images/front-page/ndp-%20 somaliland-national-development-plan%20-%20final.pdf.

Sabahi Online (2013) 'Internally displaced persons relocated from camps in Hargeisa'. 7 November. Available at http://allafrica.com/ stories/201311080091.html.

van Liempt, I. C. (2011) '"And then one day they all moved to Leicester": the relocation of Somalis from the Netherlands to the UK explained'. *Population, Space and Place* 17(3): 254–66. Available at http://dspace.library.uu.nl/handle /1874/209751.

# 4 | Pushing development: a case study of highly skilled male return migration to Ghana

Nauja Kleist

In May 2014, the Ghanaian Ministry of Foreign Affairs and Regional Integration (MFA&RI) organised a diaspora engagement forum with support from the German Society for International Cooperation (Deutsche Gesellschaft für Internationale Zusammenarbeit or GIZ). The forum targeted international migrants as well as returnees because, as Mrs Mercy Debrah Karikari, Director of Administration in the MFA&RI, explained:

> the views of Ghanaian returnees and peoples of African descent who have lived and worked in varied circumstances abroad and at home are important. They have ... re-integrated in Ghana successfully and have been able to establish viable businesses in the country (GNA 2014).

The aim of the forum was to fashion a Ghanaian diaspora policy for engagement in national development, with promoting the return of international migrants as only one of the objectives. Nevertheless, Mrs Karikari's statement reflects a widespread understanding of the benefits of return migration to Ghana. Highly skilled migrants in particular are widely seen as having the potential – and the responsibility – to contribute to development in Ghana by the Ghanaian government, international organisations and donor agencies, having been 'exposed' to life in the West, especially in relation to education, technological skills and work ethics. This perception is shared by some returnees, who see themselves as having obtained knowledge and resources through their experiences abroad and hence as being able to 'push' development processes in Ghana.

In this chapter I explore how return migrants from Western countries to Ghana are engaged in development processes and, in particular, how they perceive their engagement and the challenges they face. I address this question through a case study of 15 highly skilled male return migrants who have returned to Ghana after studying, and in many cases working, in Western countries. All of them have managed to establish professional careers or businesses or have obtained attractive positions as traditional authorities or politicians in Ghana, thereby living up to the political and public expectations of successful returnees. In focusing on this group, I do not claim to examine return migration to Ghana more generally, nor do I assess whether or not the returnees really contribute to development. Rather, I aim to scrutinise and challenge the assumption that capital acquired through migration is automatically transferred to development contributions in the country of origin – and to argue that this is not even the case with otherwise ideal returnees.

Theoretically, this study is inspired by Bourdieu's theory of fields and capital (Bourdieu and Wacquant 1992). According to Bourdieu, a field is constituted by configurations of relations between positions, where social actors struggle for various kinds of capital, guided by game-like principles of organisation and positioning (ibid.: 85), which can be termed the 'rules of the field'. When these principles are taken for granted and regarded as self-evident and unquestionable, Bourdieu calls them *doxa* – that is, the orthodoxy of the field. A person may master the rules of the field but maintain a critical stance towards *doxa* because of his or her exposure to or embeddedness in other fields, for instance through migration. The concept of capital refers to different powers 'whose possession commands access to specific profits that are at stake in the field' (ibid.: 97); these powers include economic, social, cultural and symbolic capital. In a heuristic way, capital can thus be explained as specific kinds of assets – such as skills, qualifications, networks or status – that are attractive to possess in a given field and that can be transferred to other kinds of capital.

When I write about modes of capital and fields, I thus refer to analytical tools employed to examine positions, relations and power in different socio-economic, cultural and political contexts. However, the notion of capital is sometimes appropriated in simplistic ways in policy assumptions about return migration, where it is perceived as a tangible and easily convertible asset – like money – rather than being embedded in particular fields and social relations. Whereas economic capital is characterised by its transferability, other kinds of capital are more locally grounded and cannot easily be converted or transferred (Faist 2000).

Finally, a note about scale. I use the concept of translocal to refer to relations and practices between localities across space (Brickell and Datta 2011). These localities may be situated within the same or in different countries but are characterised by their interconnectedness. However, as not all translocal connections are transnational in nature (Smith 2011), I explicitly refer to transnational relations when this is relevant in my analysis. The distinction between transnational and translocal is thus at the level of scale: translocal implies connections between localities – in this case localities in Ghana, which may or may not have a transnational dimension as well; transnational implies nation states. The usage of translocal or transnational thereby serves to indicate the scale of the informants' relations and activities and the fields and kinds of capital in play.

Based on this understanding, I present two arguments on the theoretical and empirical level. Firstly, and in line with the statement above, I contend that possessing translocal capital – i.e. forms of cultural, social and symbolic capital that work and can be converted in fields encompassing Ghana – as well as a thorough understanding and mastering of the local 'rules of the field' is a precondition for return migrants to manage the many challenges related to return and, in particular, to contribute to development processes. Secondly, I show that the group of highly skilled and elite male return migrants in this study enact and articulate their position in Ghana as 'big men': as successful, wealthy and powerful men who take responsibility for and are engaged in their local communities (cf. Lentz 1998) through both transnational and translocal connections and engagements. The ambitions of policy makers and elite returnees thus coincide to a certain degree but not entirely. While policy makers mainly focus on contributions to national development, the elite returnees tend to be driven by professional, business or chieftaincy opportunities and, at least partly, by local affiliations and obligations.

In this chapter, I start by discussing methodological considerations before I outline Ghanaian (return) migration and policies. I then go on to analyse how the returnees prepared and managed their return, and how they articulate opportunities and challenges. A case study of a returnee from Denmark and his involvement in home-town development and resource mobilisation follows, before I discuss how returnees position themselves as development agents and 'big men'.

**Methodological considerations**

This chapter is based on a total of 13 months of multi-sited fieldwork in Ghana between 2008 and 2013 carried out in relation to two research projects on Ghanaian diaspora politics and return migration. For this study, I particularly draw on interviews with 15 highly skilled male return migrants, and I also refer to findings from interviews on migration and development policies with high-ranking officials and directors from nine ministries, the Ghana Immigration Service, the Bank of Ghana, the Ghana Investment Promotion Centre (GIPC) and the International Organization for Migration (IOM) (see Kleist 2013; 2015). However, I pay most attention to the group of return migrants with whom I conducted in-depth interviews, focusing on their life and migration histories and on their reflections on return, family relations, transnational practices and development. I developed closer relationships with five of the returnees whom I met on several occasions and interviewed at various times and in different locations – in Accra and in their home town, in their offices, private homes and traditional palaces, during traditional ceremonies or political events, and in one case in Denmark. In most cases, interviews took place in private, while other interviews had a more public character, for example when talking to a traditional authority in the company of some of his counsellors. Furthermore, several interviews were supplemented by informal conversation and observation, which helped me contextualise my interlocutors' positions and practices in different contexts. All names have been changed.

The interviewed return migrants in this chapter constitute a particular group, being highly skilled, male and with successful careers. Most of them had left Ghana to study abroad in a Western country and most of them returned in the late 1990s or the early 2000s. Three went to Europe or North America in the 1960s for further studies (and returned within the same decade) and some of the interviewees migrated during the hardships of the 1970s and 1980s, but the majority left Ghana in the 1990s. While some returned relatively soon after the end of their studies, most of the interviewees had spent many years abroad, sometimes decades, working within their professional fields. Furthermore, most of them had obtained Western citizenship or a permanent residence permit in their former countries of residence – what could be termed legal capital – which facilitated transnational practices and mobility after return (cf. Eastmond 2006; Hansen 2007; Kleist 2007).

At the time of the interviews, the return migrants were aged between 40 and 75. Their origins (and hence their home towns) were dispersed throughout Ghana, but were mostly smaller towns, and while their backgrounds varied considerably – from being born into the elite to growing up in relatively poor families – all the interlocutors had tertiary education and most of them had become part of the Ghanaian elite strata after their return. The following (and in several cases overlapping)[1] levels of status and professional category were included in the sample: four politicians, including two deputy ministers (serving in 2008 and 2013); eight traditional authorities (five paramount chiefs and three senior divisional chiefs); two medical doctors; two directors in government agencies; two university professors; two lawyers; and two entrepreneurs. While less skilled return migrants tend to be self-employed (Black et al. 2003; Tiemoko 2004), this was the case for only the two entrepreneurs and one of the doctors, who had established their own companies and clinic respectively. In addition, all of the interviewees positioned themselves as agents of change, having established or facilitated development projects, mainly in relation to social services or other kinds of development projects in their home towns. Some also articulated their contributions in terms of elevating quality and providing innovative perspectives and leadership within their respective professional fields.

The interviewees were located through a mix of snowball sampling (asking interlocutors to refer me to more interviewees) and direct approach. Titles and social positions – be they professional, academic or traditional – are

_____

1 Several of the traditional authorities and two of the politicians also held civil jobs, which explain why the number of professional categories exceeds the sample number.

important for social interaction in Ghana (Nugent 1995), and my position as a Danish researcher may have facilitated access in some cases. Similarly, my focus on the possible development aspects of migration and the fact that all the interviewees were well established in Ghana at the time of the interview may also have contributed to their emphasis on development contributions and personal success. That said, the emphasis on personal contributions to development is also found in other studies on Ghanaian return migration (for example, Ammassari 2009; Asampong et al. 2013; Tiemoko 2004).

As mentioned above, my analytical focus is on the returnees' development activities and how they perceive their projects and positions. While I rely on the interlocutors' statements about their activities and achievements to a certain degree, I have been able to explore some of their projects further through observation, informal conversation and, in some cases, interviews with several people active in the same project or association. Nevertheless, I pay most attention to the 'public selves' (Lentz 1998) of the returnees: that is, how they (re)present and position themselves with regard to their surroundings and with me. Here, I am inspired by positioning theory (Davies and Harré 1990), focusing on how the interviewees articulate key notions such as development, return and migration to negotiate and constitute social positions in different contexts or fields. I thus regard returnees' accounts of opportunities, challenges and obligations as narratives or modes of positioning that reflect particular experiences and subject positions, constituting markers of social differentiation (cf. Sagmo 2014) rather than providing impartial and generalizable information on return migration.

### Return migration to Ghana

Ghana has a long history of mobility and migration, with a mix of internal, regional and international movements of both a voluntary and a forced nature, and including both highly skilled professionals and irregular migrants (Akyeampong 2000; Manuh 2005). Today, the number of international Ghanaian migrants is estimated at 1.8 million people, of whom 75 per cent live in West Africa (UNDP 2009) while approximately 20 per cent of Ghanaians live in Western Europe or North America. During the colonial era, labour migration inside the colony and to other parts of West Africa was common; equally, patterns of educational migration to the UK were established to train administrators and bureaucrats for the colonial administration and, towards independence in 1957, for the independent republic (Peil 1995). Political and economic optimism was replaced by economic hardship and political crisis from the middle of the 1960s with a series of coup d'états and Jerry Rawlings' military regime from 1983. Harsh living conditions in combination with structural adjustment programmes and political oppression led to substantial emigration of the opposition and the elite. The political situation changed again in the 1990s with the establishment of constitutional rule and multiparty democracy in 1992. Ghana was first ruled for eight years by Jerry Rawlings, followed by former opposition leader John Kufuor from 2001 to 2009 when political power changed again. The Ghanaian economy has improved since the middle of 1990s and especially since 2007, when the finding of oil in Ghanaian territorial waters spurred economic optimism (McCaskie 2008).

Return migration from Western countries started to reappear in the early to mid-1990s and increased during the 2000s. According to MAFE[2] data, return migration to Ghana in the 2000s was a fairly common phenomenon: about 65 per cent of international migrants from Europe and 72 per cent from African countries returned within ten years of their departure (Schoumaker et al. 2013). However, this data does not indicate whether the returnees have since re-migrated. There is no statistical evidence of the number or characteristics of return migrants, but the following groups have been identified: labour migrants and seasonal workers; traders; business people and entrepreneurs (Ammassari 2009; Black et al. 2003); elite professionals (Wong 2013), including doctors and other health professionals (Asampong et al. 2013); and students returning after their studies. People returning to take up a position as a traditional authority (Kleist 2011) or to pursue a political career constitute other groups. Finally, returnees also include deportees and emergency returnees who have been evacuated or fled from migration crises, such as the civil war in Libya in 2011, which led to 18,500 Ghanaian labour migrants being evacuated (Bob-Millar 2012; Kleist and Bob-Millar 2013). The latter two groups, however, are not seen as having a development potential but rather as a problem to be solved (Kleist 2013). Returnees thus include men and women, different age groups, various types of profession and educational level, and a range of time spent abroad. Nevertheless, most studies imply that a majority of returnees from Western countries are men with a relatively high level of education, although this may also reflect sample bias (Black et al. 2003; for an exception see Wong 2013).

Government interest in transnational Ghanaian migrants and return re-surfaced in the late 1990s and took off especially in the early 2000s. When newly elected President Kufuor gave his inauguration speech in 2001, he invited international migrants 'to come back home where you belong and ... join in building a new Ghana' (Kufuor 2001).[3] The invitation was further emphasised by the organisation of a 'homecoming summit' a few months later with the theme 'Harnessing the global Ghanaian resource potential for accelerated national development' (GIPC 2001). A range of policy initiatives has since been established, including: a Dual Citizenship Act in 2002; a franchise for non-resident Ghanaian

---

2 The Migrations between Africa and Europe (MAFE) project is a joint research programme on sub-Saharan African migration to Europe with a particular focus on Ghana, Senegal and Congo. See www.mafeproject.com.

3 See Mohan (2008) and Kleist (2013) for an analysis of the speech.

citizens in 2006 (which has not been implemented); and the establishment of a migration bureau in the Ministry of the Interior in 2006; a diaspora investment unit at the GIPC in 2007; and a diaspora support unit located at the Ministry of Foreign Affairs in collaboration with the IOM, initiated in 2012.

However, many of the migration policy initiatives seem to have had little effect or have not been implemented. As I have argued elsewhere, they constitute a policy spectacle where the Ghanaian government demonstrates its interest in international migrants and diaspora groups and acts as a sovereign state that aims to govern and liaise with its non-resident citizenry (Kleist 2013; 2015). In other words, it is a kind of political positioning exercise where the state shows interest but does not necessarily follow up with implementation. This does not indicate a lack of concern for international migrants, especially not in relation to investment; rather, when I talked with policy makers, they almost unequivocally expressed a strong interest in the development potential of legal migration and highly skilled return, highlighting possible triple-win scenarios but also the challenges involved (Kleist 2015). Prominent among these challenges is the fact that migrants and returnees tend not to know or care about migration development policies. Visiting or returning migrants, for their part, often complain about state bureaucracy (cf. Asampong et al. 2013; Black et al. 2003; Tiemoko 2004) and do not know about migration or return policies – or, if they do, they find them irrelevant.

### Preparing and managing return

Almost all the returnees in this study had returned on their own, without government or other kinds of institutional support, with the exception of the three graduate students in the 1960s and one IOM-assisted returnee. This did not indicate that the returnees were not well prepared: quite the contrary. As Cassarino (2004) points out in his typology of return migration, return preparedness is characterised by ample social networks and resource mobilisation as well as by a perception of positive changes in the country of origin in relation to security, livelihoods, opportunities, and so on. The returnees fit well with this ideal type: they brought savings and/or a retirement pension, typically owned a house, and had visited Ghana regularly during their migration. In this way, they resemble other Ghanaian returnees for whom sufficient economic means at the moment of return, the guarantee or prospects of a livelihood (or a retirement pension) for the future and their own house are desirable conditions for the (voluntary) return of highly and less skilled migrants alike (Asampong et al. 2013; Black et al. 2003; Smith 2007; Smith and Mazzucato 2009; Tiemoko 2004; Wong 2013). However, the interviewees in this study belong to a particularly privileged group in that they had studied abroad and, in most cases, they had worked within their professions afterwards. Furthermore, several of them had returned to high-ranking chieftaincy positions or had found attractive jobs in advance. Their situation was thus quite different to that of returnees without relevant work experience (Black et al. 2013) or less skilled individuals with the ambition to start their own businesses.

As I elaborate in this and the following section, the interviewees mainly regarded their decision to and experience of return as being characterised by both opportunities and obligations. In contrast to policy discourses about cultural sameness, kinship and autochthony in relation to return and diaspora engagement (Kleist 2013), belonging was not the central tenet in the returnees' accounts and only a few of them explained their migration and return as embedded in family concerns. Whereas both highly and less skilled people return for family-related reasons (Tiemoko 2004; Wong 2013), some studies show that less skilled migrants tend to have more contact with their families than the highly skilled ones (Black et al. 2003; Tiemoko 2004).

This does not mean that family (or cultural belonging) was unimportant for the interviewees or that it did not shape their return experience. In some cases, the whole (nuclear) family had relocated to Ghana with the returnee (see also Wong 2013), while other returnees lived transnational family lives with wives and children remaining abroad. Rather, this was not the main reason for their return. However, the returnees still had to deal with expectations from extended family and local community members. There are outspoken norms of reciprocity and expectations of wealth redistribution to kin and home town in Ghanaian society that apply to prosperous family and community members (Lentz 1994; 1998; MacLean 2010) – or to those who are perceived as being prosperous – whether they are migrants or not. Economic expectations of international and educated migrants in Western countries are often very high (Kabki et al. 2004; Mazzucato 2008), and not sending remittances in times of need will generally be viewed as a sign of indifference and alienation – and may complicate return. Indeed, studies of return migration show that most returnees sent remittances to their families before relocating to Ghana (Black et al. 2003; Black et al. 2013; Tiemoko 2004). Yet economic obligations and reciprocity patterns do not vanish after return (Arthur 2008; Kleist 2007; 2011), and returnees therefore have to find ways to deal with those expectations, especially when visiting their home town.

This emphasis on economic and social obligations implies that, for return migrants (and indeed for other Ghanaians too), social capital not only is a resource – in terms of having contacts and networks that can facilitate access to resources – but also entails economic obligations and demands. Several interviewees framed their return in terms of sacrificing a more comfortable lifestyle in Western countries and facing social pressures from family and community obligations. Nana,[4] who had been a senior manager in the US

---

4 Nana means chief in Twi, the local language spoken in the home area of this traditional authority.

before he relocated to Ghana to become a senior divisional chief in his rural home town, described his return like this:

It is a sacrifice! First and foremost it is a sacrifice of salary and comfort. The facilities are more comfortable there [in the US], the roads, the water, the electricity, etc. Because of the poverty here, when you are wealthy – or relatively wealthy – people come to you for money because they are hungry. There is poverty here and therefore it becomes an obligation to give something. It's a little bit of a drain, a disadvantage.

When Nana talked about a 'disadvantage', he positioned himself as a wealthy returnee who can compare local facilities with those in America and who is able to 'give something' to the needy local people. Similarly, he referred to norms of reciprocity, reinforced by expectations of prosperity as a returnee from the US. His sacrifice is indeed a relative sacrifice. However, not only should his statement be interpreted as an act of positioning, signalling his social position, but it also reflects widespread social and economic pressures. Indeed, concerns about how to support family and community members and how to manage sometimes unrealistic expectations of support were widely mentioned as one of the main challenges relating to return.

One of the ways in which the interviewees attempted to deal with this situation was through adopting a translocal lifestyle, living and working in Accra rather than in their home towns. This is a common strategy among highly skilled (return) migrants, while less skilled migrants tend to build houses in their home towns (Smith and Mazzucato 2009). A house in Accra provides a certain distance from the needs and demands of kin and acquaintances living in the home town. Also, a house in the capital is a good investment and there are better employment opportunities for the highly skilled in big cities than in smaller rural towns. In fact, with the exception of those originating in Accra, all the interviewees lived translocal lives, maintaining dual households: they stayed in the capital, where they pursued their professional, business or political careers, while regularly visiting or staying for shorter or longer periods of time in their home town. In this sense, their lifestyle resembled that of other highly educated Ghanaians with rural backgrounds who often live in urban centres rather than their home town. Kwame, whom I introduce in the next section, was one of them.

### Recognising and seizing opportunities

Kwame is an entrepreneur in his fifties who lived for more than two decades in Washington. When he returned to Ghana in the early 2000s, he had an MBA and an ambition to create his own business in the booming housing sector in Accra. Kwame had noticed business opportunities during previous visits and had managed to build a house in Accra while he stayed in the

US. 'This made staying in Ghana a bit easier because I had the shelter,' he explained. 'Even if I didn't have a job, I always had a place to stay.' While the first years were tough, Kwame was now comfortable, he said. Like most of the other interviewees, he emphasised opportunities as the main reason for return. Businessmen recognised economic opportunities and ambitious professionals had obtained good positions within companies, ministries and government agencies. Several interviewees talked about 'virgin' and 'untapped' opportunities waiting to be exploited in Ghana. Mr Bafour, a deputy minister (in 2013) who had studied and worked in the UK, explained that Ghana provides opportunities precisely because it is a developing country:

> There are more opportunities in a developing country than a developed one. We need to fix our tax system, we need to fix the economy, we need to fix the financial system in the country. Regardless of what you have studied – energy, education, sciences, medicine, or whatever – you can come here and together we'll fix the system.

In Mr Bafour's statement, the opportunities in Ghana can be seized by a rather particular 'we': the government, perhaps even the nation, that needs the system to be 'fixed' and educated returnees who can 'come here' and 'fix' it in collaboration with the government. This shows his belief that the capacities – or cultural capital – acquired abroad can be used for development purposes in Ghana. Being a returnee and part of the government himself, and of the nation, the deputy minister represents this 'we', emphasising his position as somebody who has a role in both fixing the system and governing it.

Such articulations are well known from other return migration studies, which document how industrious individuals see opportunities for entrepreneurship and careers in their countries of origin precisely because they 'are not finished', in contrast to Western countries where 'everything is done' (cf. Hansen 2007). The context of opportunity relates to what some interviewees defined as the unfinished nature of developing countries as well as progress and economic growth in Ghana. However, when the returnees talked about opportunities, they also highlighted their personal ability in recognising and seizing them. Kwame explained how his 'exposure' abroad had made him able to 'shoot for the skies':

> I always say, 'Look, you can think of Mount Everest and even if you only reach the middle portion, it's better than not getting to the ground in Nepal at all.' You should think big! You have to reach out. You have to ask questions and take in ideas. But if you think that 'Oh this and that and that is too difficult,' you think small, and you will fail.

Emphasising opportunity and the ability to seize it, Kwame positioned himself as a particularly resourceful person who questions *doxa* and generates new ideas – in contrast to stayers who lack this exposure. His statement thus functions as a narrative of differentiation. Other returnees, however – including very successful ones – framed opportunity in relative terms. Another deputy minister (in 2008) who had spent some years in London during his younger days explained how he had not been able to find employment there despite holding two master's degrees and being trained as a chartered accountant manager.

> After writing 75 application letters, I was called for eight interviews, and in all those interviews I was told that I was overqualified ... But I had some deficiencies, my earlier certificate was from an African university that was relatively unknown in the UK, my accent was a typical African accent, and anybody could easily see that I was a foreigner.

This deputy minister thus blamed institutional racism and ignorance in the UK for his difficult time there and had recognised that Ghana offered better career opportunities. Other returnees told similar stories of not being able to get interesting jobs abroad and, as highly skilled professionals, of finding more attractive jobs 'back home'. All of them highlighted how their careers and social positions in Ghana were equal to or better than those in their former countries of residence, at least some years after return. In this way they narrated their return as corresponding to Ghanaian masculinity ideals for highly educated men in terms of upward social mobility and professional employment, and linked to the accumulation of wealth (Arhin 1983; Wong 2013). For the interviewees, opportunity was thus a relative concept; it related to their situation both in Ghana and in the former country of residence – whether in terms of institutional racism or successful careers – and to personal dispositions. This was also the case of Kumah, a return migrant from Denmark whose story illuminates some of the overall tendencies and opportunities of return migration and engagement in development processes.

## Uncle Kumah aka Mr Cash

Kumah was born in the Volta Region in 1933 in a small rural town, here called Afé, as one of eight children in a poor family. He turned out to be an extraordinarily gifted young man who obtained scholarships for secondary and technical school and later for university. By the time of independence, Kumah had become part of the educated Ghanaian elite, driving a Mercedes-Benz that he had paid for in cash. In 1960 he was awarded a nine-month scholarship to study in Denmark. Kumah met his future Danish wife there and, when his scholarship was over, the couple moved back to Ghana where he became head of a ministerial department. He was thus one of the educated return migrants supposed to develop and modernise the young nation in the spirit of patriotism (Ammassari 2009; Lentz 1994). However, when he saw the 1965 national budget, Kumah rightly foresaw an economic and political crisis. He announced to his wife that they had to move back to Denmark, where Kumah undertook further studies and started a successful career as a development consultant and businessman, always with outspoken political opinions and always following the situation in Ghana closely. Indeed, Kumah proudly described himself as 'a proto or hard-core nationalist', preoccupied with development in Ghana.

In 1996 Kumah decided to settle in Ghana again, seeing business opportunities and wanting to spend more time in the country. His wife stayed in Denmark, visiting Kumah once or twice a year and vice versa. Kumah had thus become a transmigrant with his main base in Ghana. He set up a prosperous branch of his business in Accra, acquiring the nickname 'Mr Cash'. As a successful businessman, Kumah/Mr Cash was interested in making a profit but he also considered his business in development terms:

> I wanted to raise the standard of workmanship and to make people able to stand on their own and to be their own employer. And I succeeded. All my 32 workmen are working on their own today.

Kumah was also involved politically. During his first years in Ghana, he was close to President Rawlings, with whom he discussed the advantages of the Scandinavian welfare state.

> I told him that God gave us five fingers, food, shelter, education, employment and health; that is a welfare state. And I described what happens in Denmark, what happens in Norway, when they are on a common ground, where they have slightly different grounds, the way I know it.

Kumah thus explicitly related his experience of political and societal changes in Denmark as a kind of political capital to be transferred to Ghana. However, when Rawlings' politics did not live up to Kumah's expectations, he changed political party and quickly rose in the ranks. Between 2001 and 2003, he became a government-appointed member of the district assembly in Afé because the government 'felt that the level of knowledge here [in Afé] wasn't big enough, so they needed some people from outside to come and put some impetus into it'. Kumah thus moved back and forth between Accra, where he looked after his business, and Afé, where he took care of his political work, living a translocal life with households in both places and annual visits to Denmark. In Afé, he was now known as Uncle Kumah, a name signalling respect and familiarity. In 2006, Kumah successfully ran for one of the top posts in the district assembly. Following his political ideal of the Scandinavian welfare state, he particularly focused on improving education, encouraging school teachers to apply modern and Scandinavian-style teaching methods. He facilitated the renovation of particularly poor schools in the traditional area through collaboration with an old friend and long-term business associate who sent shipments of used equipment to the schools as well as financial support. Finally, Kumah arranged a Danish sister city, which supported an infrastructure project. He thus used his transnational connections in Denmark to further development processes in Afé as well as drawing on his Danish experience in relation to politics and business.

## Translocal and transnational citizenries

As a politician in a destitute area, promoting local development was a key priority for Kumah. Afé is widely affected by unemployment and poverty, and out-migration is common. Large numbers of youth and of educated townspeople have moved elsewhere in pursuit of better livelihoods or careers, further education, or more comfortable living conditions in larger towns in other parts of Ghana. Some also travel to neighbouring countries or even further afield to Germany, the UK, North America and Scandinavia.

One of Kumah's closest collaborators was the senior divisional chief in Afé, Togbe,[5] who also worked as a university professor in Accra while spending weekends and festivals in Afé to attend to his duties as a traditional authority. He was therefore an absentee chief (Boafo-Arthur 2003), living a translocal life. Like Kumah, Togbe was a return migrant himself. He had studied graduate and postgraduate studies in the UK before he was offered the chieftaincy position. Accepting this post was not an easy decision, he explained. He had to consider both his professional ambitions and the economic and social aspects of returning to Ghana as a chief. Taking the position would mean high social status – i.e. symbolic capital – especially in Afé, but it would also require considerable time and hence delay his academic career. It would mean a drop in living standards when living in Afé and dealing with significant expectations of economic and other kinds of support from people in the traditional area, as mentioned above. Nevertheless, Togbe accepted the chieftaincy position in 2001, explaining that 'my cousins told me that "Well, if you don't come and help us, who do you think [will get the position]? ... Not all people are as enlightened as you are, and it will not be very helpful if they are put there."' He thus articulated his choice in terms of responsibility and obligations to do something for his home town.

Togbe shared the perception that Afé needed educated individuals to return for development, explaining that the better their brains, the further away they were located:

> The human resource base of our villages, the cream of the people, they no longer reside in the villages. Life used to be better when we were younger,

---

5 Togbe means chief in Ewe, the local language spoken in Afé.

because most of the people, most of the brains stayed. Now when you go to a village, those who are there are those who are not able to make it in life ... So we rely more on people who are outside. The further away they are, the better [the brains]. I mean, if you are able to come to Accra, you are able to move out of Accra, maybe to South Africa or to Europe or the United States. So, the better or the best materials are very far away. The closer you get to home, the worse ...

Afé migrants are thus 'the cream' of society in Togbe's view, constituting the best brains and the most industrious persons through a self-perpetuating process whereby individuals with skills and resources move away from Afé to localities where they then access more or new resources. Their emigration was widely perceived as a double-edged sword. On the one hand, Afé bears the brunt of the out-migration of resources and skills: that is, a brain and a muscle drain. On the other hand, educated migrants in particular are seen as potentially contributing to development through remittances, contributions to development projects, or investment. Such expectations apply to internal and international migrants alike who form part of a transborder Afé citizenry (Schiller and Fouron 2001) that comprises Afé citizens living in Afé, in other parts of Ghana and outside the country. This citizenry includes people living in different places, under radically different living conditions, and with different access to resources; however, they are all perceived to be affiliated to Afé and hence also subject to certain expectations and obligations with regard to their kin and their home town, including contributions to development, as I show in the next section.

### Resource mobilisation

In 2006, Kumah and Togbe established the Afé Development Foundation in collaboration with local churches and the paramount chief of Afé District, a returnee from the US. The foundation had the purpose of furthering local development in the area, and it was financed through annual development levies. The plan was to save the levies until they reached 100,000 Ghanaian cedi (GhC)[6] and then use them for health and sanitation projects. In Togbe's words, the establishment of the development foundation was necessitated by the lack of state resources in Afé as 'the presence of the central government is not felt here' and taxation in Ghana is not very well developed. Therefore, the traditional authorities and the local politicians had to look elsewhere for resources.

In this case, they looked to the local, translocal and transnational citizenry of Afé, imposing a levy on all Afé citizens according to their place of residence. People living inside the traditional area were levied 4 GhC (with the option of paying in kind through communal work) and citizens living elsewhere in Ghana – i.e. the translocal citizenry – were levied 15 GhC. A major discussion

---

6 In 2008, the GhC was roughly equivalent to the US$.

followed concerning appropriate levies for international migrants, but it was decided to inform them about the graduated levy and then leave the decision about the amount to be paid to individual migrants; it was expected that they would pay significantly more than people living in Ghana. However, paying the development levy was obligatory for all citizens. If they did not pay, there would be sanctions. As Kumah explained:

> God bless you! It's just God bless you, because we have a leverage to squeeze you. We will not bury your mother; we will not bury your father, your brother. If you refuse to pay, the day will come when your mother will be lying in the mortuary for years, because we will not allow her to be buried. So far, nobody has refused to pay ... because there are sanctions and somebody is going to be embarrassed, if they don't pay.

This 'funeral squeeze' was made possible through the participation of chiefs and churches on the Afé Development Foundation committee who would know and check if the levies were paid. As traditional authorities hold custody of the land and thereby grant permissions for funerals, and churches usually have up-to-date information on the deaths of members of their congregations, this is an efficient threat. Funerals constitute very important social and cultural events for local residents and for translocal and international migrants alike, bestowing prestige or shame on the family of the deceased (Lentz 1994; Mazzucato 2008). The idea of the 'funeral squeeze' therefore demonstrates an understanding of the 'rules of the field' in Afé in relation to which capacities, events and practices generate honour – symbolic capital – or shame, as well as sufficient social capital to control and police the activities of Afé's citizens. It also shows how international migrants are expected to contribute generously to their home town.

Apart from sending remittances, many Ghanaian migrants within and outside the country are active in migrant or home-town associations. The objectives of such associations vary considerably, from social and welfare activities to developing the home town through contributions in cash or kind, for instance sending (often used) equipment such as furniture, hospital beds, computers, ambulances, books or medical kit (Crook and Hosu-Porblev 2008; Mohan 2006; Nieswand 2008). In 2008, an Afé association in London took an interest in development and donated 20 used computers to Afé to be used in an ICT centre. While the donation of computers could have been a welcome gift, they were put in storage because of the lack of appropriate premises for the ICT centre. This caused some dissatisfaction among the people in London. While Togbe was busy liaising with the London association, trying to maintain a positive relationship, Kumah was less enthusiastic. He explained that many migrant contributions are not financially substantial because the migrants are under a lot of pressure to send remittances to their families and have difficulty making ends meet. Furthermore, they are often out of touch with local needs and realities:

> We are in contact with those established Ghanaians abroad but we find it difficult ... For instance, 20 old computers were sent to us by Afé people living in London, which are just standing there. So I told them, 'Thank you very much, but it's worthless! Where are we going to keep them? Because the place we want to keep them needs to be repaired, we need to have air conditioning in that place, we need to change the locks for security. That will cost £3,000. If you don't send £3,000, come and collect your PCs! It's not enough for you to send 20 of these things and believe the next time that you're visiting home, then you see them working [in an ICT centre].' No!

The London group was now considering whether they could donate £3,000. Meanwhile, Kumah was turning down approaches from other groups wanting to donate used computers or to start other projects that would demand significant local resources. Although international migrants are presumed to have access to resources, Kumah and several others of the interviewed return migrants did not necessarily perceive them as development agents because of their lack of knowledge of local realities and their limited economic potential. Or, in Bourdieu's terms, they were characterised as people who do not know or master the local field and do not possess the desired capital to make an impact.

## Narratives of excellence and leadership

The different modes of resource mobilisation show how development potential is perceived to be located in different citizenries and at different scales, in local, translocal and transnational fields. Local Afé citizens are considered the ones in need of development, while migrants form the 'cream of the people', as Togbe explained, and hence also possess development potential – at least in terms of economic capital. However, migrants' contributions in cash and kind do not necessarily lead to development if they are not properly managed or governed, according to Kumah. That said, he and the majority of the other interviewed return migrants were explicit about the benefits of their own migration experience, emphasising how studying and working professionally abroad had taught them to pursue excellence as well as superior work ethics and personal initiative. One example is a high-ranking public official, Mr Agyeman, who went to study abroad in the 1980s and returned to Ghana in the early 1990s. Since then, he had held a range of top positions in private companies and ministries.

> I studied accounting and worked as a chartered accountant in the UK. And the work ethics and work attribute is totally different there. So everywhere I've

worked in Ghana I've excelled. When I came back to Ghana I was in the private sector and I was different from everybody else. I was very proactive; I was very vibrant. I go to work when I have to go to work and I close when I have to close. The more you put in, the more you gain. So everywhere I've gone, I have had a better approach to work.

Such statements were common among the returnees, echoing other studies of highly skilled return migrants (Ammassari 2009; Asampong et al. 2013; Tiemoko 2004). Rather than being an objective description of achievements, they constitute narratives of excellence in which the interviewees position themselves as high achievers and educated agents of change. Highlighting an enhanced understanding of societal and political processes in Western countries was another means of expressing such a position. Kumah, for instance, thanked Denmark for political inspiration. He explained his ability to provide political leadership in Ghana as being grounded in knowledge of what drives development, having witnessed the progress of the Danish welfare state from the 1960s, when he first came to Denmark. 'I know that we can get rid of poverty in a very, very short time,' he said, 'when we have good leaders, when we have good programmes, when we can explain our thoughts to the people, particularly when they accept you as a good leader.'

Talking to a Danish researcher, Kumah's emphasis on Denmark can be regarded as a co-narrative where both the interviewer and interviewee shape the content – in this case, through highlighting the benefits of the shared country of (former) residence. However, with few exceptions, almost all the interviewees accentuated their 'exposure' to Western countries, as is also shown in Mr Agyeman's statement above, explaining how it allowed them to excel in Ghana. They thus articulated their position as being characterised by superior cultural capital, leadership capacity, initiative and excellence in combination with an ability to 'push' development by occupying high (and often overlapping) positions within business, politics and the chieftaincy institution.

The 'pushes' described by Kumah and others consist of initiating new and superior practices, elevating work ethics, and inspiring Ghanaians without international migration experience to be more ambitious and open-minded – to be able to question and change *doxa*. Certainly, these pushes were not always successful and several interviewees talked about how they encountered what they perceived to be local sluggishness or lack of initiative – as did Kwame, who was frustrated by the locals not 'thinking big'. However, changing practices and mindsets in Ghana was seen as a difficult and long-term process, often aggravated by local scepticism towards change and the lack of institutional support, as shown in other studies (Arthur 2008; Asampong et al. 2013; Kleist and Vammen 2012).

### 'Big men'

Despite such challenges, the returnees accentuated their achievements, leadership, and development pushes. They thereby framed themselves as 'big men'.[7] In Ghana, as in many other places in Africa, 'big men' is an emic term, referring to personal power and central positions in networks (Utas 2012). In the Ghanaian context, a 'big man' is a person of substance who is recognised and respected for his wealth, status and power (Lentz 1998; Nugent 1995) – and increasingly also a person with international 'exposure' and transnational connections (Kleist 2011). However 'bigness' – or 'bigmanity', as Utas (2012) terms it – is not an automatic status granted by economic capital. As Lentz has pointed out, 'bigness' is related to the ability to master and combine 'different registers of power (economic, "traditional" and "modern" political)' (1998: 48) and 'skillfully craft the public image(s)' (ibid.: 59). Contributing to local development and adhering to norms of redistribution are also important aspects of 'bigness' (see also Marabello 2013; Pellecchia 2011). In Bourdieu's terms, the 'big man' position can thus be described as the abundance of symbolic, social, political and economic capital – and the ability to convert these different kinds of capital in different fields. The fact that Kumah was known as both Mr Cash and Uncle Kumah is a case in point, demonstrating how he managed to be a successful businessman as well as a politician (quite apart from the fact that economic resources can further a political career).

However, while the return migrants were explicit about the benefits of their exposure abroad, it would be utterly mistaken to perceive their engagement as a direct transfer of ideas and practices from Western countries to Ghana. Kumah was very explicit about the necessity of knowing and respecting local cultural and political realities, such as collaboration with the system of chieftaincy and the churches.

> I am with all the chiefs; you'll see me with all the chiefs. I am living in their land, they have an authority here. You cannot promote development and your own indigenous culture without the assistance of the chieftaincy institution. Likewise I am with all the churches: the Catholics, the Protestants, the Apostolic, all the smaller segments of churches. You can't do away with them. You have to collaborate with them and with the chiefs. They must never doubt your loyalty.

According to Kumah, mastering this kind of collaboration is vital for development processes and he was proud of his ability to initiate change. This ability was rooted in a thorough understanding of local institutions, power relations and cultural and political sensibilities, knowing 'how things are done'. Several other returnees expressed a similar understanding. In the

---

7 Women can achieve 'bigness' too and be 'big women'.

words of Mr Bafour, one of the two deputy ministers who had studied and worked in the UK before returning to pursue a political career in Ghana: 'If you fuse the experience of studying abroad with what you have in Ghana, then you are able to do a lot.' Similarly, the paramount chief of Afé explained how migrants abroad 'learn new ways and get new ideas ... but it is a cross-fertilisation, not a wholesale import of ideas'. Thus, while this group of highly skilled and elite returnees accentuated the cultural, social and economic capital they had accumulated abroad, their ability to use and convert such capital in Ghana is related to *also* possessing relevant 'local' forms of capital and being simultaneously embedded in and mastering both translocal and transnational fields. Merely possessing 'international' capital will not make anybody a 'big man' or development agent.

## Conclusion

This chapter analyses how highly skilled Ghanaian male return migrants involve themselves in development processes in Ghana and, in particular, how they articulate their engagement. The interviewees constitute a particular elite group, being highly educated and embedded in several transnational and trans-local fields. While studies of other types of return migrants show how policy assumptions about returnees exaggerate or misinterpret their development potential (Sinatti 2015; Åkesson 2011), the interviewees had managed to establish successful social and political positions in Ghana after return. Furthermore, they shared a discourse in which the acquisition of Western educational and professional skills, as well as exposure to Western society, enables leadership capacity and facilitates homeland development contributions. This perception mirrors popular policy notions of the development potential of return migration and diaspora groups (Kleist 2008; Turner and Kleist 2013). It also reflects how return migration, and more broadly development, has been discussed in Ghana in political and policy circles since the 2000s, constituting a public discourse that is taken up by return migrants, traditional authorities and policy makers (Ammassari 2009; Kleist 2011; Lentz 1998; Pellecchia 2011).

However, the positioning of the interviewees as development agents is not merely a reflection or reproduction of a development lingo that has become widespread in Ghana – and which may be emphasised further when talking to (Western) researchers or policy makers. When examining the 'public selves' of a group of successful, educated and self-assured elite men, their positioning as enterprising development agents is to be expected (cf. Lentz 1998). Their involvement and positions are in accordance with long-established ideals in Ghana of successful returnees as 'upper-class citizens' (Akyeampong 2000) and notions of being 'big men', being able to combine and convert different forms of capital, showing off wealth and superiority, exercising leadership, and – especially for politicians and traditional authorities – contributing to home-town development. International experience and transnational connections may add to this status but do not guarantee it. Indeed, the interviewees become part of a translocal elite upon their return, living translocal lives with households in both Accra and their rural home town, making it possible to maintain relations and respond to obligations in the home town while pursuing professional and business opportunities in Accra, and often maintaining transnational practices as well. This also implies that the development involvement of international return migrants could fruitfully be approached as part of translocal elite practices and positions, rather than as a separate phenomenon.

Finally, the chapter has demonstrated that, in spite of the success of the returnees and their articulations of exposure and leadership capacity, the assumption of an almost automatic link between capital acquired abroad and its smooth conversion to contributions to development processes in Ghana is fundamentally flawed at both the empirical and theoretical level. While the interviewees adhered to the notion of having enriched their cultural capital through their time in Western countries, they emphasised the fact that a thorough understanding and mastering of local realities and power positions are required in order to initiate change and exercise leadership. They need to master 'the rules of the field', so to speak, including having translocal social, cultural, symbolic and political capital. I will therefore end with a caveat: we should remember that social, political and symbolic capital are not easily convertible assets but rather constitute assemblages of skills, networks and positions that are specific to different fields and contexts. If used in over-simplified ways, the vocabulary of capital risks producing yet another distorted model for linking migration and development, while ignoring one of the most important factors: that much successful return migration (in the logic of return migration and development) is characterised by a thorough embeddedness in both translocal and transnational fields.

## Acknowledgements

I thank all interviewees for time, help and kindness, and the editors and other contributors to this book for constructive comments to earlier versions of this chapter. The research has been funded by two grants, one from the Danish Council for Social Science (2008–11) and one from the Danish Council for Independent Research – Culture and Communication (2012–15).

## Bibliography

Åkesson, L. (2011) 'Making migrants responsible for development: Cape Verdean returnees and northern migration policies'. *Africa Spectrum* 41(1): 61–93.

Akyeampong, E. (2000) 'Africans in the diaspora: the diaspora and Africa'. *African Affairs* 99: 183–215.

Ammassari, S. (2009) *Migration and Development: Factoring return into the equation.* Newcastle upon Tyne: Cambridge Scholars Publishing.

Arhin, K. (1983) 'Rank and class among the Asante and Fante in the nineteenth century'. *Africa* 53(1): 2–22.

Arthur, J. A. (2008) *The African Diaspora in*

the United States and Europe: The Ghanaian experience. Aldershot: Ashgate.

Asampong, E., J. A. Harrison, L. Yarney,
K. Opuku-Mensah, A. S. Karim and
J. N. Fobil (2013) 'Back to my roots: a
study of "returning" emigrated health
professionals in the Greater Accra
Region of Ghana'. Africa Today 59(4):
119–30.

Black, R., R. King and R. Tiemoko (2003)
'Migration, return and small enter-
prise development in Ghana: a route
out of poverty?' Working Paper 9.
Brighton: Sussex Centre for Migration
Research, pp. 1–21.

Black, R., P. Quartey, E. Castagnone,
T. Nazio, B. Schoumaker and
N. Rakotonarivo (2013) 'Understanding
Afro-European labour trajectories:
integration of migrants into the
European labour market and reinteg-
ration into the country of origin: the
case of Ghana'. MAFE Working Paper
8. Paris: Institut National d'Études
Démographiques (INED), pp. 1–30.

Boafo-Arthur, K. (2003) 'Chieftaincy in
Ghana: challenges and prospects in
the 21st century'. African and Asian
Studies 2(2): 125–53.

Bob-Millar, G. M. (2012) 'Rescuing
migrants in Libya: the political
economy of state responses to migration crises – the case of Ghana'. DIIS
Working Paper 16. Copenhagen:
Danish Institute for International
Studies (DIIS), pp. 1–28.

Bourdieu, P. and L. Wacquant (1992)
An Invitation to Reflexive Sociology.
Cambridge: Polity Press.

Brickell, K. and A. Datta (eds) (2011)
Translocal Geographies: Spaces, places,
connections. Farnham: Ashgate.

Cassarino, J.-P. (2004) 'Theorising return
migration: the conceptual approach
to return migrants revisited'. International Journal on Multicultural
Societies 6(2): 253–79.

Crook, R. and G. Hosu-Porblev (2008)
'Transnational communities, policy
processes and the politics of development: the case of Ghanaian hometown

associations'. NGPA Research Paper
13. London: Economic and Social
Research Council, Non-Governmental
Public Action (NGPA) Programme,
pp. 1–45.

Davies, B. and R. Harré (1990) 'Positioning: the discursive production of
selves'. Journal for the Theory of Social
Behaviour 20(1): 43–63.

Eastmond, M. (2006) 'Transnational
return and reconstruction in post-war
Bosnia and Herzegovina'. International
Migration 44(3): 141–64.

Faist, T. (2000) The Volume and Dynamics
of International Migration and Transnational Social Spaces. Oxford: Clarendon
Press.

GIPC (2001) Action Plan. Homecoming
summit recommendations. Accra: Ghana
Investment Promotion Centre (GIPC).

GNA (2014) 'Diaspora engagement forum
opens', Ghana News Agency, 8 May.
Available at www.ghananewsagency.
org/social/diaspora-engagement-
forum-opens-74499.

Hansen, P. (2007) 'Revolving returnees in
Somaliland'. In N. Nyberg Sørensen
(ed.) Living Across Worlds: Diaspora,
development and transnational engagement. Geneva: International Organization for Migration, pp. 129–47.

Kabki, M., V. Mazzucato and E. Appiah
(2004) '"Wo benane a eye bebree": the
economic impact of remittances of
Netherlands-based Ghanaian migrants
on rural Ashanti'. Population, Space
and Place 10: 85–97.

Kleist, N. (2007) 'Somali-Scandinavian
dreaming: when "the diaspora"
returns to the desert'. In N. Nyberg
Sørensen (ed.) Living Across Worlds:
Diaspora, development and transnational engagement. Geneva: International Organization for Migration,
pp. 107–28.

— (2008) 'In the name of diaspora:
between struggles for recognition and
political aspirations'. Journal of Ethnic
and Migration Studies 34(7): 1127–43.

— (2011) 'Modern chiefs: tradition, development, and return among traditional

authorities in Ghana'. *African Affairs* 110(441): 629–48.

— (2013) 'Flexible politics of belonging: diaspora mobilization in Ghana'. *African Studies* 72(2): 285.

— (2015) 'Policy spectacles: promoting migration-development scenarios in Ghana'. In J. Quirk and D. Vigneswaran (eds) *The State and Mobility in Africa*. Pennsylvania PA: University of Pennsylvania Press, pp. 125–46 (in press).

— and G. M. Bob-Millar (2013) 'Life after deportation and migration crisis: the challenges of involuntary return.' DIIS Policy Brief. Copenhagen: Danish Institute for International Studies (DIIS), pp. 1–4.

— and I. Vammen (2012) *Diaspora Groups and Development in Fragile Situations.'* Copenhagen: Danish Institute for International Studies (DIIS), pp. 1–84.

Kufuor, J. A. (2001) 'Ghana: inaugural speech by Ghana president', AllAfrica, 7 January. Available at http://allafrica.com/stories/200101070055.html.

Lentz, C. (1994) 'Home, death and leadership: discourses of an educated elite from north-western Ghana'. *Social Anthropology* 2(2): 149–69.

— (1998) 'The chief, the mine captain and the politician: legitimating power in northern Ghana.' *Africa* 68(1): 46–67.

MacLean, L. M. (2010) *Informal Institutions and Citizenship in Rural Africa: Risk and reciprocity in Ghana and Côte d'Ivoire*. Cambridge: Cambridge University Press.

Manuh, T. (ed.) (2005) *At Home in the World? International migration and development in contemporary Ghana and West Africa*. Accra: Sub-Saharan Publishers.

Marabello, S. (2013) 'Translating and acting diaspora: looking through the lens of a co-development project between Italy and Ghana'. *African Studies* 72(2): 207–27.

Mazzucato, V. (2008) 'The double engagement: transnationalism and integration. Ghanaian migrants' lives between Ghana and the Netherlands'. *Journal of Ethnic and Migration Studies* 34(2): 199–216.

McCaskie, T. C. (2008) 'The United States, Ghana and oil: global and local perspectives'. *African Affairs* 107(428): 313–32.

Mohan, G. (2006) 'Embedded cosmopolitanism and the politics of obligation: the Ghanaian diaspora and development'. *Environment and Planning A* 38: 867–83.

— (2008) 'Making neoliberal states of development: the Ghanaian diaspora and the politics of homelands'. *Environment and Planning D: Society and Space* 26: 464–79.

Nieswand, B. (2008) 'Ghanaian migrants in Germany and the social construction of diaspora'. *African Diaspora* 1: 28–52.

Nugent, P. (1995) *Big Men, Small Boys and Politics in Ghana: Power, ideology and the burden of history, 1982–1994*. London and New York NY: Pinter Publishing.

Peil, M. (1995) 'Ghanaians abroad'. *African Affairs* 94(376): 345–67.

Pellecchia, U. (2011) 'The power of abundance: local meaning of authority among traditional and state elites in Sefwi, Southern Ghana'. *Universitas: University of Ghana Inter-Faculty Journal* 12: 69–87.

Sagmo, T. (2014) 'Return visits as a marker of differentiation in the social field'. *Mobilities* 1–17.

Schiller, G. N. and G. Fouron (2001) *Georges Woke Up Laughing: Long-distance nationalism and the search for home*. Durham NC and London: Duke University Press.

Schoumaker, B., M.-L. Flahaux, D. Schans, C. Beauchemin, V. Mazzucato and P. Sakho (2013) 'Changing patterns of African migration: a comparative analysis'. MAFE Working Paper 18. Paris: Institut National d'Études Démographiques (INED), pp. 1–24.

Sinatti, G. (2015) 'Return migration as a win-win-win scenario? Visions of return among Senegalese migrants, the state of origin and receiving countries'. *Ethnic and Racial Studies* 38(2): 275–91.

Smith, L. (2007) 'Tied to Migrants: Transnational influences on the economy of Accra, Ghana.' PhD thesis, Faculty of Social and Behavioural Sciences, University of Amsterdam.

— and V. Mazzucato (2009) 'Constructing homes, building relationships: migrant investments in houses'. *Tijdschrift voor Economische en Sociale Geografie* 100(5): 662–73.

Smith, M. P. (2011) 'Translocality: a critical reflection'. In K. Brickell and A. Datta (eds) *Translocal Geographies: Spaces, places, connections*. Farnham: Ashgate, pp. 181–98.

Tiemoko, R. (2004) 'Migration, return and socio-economic change in West Africa: the role of family'. *Population, Space and Place* 10(2): 155–74.

Turner, S. and N. Kleist (2013) 'Agents of change? Staging and governing diasporas and the African state'. *African Studies* 72(2): 192–206.

UNDP (2009) *Human Development Report 2009. Overcoming barriers: Human mobility and development*. New York: United Nations Development Programme (UNDP).

Utas, M. (2012) 'Introduction: bigmanity and network governance in Africa'. In M. Utas (ed.) *African Conflicts and Informal Power: Big men and networks*. London: Zed Books, pp. 1–34.

Wong, M. (2013) 'Navigating return: the gendered geographies of skilled return migration to Ghana'. *Global Networks* 14(4): 438–57.

# 5 | 'Come back, invest, and advance the country': policy myths and migrant realities of return and development in Senegal

Giulia Sinatti

## Introduction

Since the early 2000s, policy debates and academic research on the links between migration and development have blossomed. Within this discussion, a particular focus is on the potential of return migrants' investment in home economies. In origin countries, scholars have observed growing policy interest in emigrant communities (Barry 2006; Delano 2009; Fitzgerald 2008; Gamlen 2008; Guarnizo 1998; Itzigsohn 2000; Levitt and de la Dehesa 2003; Naujoks 2013; Ragazzi 2009; Sherman 1999; Ho 2011; Østergaard-Nielsen 2003; Waterbury 2010), highlighting that Southern governments 'have increasingly moved to intensify their contacts with their diasporas and involve them in various forms in national life' (Nyberg-Sørensen et al. 2002: 23). Migrants are progressively 'being courted ... for their contributions to development in their countries of origin, praised for their remittances, investments, knowledge transfer' (Turner and Kleist 2013: 192).

Senegal is no exception to this trend. The prevalent view among policy makers is that migrants should 'Come back, invest and help advance the country', as a Senegalese government official observed in a conversation with me. Portes (2001) indicates that the main factors justifying the interest of third world governments in their diasporas lie in the significant resources transferred through remittances and their potential for investment in home economies. Not surprisingly, studies of origin country policies advocating the return of their emigrants find that such policies are often driven by state interest and concerned less with the return of migrants than they are with the repatriation of skills and resources (Boccagni 2011; Cohen 2009; Flahaux and Kabbanji 2013; Sinatti 2014; Strachan 1980; Tsuda 2010). Policy focus on migrant economic investment is paralleled by research analysing the traits and economic successes of migrant businesses. Ethnographic knowledge about the social dynamics in which these investments take place, however, is lacking.

I argue that widespread policy optimism about return, investment and development is based on a number of misconceptions. I defend this argument with reference to the case study of Senegal, because of its long history in developing diaspora return policies. As one of the first African countries to establish an institution at the ministerial level dedicated to relations with its diaspora, Senegal's experience is considered a model to be replicated elsewhere in Africa. Senegal has an important emigrant community, made up primarily of low-skilled economic migrants who generally migrate as single male breadwinners and leave their families behind. These migrants are target savers whose aspiration is to finance specific goals back home.

In this chapter, I offer a critical examination of current official policy discourse about the return and development nexus in Senegal and uncover key underlying myths. The main questions I address are: what assumptions lie behind policy documents? How do migrant experiences of return and business investment compare with the assumptions contained in policy? What are the expectations of policy makers and how do they relate to those of migrants? Comparing return and investment, as they are understood in governmental policies and by migrants, I reveal significant inconsistencies between returnees' experiences and the implicit understandings and expectations contained in policy documents.

I base this analysis on governmental documents that outline Senegalese policy on migration, poverty reduction and economic growth.[1] Additional interviews conducted with 12 officials engaged in return migration programmes and policy making ensure a rigorous account of the policy perspective. In order to compare policy expectations with migrant experiences of return and investment, I also rely on semi-structured interviews with 30 Senegalese migrants who were economically active in Senegal upon return from Italy or Spain. Another 29 migrant interviewees were preparing their return and were at different stages of setting up economic investments in Senegal from a distance. I therefore adopt a broad notion of returnee that incorporates those who have definitively resettled in the country of origin and others who come and go between worlds.

In addition to interviews, this research benefited extensively from several years of ethnographic fieldwork among Senegalese migrants, including repeated contacts with a number of returnees. I used this background experience to guide the selection of migrant interviewees. In sampling, I aimed to include a range of profiles, particularly in terms of respondents' social background, the nature of their economic investments and their success as business owners. The first two criteria were relatively straightforward. Interviewees had different educational backgrounds, had emigrated with or without previous professional

---

1 I analysed the following policy documents: the *Sector Policy for Overseas Senegalese*, first issued in 2006 and later updated in 2011 (MSE 2011) and the *National Strategy for Economic and Social Development* for the period 2013–17 (RS 2012). I also systematically consulted governmental websites and documentation from official initiatives encouraging migrant return and investment.

experience in Senegal, and faced varying economic responsibilities in relation to their families. Despite a definitive clustering in commercial retail and wholesale trade and transport, they had established businesses in different sectors, ranging from animal breeding and agriculture to service provision and small craftsmanship workshops, including printing, carpentry, welding, shoemaking and tailoring.

The third criterion, which relates to the success of migrant investors, proved trickier. First, exactly what constitutes 'success' is debatable. The migrants I spoke with attached different worth to various aspects of their businesses, self-evaluating their achievements on the basis of different measures. In interviews, some spoke about economic aspects of their business accomplishments and failures, while others highlighted the social rewards of being business owners in their own country. Second, and linked to this first point, talking about success clearly reflects the researcher's and interviewees' respective positionalities. During interviews, there was a frequent awareness that migrants chose which aspects to highlight and which to minimise on the basis of what they wished to convey to the interviewer, or what they assumed the interviewer expected to hear. For instance, some interviewees seemed to be searching for the researcher's approval when applauding 'Western' work ethics they brought back from their experience as immigrant workers, or when lamenting the difficulties of running a business in the 'backward' Senegalese environment. At times, interviewees appeared keen to impress with their entrepreneurial abilities because I, a European, might put them in contact with interested foreign investors. Nevertheless, by reflecting migrants' views as they choose to express them, this chapter does justice to Oxfeld and Long's (2004) call for ethnographies of return migration that reflect people's own understandings and experiences.

The rest of this chapter is divided into five sections. In the next section, I outline three fundamental myths underlying Senegalese migration policy: that migrants privilege consumption over economic investment, that they acquire capital abroad that is useful for development, and that they fail to pursue their natural commitment to the development of their home country. Three sections then challenge each of these myths with ethnographic insight into the perspectives of return migrant investors. I first show that migrants engage significantly in economic investment at home, and distinguish between the investment logics of 'survival-' and 'growth-oriented' businesses. I then contrast the argument that migrants bring back useful capital exclusively from overseas and argue, through ethnographic insight, that the social capital they hold at home shapes their business logics to a substantial extent. I subsequently stress that there is a significant mismatch between understandings of success by policy and migrants. Finally, I offer some general conclusions in the last section.

## Economic advancement expectations and Senegalese policy myths

The Senegalese government has been actively reaching out to its emigrant community since the 1970s, earning itself a reputation as a frontrunner in the field of diaspora policies. Since then, return has been a central policy concern. The first protocol to promote the voluntary return of migrants was signed between France and the Republic of Senegal in 1975. In the 1980s, a joint 'reinsertion–return' programme was integrated with a fund providing credit to migrant workers who wished to invest economically. In the 1990s, a negative review of migrant businesses funded through these schemes led to the tightening of the qualifying requirements for support and to greater assistance for those who made it over the threshold. In 1993, the establishment of a Ministry for Overseas Senegalese (Ministère des Sénégalais de l'Extérieur or MSE) marked a new orientation in return policies. As noted by Diatta and Mbow (1999: 250), preference was 'henceforth given to the concept of "participation" by Senegalese Resident Abroad in the national effort to promote economic advancement, the initial concept of "reinsertion-return" having become viewed as overly restrictive'. In practice, this translated into a further narrowing of the eligibility criteria for return and business support schemes, revealing ideas about the 'ideal type' of migrant returnee: resourceful, experienced, and eager to initiate innovative and profitable enterprises that would allow new economic sectors to boom.

The Senegalese government's latest thinking on migration and return is best illustrated through an analysis of its policy. The National Migration Strategy and Action Plan was first adopted by the MSE in 2006 and updated in 2011. This document reveals the three underlying myths mentioned above. First, migrants are understood as being conspicuous consumers who do not engage in economic investment. Second, migrants are assumed to automatically acquire useful capital – particularly economic capital – while abroad. Third, migrants are seen as failing to pursue their commitment to homeland development. Each of these myths is further discussed below.

The first myth emerging from Senegal's migration policy concerns migrants' presumed preference for conspicuous consumption over savings and investment as a major obstacle preventing the exploitation, for the benefit of development, of the capital they bring back from abroad:

> Emigrants play an important role in terms of private and collective investments
> ... the resources and potential of this overseas Senegalese community are
> however insufficiently exploited, particularly in the economic sphere, as they
> are geared towards the satisfaction of consumption needs for families rather
> than towards the achievement of economic goals (MSE 2011: 29).

Senegal's *National Strategy for Economic and Social Development* (which overrides the migration policy analysed here) estimates that over 90 per cent of remittances, worth a yearly average of 800 billion CFA francs (€1.2 billion), is used for consumption purposes (RS 2012: 10). Alongside a preference for consumption, migrants' lack of information about supposedly promising and productive investment sectors is noted as being another barrier that 'prevents moving from a subsistence emigration to an emigration of accumulation' (MSE 2011: 11). Migrants are described as 'simply hoarding savings or ... putting their money into anarchical socio-economic constructions' (Diatta and Mbow 1999: 253). Recent schemes designed to promote migrant investment and entrepreneurship further reveal this interpretation. The Support Fund for the Investments of Overseas Senegalese (FAISE), for instance, offers financial and technical assistance to migrant investors in different sectors, albeit with the exclusion of those sectors in which most migrants prefer to invest (Sinatti 2014). Favoured investments in real estate, commerce and transport are dismissed in Senegalese policy, which labels these as being saturated or economically unattractive sectors.

The second myth in Senegalese policy is the idea that migration is automatically an enriching experience, intrinsically linked to the acquisition of capital that is useful for the homeland. As illustrated in the following quotation, important expectations are placed on the transfers of resources from migrants with regard to improving Senegal's prospects on the global scene:

> With the aim of making of Senegal an emerging country, it is necessary to promote a migration ... that hinges on the development of human resources and the capacity to accumulate wealth, which can lead to productive investment in our country (MSE 2011: 19).

While the policy does mention the importance of cultural capital transfers via Senegal's few 'intellectual' migrants, it also recognises that:

> The return of the scientific and highly skilled diaspora is rare. It claims not to find, in Senegal, a professional environment that invites [it] to come back and work in the country ... compared to the considerable means and conditions offered by Northern countries (ibid.: 8).

The main policy focus is, rather, on the significant economic capital acquired abroad by the majority of migrants: young, scarcely educated men migrating on their own for economic reasons. The policy states: 'The first asset of the overseas Senegalese lies in their financial capacity' (ibid.: 12).

Contrary to Faist's (2009) argument that current migration development policies mainly emphasise the transfer of cultural and social capital, Senegalese policy overwhelmingly focuses on the repatriation of economic capital. It refers to remittances as a 'financial manna', equal in 2008 to two and a half times public development assistance and 14 per cent of the country's gross domestic product (MSE 2011: 29). In a review of Senegalese policies and programmes designed to involve migrants in national development, Diatta and Mbow indicate that it became 'clear that their participation ... would essentially be through repatriation of their savings to Senegal' (1999: 252). Migration is seen as an enriching experience that makes (especially financial) capital potentially available for the benefit of the home country. Lastly, the following quotation sums up the third myth that underpins Senegalese migration policy and reveals other related implications:

> Overseas Senegalese ... encounter multiple difficulties in their *will* to play a positive role in the *economic development* of their *country* of origin (MSE 2011: 11, emphasis added).

In accordance with an argument I have made elsewhere (Sinatti 2014: 281), this quotation refers to migrants' 'will' to take part in the development of their country of origin, suggesting that this should be an unequivocal aspiration among Senegalese migrants. According to Turner and Kleist (2013: 196), developmentalist diaspora discourse is rooted in the idea 'that members of diasporas have an inherent desire to assist their "homeland"' and, in line with the first policy myth, 'that they hold particularly advantageous positions to do so because of their lives in western countries'.

The quotation above underscores important implications resulting from all three policy myths. By referring to the 'country' of origin, the policy stresses a concern for development on the national scale. In addition, a restrictive focus on development as national economic growth is adopted persistently throughout Senegalese policy. Understanding development as a primarily economic affair in turn leads to a restrictive interpretation of *which* investments may be favourable and the subsequent construction of the image of the 'ideal returnee'.

The myths contained in Senegalese migration policy and their implications are interesting not only in their own right but even more so when confronted with migrants' actual experiences of return and investment. The three sections that follow contrast each of these myths with ethnographic insight, showing that policy expectations are ill fitted to the reality of return migration to Senegal.

### The business logics of return migrant investors in Senegal

The policy myth that sees Senegalese migrants as conspicuous consumers contrasts with their prevalent aspirations for investment, followed by return (Sinatti 2011). Most Senegalese migrants cultivate the idea of one day returning for good to their country of origin. This dream does not falter throughout the period of migration, even if that period lasts many years; during this time, migrants continuously think about when and how their return might be possible. They explore and plan investment ideas, and they initiate small business projects at a distance. While carrying out ethnographic fieldwork for this research, I found that business creation efforts in Senegal are extensive, not only among returnees but also among those who hope to prepare the ground for a sustainable resettlement back home while still an emigrant. Some respondents had returned to Senegal definitively, giving up their residency rights in the country of immigration, and took care of their businesses by staying put. Others had invested in activities that required regular alternation of periods abroad and periods back home, as with those involved in selling imported goods.

The migrants interviewed for this research had initiated a variety of businesses. Activities covered different sectors: commerce – for example, selling imported goods such as ceramic tiles, electrical appliances, spare vehicle parts and second-hand furniture, or selling locally consumed everyday foodstuffs and consumer goods in small boutiques and hardware shops; local craftsmanship – welding and carpentry workshops, tailors, printing workshops, bakeries, and so on; services – such as cyber cafés, taxi services, domestic and international logistics and transport businesses; and agriculture – including farming and animal breeding.

In several countries, migrants' high propensity to invest back home is supported by literature investigating migrants' occupational choices after return. Evidence from Algeria, Tunisia and Morocco (Gubert and Nordman 2011), Egypt (Wahba and Zenou 2012), Turkey (Dustmann and Kirchkamp 2002), Mozambique (Batista et al. 2014), Pakistan (Ilahi 1999), Albania (Kilic et al. 2009) and China (Démurger and Xu 2011) indicates that migrants invest significantly in business creation both in absolute terms and (where this distinction is made) compared with non-migrants. In Senegal, recent findings from a representative quantitative sample in the region of Dakar confirm that migration does indeed stimulate investment in assets at home (Mezger Kveder and Beauchemin 2014). In policy circles, these findings have led uncritically to the conclusion that, through investment, migrants can trigger the economic development of their countries of origin.

Nonetheless, migrant investments are extremely varied. Academic research on migrant business creation displays a key concern with the size and degree of formalisation of their initiatives. A distinction is introduced between 'self-employment' and 'entrepreneurship'. Whereas the former creates an occupation for the individual investor, the latter requires the use of additional workers, thus generating employment and contributing to economic growth. Self-employment is understood as a last resort option for returnees, and one that carries little developmental impact. This is Mezger Kveder and Flahaux's (2013) conclusion about migrant business investment in Dakar. Studies from different countries find that limited overseas savings are sufficient for illiterate or low-skilled returnees to invest in self-employed businesses, whereas qualifications and the duration of migration are important in facilitating the creation of enterprises (McCormick and Wahba 2001; 2003; Mesnard 2004; Piracha and Vadean 2010). Other scholars believe that, rather than the number of jobs generated by a business, more significant implications for development depend on whether investments are made in the formal or informal economy. In their analysis of entrepreneurship among return migrants to Ghana and Côte d'Ivoire, for instance, Black and Castaldo (2009) investigate the relationship between return, entrepreneurship and development by focusing on migrants who registered a business after their return, since this is considered to play a part in entrepreneurial growth and the home economy through taxation and its contribution to gross domestic product.

I argue that distinctions based on size and formalisation do not do sufficient justice to the diversity of migrant businesses or to their development repercussions. Cases studied in this research, for example, often combined formal and informal characteristics: a commercial activity might be registered officially as a one-man business and still rely on informally paid labourers or family members. Important aspects of migrant businesses are better understood by distinguishing between 'survivalist' and 'growth-oriented' investments. Introduced by Berner, Gomez and Knorringa (2012), this idea suggests that differences between businesses are qualitative in nature and relate to the underlying logics of investment strategies. I understand survivalist and growth-oriented businesses as ideal types lying on a continuum. At one extreme, survivalist businesses are driven by necessity; require limited skills, capital and technology; are easy to enter; are part of household diversification strategies; and aim at maximising security. At the other extreme, growth-oriented businesses are opportunity-driven; face entry barriers; require specialisation; and involve risk taking. The latter are closer to the ideal type of investment on which policy thinking is based.

My argument is conveyed more clearly using ethnographic examples. The most unequivocal case of a growth-oriented business among my interviewees was the one established by Tapha. When I first met him, this enterprising returnee was running a rapidly growing chicken-breeding business on the outskirts of Dakar, along with two Italian partners. Before this, Tapha had been involved in other investments. Like many others, he had started off importing spare vehicle parts to Senegal, and he combined this with regular employment in an Italian factory. Among his spare part suppliers, two Italians had approached him with an investment idea: they wanted to set up a pellet production plant in Senegal, exploiting sawdust from local carpentry workshops and exporting the final product to Italy. The Italians had the financial means, while Tapha had knowledge of the country and experience in dealing with administrative matters gained through his own import business. This investment relied on an innovative concept, financial resources, imported technology, and contracts with buyers in Italy secured ahead of production. From a policy perspective, this idea had the features of a pioneering and productive ideal-type investment. However, the sawdust contained high levels of sand, which resulted in poor-quality pellets and therefore buyers dropped out, rapidly leading to the closure of the business. Determined to remain in Senegal, Tapha fell back on the vehicle parts trade, alongside which he also started up a small poultry-breeding venture. His former Italian partners initially frowned upon this idea. Later, they decided to join. Today, the poultry farm has grown into a medium-scale business and has secured financial support from institutional funders. In Tapha's words:

> In the beginning the guys didn't believe in chickens, you see? So I started on my own, slowly slowly. Then they saw what I was doing and decided it could become a big company, with thousands and thousands of chickens, with a slaughterhouse and all those kinds of things. Now we have modern chicken feeding lines, each costing more than 50 million francs [€76,000]. We invested a lot of money but we also earn more money, because we increased our production. It's going very well.

The activity formally hires ten full-time employees and 30 workers contracted on a daily basis. Moreover, Tapha points out with pride that dozens of other people are making a living by reselling his chickens for a small profit: 'I more or less created those: I gave them the idea. They come here and go out to places where they can sell. There are many of them, really many.'

Stories like Tapha's are far from common among returnees. While his is an outlier case, however, I interviewed and visited the businesses of several other returnees who showed a noticeable entrepreneurial spirit, even when their investment choices were more common. In the commercial sector, for instance, the retail trade of ceramic tiles has boomed in Senegal and is a favoured investment among migrants returning from Italy and Spain. Several interviewees had entered this line of business, reinventing themselves as retail sellers of low-quality imports and largely employing family members as underpaid, informal labourers. Khadim and Balla, however, stood out from this crowd. They had set up impressive showrooms and specialised in *haut de gamme* (top of the range) products imported from selected Italian dealers. Khadim regularly competes in public tenders and supplies large building sites with expensive imported marble. Balla's commercial strategy, on the other hand, explicitly targets affluent clients from Dakar's most exclusive neighbourhoods. Between them, Khadim and Balla employ a few local professionals, who ensure the smooth running of their businesses during their regular trips to Europe.

Another outlier case is that of Makhou, a middle-aged returnee to a rural Senegalese village who runs a lucrative transport business, albeit in the informal sector of the economy. A vehicle that is entrusted to a driver in exchange for a daily fee is considered a safe investment, and one that several of my interviewees had chosen. In Dakar and elsewhere, clandestine taxis are often owned by migrants and returnees. Based on this principle, Makhou had various people working for him, driving a fleet of several lorries. He had started off with a couple of vehicles, purchased with savings built up over 25 years of migration. While others did the driving, Makhou was free to seek commissions, manage the rotation of staff, oversee vehicle maintenance, gradually purchase more lorries and see his business thriving.

The stories outlined above are typical of businesses displaying growth-oriented characteristics. However, the majority of Senegalese migrant investors better fit the profile of survival entrepreneurs. These investors are interested not so much in business expansion, but rather in business diversification. Like many returning Congolese investors (see Chapter 2), several of the returnees I spoke with ran more than one business. Babacar, for instance, fills idle moments of the year from his agricultural business with investments in the transport sector, while also overseeing a family-run grocery store. Similarly, once his dream investment in a bakery was running smoothly, Cheikh opened another bakery in a different location.

It would be wrong to assume that migrants returning to Senegal all succeed in setting up at least a survivalist business. While my interviewees were all making a living somehow, many of them were simply playing it safe by still keeping a foot in migration (Sinatti 2011). Many had lived through investment failures as well. Taken collectively, however, their stories challenge the policy myth that returnees do not invest. Nonetheless, because migrants engage in investments that are not aligned with the ideal types that might pursue the government's national economic growth goals, policy makers downplay their efforts and dismiss them as 'conspicuous consumption'.

Tapha's failed attempt to set up a pellet production plant shows that an innovative and productive business idea does not in itself guarantee that the activity will take off and generate economic returns. Government policy under-estimates the fact that, even in economic sectors that it labels 'saturated' or in the informal economy, some migrant businesses stand out. The examples given above of transport businesses and tile retailers indicate that businesses that are unattractive to policy makers and are run in a different way may in fact thrive economically and generate employment both directly and through multiplier effects. I have argued that differences between businesses are explained more appropriately by referring to the distinction between survival and growth-oriented entrepreneurs. As will become clear in the next section, migrants' ability to mobilise bridging and bonding social capital is one essential ingredient marking the difference between these two extremes.

### Capital repatriation or home-held capital? Business logics and social networks

The policy view of migrants is that they come back with useful capital acquired overseas. In much of this discourse, however, 'inadequate attention has been given to selectivity in terms of returnees' personal characteristics, duration of stay abroad, and the motivations underlying different types of return' (Nyberg-Sørensen et al. 2002: 22). Even some of the academic evidence indicating that migrant investors have positive impacts on their countries of origin is biased towards highly skilled individuals. Ammassari (2009), for instance, concludes that in Côte d'Ivoire and Ghana, migrant investors favour economic growth by bringing back skills and capacities. Her research, however, is based on a sample of elite return migrants, who may not be representative of the larger migrant population.

Among low-skilled migrants, a review of the available evidence suggests that the duration of their stay abroad is a key determinant in the achievement of target savings goals (Nyberg-Sørensen et al. 2002). Nevertheless, whether returnees' investments lead to development still remains questionable. Based on worldwide examples of 'migrants from poorer rural areas spending time abroad before returning to invest in small businesses', Black and Castaldo (2009: 46) interrogate their development potential and conclude that they 'are often seen as having limited economic impact'. In the African context, the same authors indicate that research evidence about migrant investment in small-scale businesses and economic growth 'does not provide – at first sight – an unambivalent case for believing that migrants are either likely to invest in business activity, or that such activity is likely to have positive effects on development' (ibid.: 46).

In this section, I challenge this narrow focus on the economic impact of migrant businesses. In line with policy preoccupations about repatriated financial capital, this view fails to acknowledge the role of other forms of capital that are also held at home. Specifically, I argue that survival and growth-oriented businesses are embedded in different types of social capital. Whereas the former depend on 'family and kin networks' that 'require sharing the resulting income' (Berner et al. 2012: 387), growth-oriented businesses rely on 'business networks' and 'allow accumulation of the generated income' (ibid.). Put differently, migrant businesses are closer to survivalist or growth-oriented extremes in relation to investors' capacity to mobilise 'bonding' and 'bridging' social capital to their own advantage.

In line with other cases in this book (see Chapter 6), trust is a serious concern in Senegal. It poses a significant constraint to migrant investors, even when they return with significant financial resources. As one of the returnees I spoke with explained: 'It is difficult to have partners. The main problem is trust, because there are few dynamic and trustworthy people. This makes it very difficult to work in Senegal with someone on a project.' For most migrants, trust is strongest among their close social ties, which they rely on heavily for their investments. Unlike returnees to Congo (see Chapter 2), the Senegalese turn mainly to family members and sometimes to immediate friends, who provide support in studying the market, acquiring the necessary skills, and running their businesses.

Returnees with no earlier professional experience in Senegal ask relatives for help in choosing an investment project and acquiring the necessary knowledge. Having left Senegal when he was not much older than a boy and after 20 years living in Italy, for instance, Gallaye explains how his choice developed of running a self-employed wholesale business selling imported clothing from China:

> When I came back to Senegal I didn't know how to do this job well ... I started working with my brothers, who had always been here. I gave them the money I had after 20 years – it wasn't a lot – and they helped me out ... They know things better than me, so I followed them. I give them what I have and they go to China and buy stuff also for me. Then they tell me: 'This you sell at so much, this at so much ...' And that's how you learn.

Gallaye underlines the importance of capital within the family, indicating that his brothers are the ones to be praised for his achievements: 'Had it been only up to me, on my own, I don't know how to do things. It's a good job my brothers were there ... Without them I wouldn't have made it, because I don't know how to do things.' Gallaye's words resonate with those of many others, whose reliance on those same close networks from which they had emigrated results in largely imitative business ventures.

While Gallaye needed to train in a job that was new to him, those who had a profession before leaving Senegal prefer to invest in the same sector. Many of those who establish sustainable businesses back home, in fact, were already business owners before emigrating. Modou, a welder, and Mawa, a carpenter, had both worked in Italy in low-skilled factory jobs unrelated to their earlier experience. Upon return, they turned to their former professions, highlighting that they already had the necessary skills and could easily recruit additional workers through their bonding networks:

> When I came back, I continued what I did before. When I left, I was a welder. I was in sheet metal work. It's what I know, the metal profession.
>
> When I came back here, I had just one thing on my mind: taking up my job again. Also, I had my nephews here who I had already trained before I emigrated. I knew that once back here, I wouldn't lack people with whom to work.

Similarly, Daouda, who ran a tailoring business that he handed over to a cousin during his 15 years of migration, comments: 'Migration has very much improved my life. I was able to buy additional sewing machines and enlarge my tailoring activity.'

Modou, Mawa and Daouda resumed or expanded pre-existing businesses thanks to economic capital acquired abroad. Other returnees leapfrog forward, moving up the social ladder from the apprentice position they had held before to being business owners upon their return. Makhou's transport business mentioned in the previous section is a case in point. Before emigrating from

Senegal, he had been an apprentice in this trade, helping with the loading and unloading of vehicles in the vain hope of one day obtaining a driver's licence and moving up the ranks. If migrants invest in the same sector in which they were involved prior to emigration, this confirms the interpretation proposed by the new economics of labour migration, according to which migration, followed by return, is often a household strategy to acquire investment capital in order to expand or upgrade a family business (see also Ma 2002).

In the development of their businesses, most returnees prefer to rely on social capital rather than on formal schemes offering technical or financial assistance. Some returnees who came back with limited savings told me that they even raised additional investment capital through relatives. They claimed that the family is a safer source of funding than banks, which would impose on them strict and non-negotiable repayment obligations. In general, migrants expressed general suspicion towards official schemes supporting business creation, viewing them as something out of reach and too distant from their needs.

The above shows that, for most migrant investors, trusted relations and social capital are a precious resource. Nonetheless, the downside of social capital (Portes and Landolt 1996) also poses threats to businesses. Even when they relied on supposedly trusted relationships, migrant investors told me many tales about fund detours,[2] insolvent debtors and business failures. Those investing from overseas are especially exposed to these risks, which leads many to prefer return and direct supervision of their businesses (Sinatti 2011).

When returnees succeed in achieving economic returns, they are expected to use their better-off position to solve the problems of others in their network (offering medical care to family members, employment to unqualified relatives, credit to customers, and so on). Irrespective of the economic condition of their families, all migrants reported being exposed to similar pressures. This erodes the possibilities for profit for many returnee businesses, pushing them towards survivalism:

> When I give money to buy new supplies for the business some of it is always used to fix another problem. It is not stealing. They use it because they need it, but the problem is that they never give it back.
>
> I don't make much, but I still help many other people. I love helping other people. It is something I really like a lot.

Controlling the dark side of social capital is difficult, but migrant entrepreneurs who display growth potential master this ability well. Coming from an extremely humble background and exposed to constant pressures to share his fortune, Tapha (the poultry farm owner) explains:

---

2 That is, funds that a migrant intended for an investment are spent (by his 'collaborators' and without him knowing) for other purposes.

Do you know how I deal with this? If someone asks me for 10,000 francs [€15], I give them 2,000 [€3]. And I make a difference between those who *need* help and those who *want* it. You need to distinguish between the two, that's all. I help a lot of people in the end. I just know how to do it.

Equally important in marking the growth-oriented character of some businesses is returnees' capacity to activate bridging ties. A bakery owner shared with me the dream of expanding his business and introducing all sorts of new products. During the interview, he commented: 'Partners we look for in the country of destination, not here. Even if they don't want to invest money directly, they can give us advice and competences that can help us realise our project.' Many other interviewees who were keen to see their businesses expand further hoped to meet potential partners during their trips to Europe. Having realised this goal with his poultry farm, Tapha says:

To be honest, without the help of the Italians I would never have got to where I am. They work hard. We have the same ambition of not depending on anyone. We work for ourselves. We get our hands dirty like our workers. We are not big bosses driving around in fancy cars ... Most other migrants in my position would have a nice car, wear a suit and tie. For me, success comes with modesty.

In Tunis, Cassarino (2000) concluded that continuous involvement in cross-border social and economic networks allowed returnee *new entrepreneurs* to transfer skills and promote development at home. My ethnography among the Senegalese highlights that the ability to mobilise bridging ties involves more than establishing useful contacts transnationally or attracting foreign partners to Senegal. Several growth-oriented investors also connect to the 'right' networks in Senegal. The success of Tapha's poultry farm depended equally on his ability to reach out to potential regular clients among restaurant and supermarket owners in Dakar, which he manages despite having no former personal contacts in this field. Balla emphasises that commercialising his exclusive marble tiles is a question of bridging social capital:

I know a lot of people. Social relations are very important. Though it depends what kinds of relations. Relations mean rich people, important people. I sell prestige tiles; I am one of the most expensive sellers in Dakar. There are already too many selling rubbish; I wanted to make a difference and sell good quality. To succeed in this, I cultivate relations among those who can afford to buy.

The stories outlined in this section suggest that current policy debates tend to overlook the significance of capital mobilised by migrants at home in shaping their business endeavours. An interpretation that sees migrants as coming back with useful resources on the one hand, while on the other lacking the capacity to exploit them, is inherently contradictory. Furthermore, placing the responsibility on migrants diminishes governmental responsibilities for removing barriers to investment. Returnees in this research cited numerous infrastructure, bureaucratic and administrative hurdles when starting up their businesses that the state should be addressing. As others have rightly noted, the structural context in the country of origin plays an important part in affecting migrants' capacity to implement developmental change (Åkesson 2011; de Haas 2010; Faist 2008).

Unlike Cape Verdean migrants, who are able to return with pension guarantees from their labour in Europe (Chapter 8), the Senegalese do not benefit from the transferability of social security after returning to their country of origin. Success in business is therefore extremely relevant, insofar as it strongly affects migrant livelihoods and the sustainability of return for them and their families (van Houte and Davids 2008). While still recognising the importance of economic performance, the distinction between survivalist and growth-oriented investments reveals the importance of local social capital for business outcomes. By offering an insight into returnees' abilities to mobilise bridging and bonding ties, ethnography provides an essential step forward in our understanding of the relationship between return, investment and development.

### Understandings of success and commitment to personal and national good

The previous two sections shed light on Senegalese migrants' businesses, their investment logic and the networks in which they are embedded. What remains to be seen is how return and investment are linked to a commitment to homeland development.

When asked what induced them to go back to Senegal, most migrants mention a mixture of motivations. The desire to invest economically is seldom the first priority. Instead, returnees indicate their wish to reunite with families and take up positions of responsibility as heads of households, to occupy a senior position in home communities, and to no longer endure the hardships of immigration. These motivations compensate for the fact that, for most, return corresponds to a significant loss in earnings compared with those when they were abroad, even among the most growth-oriented investors. For the majority, investment is simply a means to return rather than an independent goal (see Chapter 8; Sinatti 2011).

Migrants' motivations for return are reflected in their perceptions of the success or failure of their return. Remarkably, those whose businesses barely make it economically tend to be those who express the highest levels of personal satisfaction. Survivalist entrepreneurs spoke to me with pride about their investments. They described themselves as having become respected men in their families and home communities. At the other extreme, growth-oriented entrepreneurs, like Tapha, are driven by further ambition:

I still do not see success in where I am today. Where I want to be is still far away. Not because I need a lot of money, but because I am not yet the number one chicken breeder in Senegal ... I still have a long way ahead.

The different investment logics of survival and growth-oriented returnees explain not only their interpretations of success, but also their attitudes towards the contributions that their investments make to Senegal. A majority of respondents declared that they felt little commitment to their country's development. Some even expressed resentment against the government, confirming that 'mistrust is inherent in most of the relations between states and their diasporas' (Turner and Kleist 2013: 202):

Every one of us had to cater for himself to go abroad. We didn't get a bean from the government. Therefore if we emigrate, we emigrate out of our personal account and if we return, we return out of our personal account.

Among survivalist returnees in particular, personal well-being takes precedence over their desire for national advancement. Growth-oriented investors, however, demonstrate a different disposition. As two respondents reveal:

I think we must all do something to repay the Senegalese state.
    I always thought of one day coming back to help my country, develop my country like others have done. This idea was always popping up in my head.

It is again Tapha, the poultry farm owner, who is most explicit in speaking about investment as fulfilling his personal ambitions while also representing a feasible way to do something for his country:

Since leaving Senegal I had always had the idea of returning, investing and giving work to other people. This was my idea ever since I was a boy ... I don't have a diploma to become a minister, or a director general, or something like that. But I still want to contribute to the development of my country. Even if I am not a great man, I want to become somebody who can do something for his country and for himself. This is an idea that came to me just like that, but I had it already as a child. I have always imagined this. I have never wanted to be someone who just stays where he always was.

While Tapha clearly matches policy ideals, migrants investing in sectors that are downplayed in policy also see themselves as contributing to the country's economy. Cheikh, who owns a small bakery with five employees, says:

At least some Senegalese who were unemployed now have a job. Today they work with me and I pay them every month. By paying them and paying taxes ... it may not be much, but I like to think that I am doing something for Senegal too.

These quotations reflect the fact that the expectation of Senegalese policy that all migrants should be committed to national development is unrealistic.

The desire and capacity to contribute to the advancement of their country is instead tied to migrants' different abilities to mobilise financial, cultural and social capital in the establishment of survival- or growth-oriented businesses.

Policy aspires to gear the financial capital repatriated by migrants towards centrally defined economic development goals. This, however, ignores the nature of these financial flows and the fact that they are distinct from public flows, such as Overseas Development Assistance (ODA).

> As opposed to ODA expenditure, which is directed towards and evaluated in relation to economic goals at the national level, both the migrants who send remittances and the relatives who receive them have their own micro-level interests as their first priority (Horst et al. 2014: 521).

By adopting a restrictive idea of the development outcomes that should derive from migrant investment, Senegalese policy fails to acknowledge that these businesses may indeed have development effects, but on a different scale. As Boccagni notes about returnees to Ecuador, 'even when they do make personal progress, they generally have neither the resources nor the critical mass necessary to induce wider social changes' (Boccagni 2011: 476–7).

**Conclusion**

I have shown that migrant businesses are inspired by different investment logics, that they differ in the ways in which they mobilise capital from overseas and social capital held at home, and that they reflect different personal dispositions towards national development goals.

This chapter challenges the idea that development may be promoted in Senegal through migrant return and investment. Rather than challenging such an idea per se, however, I challenge the way in which it is predominantly formulated in current policy making. Three main criticisms can be made against such policy thinking.

First, the aspirations of origin countries to promote development through the return of its nationals resonate with broader migration and development discourses and largely suffer from the same problems and limitations. Officials designing return migration policies and programmes in Senegal blame migrants for the limited advantages that result from the significant financial resources they transfer to Senegal. As highlighted by Turner and Kleist (2013: 199), placing the responsibility for promoting development on individual migrants 'fits well with neoliberal policies' and offers an alternative to the 'failures of state-centred development approaches'. It also alleviates state responsibilities for addressing structural barriers to economic investment, which the state should be addressing. Furthermore, the idea that the state can control individual migrant action to achieve narrowly defined developmental aims is inherently problematic. Senegalese policy aspires to control private initiative and direct it towards centrally identified target sectors, with the aim of stimulating the market economy under the guidance and rules of the state. Migrant remittances, savings and investments, however, are private resources. Interpretations that tie these resources to national development goals question the legitimacy of migrant loyalties in other spheres and reveal normative assumptions about the ways in which migrant capital should be used (Horst et al. 2014).

Second, an interpretation that sees migrants as carrying various forms of useful capital on the one hand, while on the other lacking the capacity to exploit that capital, is inherently contradictory. Policy discourse overemphasises the financial capital flowing to Senegal via its migrants and ignores the importance of social capital held at home before and after migration in shaping investment outcomes. As aptly put in an interview by a practitioner, highly critical of governmental policies on return and investment: 'People speak of financial transfers, but really this is the least important ... Money is the last factor, yet all is spoken about here is migrants' money.'

Ethnographic insight offered in this chapter shows that migrants' ability to rely on bonding and bridging ties is crucial in developing business ideas, acquiring the necessary skills and generating profit. Migrants' ability to exploit social capital affects their capacity to translate their savings and business ideas into a functioning investment:

> I tell you the truth. In Senegal with no money you can't do anything. If you
> don't have a clear idea you won't do anything. If you are on your own you won't
> get anywhere ... You need all these things together to make it.

Third, the idea that migrants rarely engage in productive investment is heavily challenged by the migrant stories in this chapter. Because migrants invest in activities that are not considered attractive for the pursuit of the government's own goals of national economic growth, policy makers downplay migrant businesses and dismiss them as 'conspicuous consumption'. This confirms that in 'the case of African states reaching out to diasporas as agents of change, they are implicitly reaching out to those expatriates whom they assume have the desired resources in terms of economic and human capital' (Turner and Kleist 2013: 201). Evidence from diaspora engagement policies of migrant sending states around the world confirms that state policy making with regard to diaspora groups is often designed in pursuit of domestic political interests. Research in India and Israel shows that, while the policies of these two governments generically appeal to Indians living abroad (Varadarajan and Mani 2005) and to members of the Jewish diaspora (Cohen 2009), they are actually targeting professional individuals living in the West. Similarly, Kleist (2013) finds that diaspora engagement policies in Ghana combine ambivalent claims of belonging with a state focus on economic interest. Ho (2011: 759) refers to 'analytical slippage' when origin countries universally reach out to their diasporas, while in reality attempting to maintain relationships with elite business and professional emigrants who can help develop global economic opportunities and enhance the country's competitiveness. Waterbury (2010: 135) confirms that 'while states often utilise a rhetoric of engaging the "global nation", their policies target specific populations abroad, depending on what these populations can offer the homeland state'. The situation in Senegal is analogous: migration policy is subordinate to higher political strategies. Migration policy and programmes are in fact geared towards the achievement of goals and visions set in the *National Strategy for Economic and Social Development* (RS 2012), which has a declared aim of turning Senegal into an emergent economy by 2035.

Channelling migrant resources towards such centrally defined aspirations is likely to lead to disappointment, if not failure. Senegalese and other origin states' policies towards their returnees ignore the fact that migrants' measures of success may differ from the institutional ones. While it is true that migrants who have largely emigrated for economic reasons do have economic goals, it is simplistic to reduce their aspirations exclusively to rational economic thinking. The policy focus on national economic growth fails to understand that businesses may also thrive and trigger (economic) development in sectors that are not prioritised by the government, or when they combine assets in formal and informal markets. Examples given in this chapter show that business ideas in sectors labelled by policy makers as innovative or productive (Tapha and his partners' pellet production) may lead to failure. At the same time, businesses in sectors pigeonholed as being saturated, such as commerce and transport, can generate employment and enhance tax revenue (Balla's and Khadim's selling of marble and tiles, Cheikh's bakery, and Makhou's informal transport business). Origin state migration policies would do better to acknowledge the significance of survival-oriented businesses; if nothing else, they can act as a buffer against people slipping into worse conditions of poverty. The idea that all migrant investors could become growth-oriented entrepreneurs is highly unrealistic. Policy interpretations identify barriers in migrants' lack of key ingredients, such as access to credit and business skills. This is translated into programmes and practices that assist migrant investors in accessing these missing ingredients. Instead, Senegalese policy and practice should recognise that survival businesses are qualitatively different from those presenting growth potential. Aspirations of the home country to directly manage the resources flowing into Senegal by way of its diaspora towards centrally defined goals would be better served by a less restrictive understanding of development and by efforts to create improved opportunities that will encourage migrants' own independent initiatives.

## Bibliography

Åkesson, L. (2011) 'Making migrants responsible for development: Cape Verdean returnees and Northern migration policies'. *Africa Spectrum* 41(1): 61–83.

Ammassari, S. (2009) *Migration and Development: Factoring return into the equation*. Newcastle upon Tyne: Cambridge Scholars Publishing.

Barry, K. (2006) 'Home and away: the construction of citizenship in an emigration context'. *New York University Law Review* 81(11): 11–59.

Batista, C., T. McIndoe-Calder and P. C. Vicente (2014) 'Return migration and entrepreneurship in Mozambique'. IZA Discussion paper. Available at http://ssrn.com/abstract=2441491 (accessed 14 April 2015).

Berner, E., G. Gomez and P. Knorringa (2012) 'Helping a large number of people become a little less poor: the logic of survival entrepreneurs'. *European Journal of Development Research* 24: 382–96.

Black, R. and A. Castaldo (2009) 'Return migration and entrepreneurship in Ghana and Côte d'Ivoire: the role of capital transfers'. *Tijdschrift voor Economische en Sociale Geografie* 100(1): 44–58.

Boccagni, P. (2011) 'The framing of return from above and below in Ecuadorian migration: a project, a myth, or a political device?' *Global Networks* 11(4): 461–80.

Cassarino, J.-P. (2000) *Tunisian New Entrepreneurs and their Past Experiences of Migration in Europe: Resource mobilization, networks, and hidden disaffection*. Aldershot: Ashgate.

Cohen, N. (2009) 'Come home, be professional: ethno-nationalism and economic rationalism in Israel's return migration strategy'. *Immigrants and Minorities* 27(1): 1–28.

de Haas, H. (2010) 'Migration and development: a theoretical perspective'. *International Migration Review* 44(1): 227–64.

Delano, A. (2009) 'From limited to active engagement: Mexico's emigration policies from a foreign policy perspective (2000–2006)'. *International Migration Review* 43(4): 764–814.

Démurger, S. and H. Xu (2011) 'Return migrants: the rise of new entrepreneurs in rural China'. *World Development* 39(10): 1847–61.

Diatta, M. A. and N. Mbow (1999) 'Releasing the development potential of return migration: the case of Senegal'. *International Migration* 37(1): 243–64.

Dustmann, C. and O. Kirchkamp (2002) 'The optimal migration duration and activity choice after re-migration'. *Journal of Development Economics* 67(2): 351–72.

Faist, T. (2008) 'Migrants as transnational development agents: an inquiry into the newest round of the migration-development nexus'. *Population, Space and Place* 14(1): 21–42.

— (2009) 'Transnationalization and development: toward an alternative agenda'. *Social Analysis* 53(3): 38–59.

Fitzgerald, D. (2008) *A Nation of Emigrants: How Mexico manages its migration*. Berkeley and Los Angeles CA: University of California Press.

Flahaux, M. L. and L. Kabbanji (2013) 'L'encadrement des retours au Sénégal: logiques politiques et logiques de migrants'. In C. Beauchemin, L. Kabbanji, P. Sakho and B. Schoumaker (eds) *Migrations Africaines: le co-développement en questions. Essai de démographie politique*. Paris: Institut National d'Études Démographiques (INED) and Armand Colin, pp. 241–79.

Gamlen, A. (2008) 'The emigration state and the modern geopolitical imagination'. *Political Geography* 27(8): 840–56.

Guarnizo, L. E. (1998) 'The rise of transnational social formations: Mexican and Dominican state responses to transnational migration'. *Political Power and Social Theory* 12: 45–94.

Gubert, F. and C. J. Nordman (2011) 'Return migration and small enterprise development in the Maghreb'. In

S. Plaza and D. Ratha (eds) *Diaspora for Development in Africa*. Washington DC: World Bank, pp. 103–26.

Ho, E. L. E. (2011) '"Claiming" the diaspora: elite mobility, sending state strategies and the spatialities of citizenship'. *Progress in Human Geography* 35(6): 757–72.

Horst, C., M. Bivand Erdal, J. Carling and K. Afeef (2014) 'Private money, public scrutiny? Contrasting perspectives on remittances'. *Global Networks* 14(4): 514–32. doi: 10.1111/glob.12048.

Ilahi, N. (1999) 'Return migration and occupational change'. *Review of Development Economics* 3(2): 170–86.

Itzigsohn, J. (2000) 'Immigration and the boundaries of citizenship: the institutions of immigrants' political transnationalism'. *International Migration Review* 34(4): 1126–54.

Kilic, T., C. Carletto, B. Davis and A. Zezza (2009) 'Investing back home: return migration and business ownership in Albania'. *Economics of Transition* 17(3): 587–623.

Kleist, N. (2013) 'Flexible politics of belonging: diaspora mobilisation in Ghana'. *African Studies* 72(2): 285–306.

Levitt, P. and R. de la Dehesa (2003) 'Transnational migration and the redefinition of the state: variations and explanations'. *Ethnic and Racial Studies* 26(4): 587–611.

Ma, Z. (2002) 'Social-capital mobilization and income returns to entrepreneurship: the case of return migration in rural China'. *Environment and Planning A* 34(10): 1763–84.

McCormick, B. and J. Wahba (2001) 'Overseas work experience, savings and entrepreneurship amongst return migrants to LDCs'. *Scottish Journal of Political Economy* 48(2): 164–78.

— (2003) 'Return international migration and geographical inequality: the case of Egypt'. *Journal of African Economies* 12: 500–32.

Mesnard, A. (2004) 'Temporary migration and capital market imperfections'. *Oxford Economic Papers* 56: 242–62.

Mezger Kveder, C. and C. Beauchemin (2014) 'The role of international migration experience for investment at home: direct, indirect, and equalising effects in Senegal'. *Population, Space and Place* (published online). doi: 10.1002/psp.1849.

Mezger Kveder, C. and M. L. Flahaux (2013) 'Returning to Dakar: a mixed methods analysis of the role of migration experience for occupational status'. *World Development* 45: 223–38.

MSE (2011) 'Lettre de politique sectorielle des Sénégalais de l'Extérieur'. Dakar: Ministère des Sénégalais de l'Extérieur (MSE), Direction des Sénégalais de l'Extérieur.

Naujoks, D. (2013) *Migration, Citizenship, and Development: Diasporic membership policies and overseas Indians in the United States*. Oxford: Oxford University Press.

Nyberg-Sørensen, N., N. van Hear and P. Engberg-Pedersen (2002) 'The migration–development nexus: evidence and policy options. State-of-the-art overview'. *International Migration* 40(5): 3–43.

Østergaard-Nielsen, E. (ed.) (2003) *International Migration and Sending Countries: Perceptions, policies and transnational relations*. Basingstoke: Palgrave Macmillan.

Oxfeld, E. and L. D. Long (2004) 'Introduction: an ethnography of return'. In L. D. Long and E. Oxfeld (eds) *Coming Home? Refugees, migrants, and those who stayed behind*. Philadelphia PA: University of Pennsylvania Press, pp. 1–15.

Piracha, M. and F. Vadean (2010) 'Return migration and occupational choice: evidence from Albania'. *World Development* 38(8): 1141–55.

Portes, A. (2001) 'Introduction: the debates and significance of immigrant transnationalism'. *Global Networks* 1(3): 181–94.

— and P. Landolt (1996) 'The downside of social capital'. *American Prospect* 7(26): 18–21.

Ragazzi, F. (2009) 'Governing diasporas'. *International Political Sociology* 3(4): 378–97.

RS (2012) *SNDES 2013–2017. Stratégie Nationale de Développement Economique et Social: Sur la rampe de l'émergence.* Dakar: République du Sénégal (RS).

Sherman, R. (1999) 'From state introversion to state extension in Mexico: modes of emigrant incorporation, 1900–1997'. *Theory and Society* 28(6): 835–78.

Sinatti, G. (2011) '"Mobile transmigrants" or "unsettled returnees"? Myth of return and permanent resettlement among Senegalese migrants'. *Population, Space and Place* 17(2): 153–66.

— (2014) 'Return migration as a win-win-win scenario? Visions of return among Senegalese migrants, the state of origin and receiving countries'. *Ethnic and Racial Studies* 38(2): 275–91. doi: 10.1080/01419870.2013.868016.

Strachan, A. J. (1980) 'Government sponsored return migration to Guyana'. *Area* 12(2): 165–9.

Tsuda, T. (2010) 'Ethnic return migration and the nation-state: encouraging the diaspora to return "home"'. *Nations and Nationalism* 16(4): 616–36.

Turner, S. and N. Kleist (2013) 'Introduction: agents of change? Staging and governing diasporas and the African state'. *African Studies* 72(2): 192–206.

van Houte, M. and T. Davids (2008) 'Development and return migration: from policy panacea to migrant perspective sustainability'. *Third World Quarterly* 29(7): 1411–29.

Varadarajan, L. and B. Mani (2005) '"The global Indian family": nationalism, neoliberalism and diaspora at Pravasi Bharatiya Divas'. *Diaspora: Journal of Transnational Studies* 14(1): 45–74.

Wahba, J. and Y. Zenou (2012) 'Out of sight, out of mind: migration, entrepreneurship and social capital'. *Regional Science and Urban Economics* 42(5): 890–903.

Waterbury, M. (2010) 'Bridging the divide: towards an analytical framework for understanding kin state and migrant-sending state diaspora politics'. In R. Baubock and T. Faist (eds) *Diasporas and Transnationalism: Concepts, theories and methods.* Amsterdam: Amsterdam University Press.

# 6 | The role of social capital in post-conflict business development: perspectives from returning migrants in Burundi

Tove Heggli Sagmo

## Introduction

People in Burundi typically believe that returnees from the global North are 'leaving paradise and coming back to the fire', as one person expressed it. This perception is built on two elements. On the one hand, it signals profound scepticism at the returnees' improbable decision to leave paradise; on the other, it reveals expectations of wealth and resources that the returnees will bring back. This combination of scepticism and expectations from the local population affects the process of building social capital, which is central to becoming an agent of change in Burundi.

Returnees often view the economic sector – private business entrepreneurship in particular – as a critical arena in which to gain sufficient income and at the same time maintain independence and influence society. Opportunities are considered to be abundant for those with sufficient financial capital. What returnees often underestimate, however, is the central role of *social* capital in the economic sector. Social capital plays a key role in dealing with practical challenges in relation to business development, such as obtaining information, hiring employees and attracting customers. Furthermore, social capital is central for developing intangible knowledge about the unwritten rules and the power dynamics within the economic sector – a certain feel for the game. The landscape of power has changed dramatically over the last 20 years, and a returnee's pre-migration networks will not always be able to provide the necessary assistance upon return, when building new networks becomes a crucial but complicated task.

Like many other post-conflict settings, Burundi is characterised by high levels of mistrust between individuals, groups and institutions (Uvin 2009). This chapter explores some of the challenges involved in building networks in a society recovering from decades of political and social instability. More specifically, I ask two questions: how are the rules of the game in the economic sector in Burundi perceived by returnees? And what are common strategies for building social capital among returnees?

An individual's capacity to contribute is not just shaped by capital acquired during the time in exile; pre-migration and post-return experiences also shape such capacities in important ways. Hence, I understand return as a process whereby returnees 'establish the social, political and economic ties that define them in a meaningful way as members of a community' (Hammond 2004: 188). Such a definition of return includes the process leading up to the return (Long and Oxfeld 2004) and extends for a long time after arrival. Accordingly, the label 'returnee' will be used both for returnees who have come back to Burundi and for potential returnees abroad.

This chapter builds on 26 semi-structured interviews and two focus group discussions conducted among returnees from the West, now residing in Bujumbura, in addition to 17 interviews with Burundians currently living in various cities in Norway and the UK but engaged in business activities in Burundi.[1] I will also draw on two focus group discussions with members of the local population in Burundi, along with a number of informal conversations, interviews with key informants and observations. All interviews were conducted between 2011 and 2013. The informants were recruited through numerous entry points, including various types of organisation, as well as through personal contacts, to ensure a range of experiences and opinions. The majority of the informants living in Norway and the UK had come to the country of settlement as asylum seekers or quota refugees and held residence permits at the time of the interview. Some had fled Burundi because of threats or direct attacks on themselves or their families, generally related to their ethnic affiliation. Others had fled because of the protracted nature of the generalised violence. Most of the informants were in the 20 to 40 age group; about one-third were female. Both Hutus and Tutsis were included, but, owing to the sensitivity of this issue, I did not systematically ask about ethnic identity. A variation in individuals' socio-economic status (before and after migration) and return intentions was also ensured.

Returnee informants in Bujumbura were as diverse as members of the diaspora in terms of socio-economic characteristics, and their motivations for returning varied along the forced–voluntary axis. The scope of this chapter does not allow for in-depth elaboration of particularities within the various socio-economic and gender categories. Furthermore, I will not differentiate between interviews with returnees and diaspora, mainly because the two groups tend to have rather similar views on the economic field. Instead, I concentrate on these individuals' main perceptions and experiences as actors in the economic arena. The narratives presented are subjective, influenced in part by the interview situation and by my being a female Norwegian. All the same, accounts from the interviews with returnees and other key informants,

1 The Burundian case study is part of the international cross-disciplinary project 'Possibilities and Realities of Return Migration', based at the Peace Research Institute Oslo (PRIO).

combined with observation data and informal discussions, should provide a general impression of the power dynamics in the economic sector in Burundi, although particular details in the narratives might be contested.

I begin the chapter with a brief presentation of the migration context before describing the theoretical framework that guides the analysis. Here, I emphasise that the value of an individual's cultural capital depends on the size and composition of his or her social capital. After a brief analysis of the post-war economy in Burundi and of returnees as actors in the economic arena, I explore the role that social capital plays in three aspects indicated by my informants as being crucial for establishing a successful business: finding employees, assessing the market and attracting customers. I argue that a return to a post-conflict society in which people are struggling with high levels of mistrust is particularly challenging for efforts to build various types of social capital. The chapter ends with a discussion of strategies related to strengthening social capital.

## The history of migration

Burundi's history of migration is intertwined with the political evolution of the Great Lakes area. Like most countries in the region, Burundi has been both a producer and a receiver of various flows of migration, mostly induced by conflict (Fransen and Ong'ayo 2010), although Bakewell and Bonfiglio (2013: 23) correctly point out that mobility in the Great Lakes region is also influenced by 'social processes of education, urbanization and family formation'. In the history of out-migration, the years 1972 and 1993 represent important milestones. In 1972, a Hutu uprising was followed by genocidal reprisals by the Tutsi army (Lemarchand 1994), resulting in 200,000 deaths and 300,000 refugees (Ngaruko and Nkurunziza 2005). The political crisis in 1993 was sparked by the assassination of the newly elected Hutu President Melchior Ndadaye in an attempted military coup. Years of political instability, communal violence and civil war followed, and it is estimated that 300,000 died as a direct result of the war (Lemarchand 2009). Around 700,000 people fled to Tanzania, Rwanda and the Democratic Republic of the Congo (Reyntjens 1995; Lemarchand 2009). Some fled because of threats or direct attacks on themselves or their families, usually based on their ethnic affiliation. Others fled because of the protracted and generalised nature of the violence. Several hundred thousand people were also displaced within Burundi itself. Fewer than 50,000 Burundians found their way to Europe.[2] A small fraction of these were resettled through the United Nations High Commissioner for Refugees (UNHCR), while the majority applied for asylum upon arrival in Europe.

Burundi started the new millennium with the conclusion of ongoing peace negotiations and a framework for the transition period up to 2005. With

---

2 Figures are taken from the UNHCR Statistical Online Population Database: http://popstats.unhcr.org/Default.aspx.

political stability improving in the country, a large-scale repatriation movement from the surrounding region was organised by the UNHCR (UNHCR 2009). Close to 600,000 refugees have since returned from the neighbouring areas, according to the UNHCR's statistical database. This repatriation has caused significant challenges relating to access to land, particularly in the south of Burundi. The number of returnees from Europe is not known but is thought to be small compared with the large-scale return from neighbouring countries.

Burundi's Ministry of Foreign Affairs (MFA) has established a section for diaspora affairs, one of whose tasks is to develop a policy aimed at encouraging members of the diaspora to invest in Burundi and to contribute to the country's national development by returning. However, limited resources have so far prevented this policy from materialising.[3] However, the Burundian government has developed bilateral readmission agreements with several Western countries.

## The theoretical framework

The debate on the impact of return migration on development is well established, but far from conclusive. Differences in methodologies and in definitions of the concept of 'development' as well as variations in scales and in the geographical focus of the studies conducted are some of the reasons why the literature has so far failed to offer definitive answers. Instead of attempting a comprehensive overview of the relevant literature, I will simply highlight the work of three central contributors. The first of these is Francesco P. Cerase (1974), whose typology of return migrants has greatly influenced academic and non-academic thinking on the relationship between return migration and development. By distinguishing between return of failure, return of conservatism, return of innovation and return of retirement, Cerase believed that he could map the development implications of returnees and predict future contributions. Innovative returnees proved hard to find in the case of southern Italy, and Cerase blamed the economic and social structure of the region of origin for the lack of economic innovation and development. Building on Cerase's typology, Bimal Ghosh (2000b) presented three conditions that would have to be met before a society could benefit from the human capital brought by returnees; that is, the skills brought back must be: 1) unique; 2) relevant; and 3) accepted by the country of origin. However, although his identification of these criteria seems useful, Ghosh fails to explain why some skills may be considered unique and relevant and might be accepted, while others are not. I believe that unequal access to social networks may provide part of the explanation. Thirdly, Jean-Pierre Cassarino (2004) presents a different perspective, arguing that the key to successful return lies in the opportunity to accumulate resources from abroad and in the level of preparedness for

---

3 Interview with the MFA, Burundi, 2012.

return. This chapter builds on insights from these three contributors when exploring the role of social capital in business development.

The importance of networks in the migration cycle, including return, is by now well established. However, as Harpviken (2006: 137) has argued, 'the fundamental research challenge is to move beyond the mere contention that networks play an essential role in reintegration and to determine the exact roles – both integrative and disruptive – played by networks of various kinds'. Bourdieu's (1990) theory of social practice, in particular the concept of field and social capital, offers a useful framework for efforts to understand how social networks affect individuals' opportunities in a given context. In the present chapter, combining economic field with social capital is useful for explaining how challenges and opportunities in Burundi are unequally distributed among returnees.

The term 'economic field' is here understood as the arena in Burundi for people involved in business activity of any kind. Such actors compete for investors, location, customers and information. They also compete for power, control and influence over other actors in the field. In the economic field there are unwritten rules for how the actors should behave, and also how they can increase their power and influence. In the Burundian economic field, I argue, a person's legitimate authority is partly defined by the value of his or her social capital. Bourdieu (1986: 249) has claimed that the volume of an individual's social capital 'depends on the size of the network of connections that he can effectively mobilise'. Furthermore, he emphasises that differences in social capital, as well as other types of capital, explain social differentiation in a particular field. Such an understanding of social capital differs from Putnam's functionalistic view of social capital, in which more is better and social capital is linked to voluntary participation and civic engagement (for a full outline of the distinction between Putnam and Bourdieu, see Siisiainen 2003). Nevertheless, I feel that, despite their differing understandings of social capital, Putnam's distinction between bonding and bridging capital can enhance a Bourdieusian analysis of social capital. Bonding is understood as networks among likeminded individuals, and bridging as networks between people belonging to different social strata within a given society (Putnam 2000). This distinction between types of social capital is useful for understanding how diverse types of social networks affect opportunities in the economic field in different ways.

The relationship between the field and individual resources is often compared to a game of cards, where the outcome depends not only on the hand held by each individual player (the resources), but also on how well he or she plays that hand. Having an MBA does not necessary translate into running a successful business. However, in combination with useful networks (social capital) and a comprehensive understanding of the context (the field), it is easier to develop a good business plan. This contextual understanding entails a:

constant awareness of and responsiveness to the play of all the actors involved. It requires assessment of one's own team-mate/s' resources, strength and weaknesses and also those of the opponent/s. It requires improvisation and flexibility and above all, it requires use of anticipation as to what one's team-mate/s and one's opponent/s will do. Behaviours cannot be reduced simply to theoretical rules (Hillier and Rooksby 2005: 23).

The level of trust is one element that characterises any field, as it influences the value of interpersonal relationships and defines the nature of a network (Bourdieu and Thompson 1991; Siisiainen 2003). In the economic field, trust is often referred to as the currency of the new economy in the world, as it influences efficiency and productivity. As Fukuyama (1995: 90) writes:

> trust can dramatically reduce what economists call transaction costs – costs of negotiations, enforcement and the like – and makes possible certain efficient forms of economic organization that otherwise would be encumbered by extensive rules, contracts, litigations, and bureaucracy.

The issue of trust seems particularly relevant in the Burundian case, and the current deficit of trust – both horizontal and vertical – in Burundi is partly linked to the social transformative effect of the civil war (Uvin 2009). On the other hand, mistrust was an inherent property of the patron–client network in Burundi long before the civil war in the 1990s (Trouwborst 1973). When analysing the role and value of social capital in the economic field in Burundi, it is essential to acknowledge the existence of different types of social networks.

## The economic field in Burundi

Burundi's economy is still in a post-war mode. In addition to being one of the world's poorest countries, as well as one of the most corrupt, Burundi has been characterised as a 'low-opportunity economy' (Transparency International 2012; World Bank 2012; Nkurunziza and Ngaruko 2008). Structural conditions such as land scarcity, the country's landlocked location, and being surrounded by unstable neighbours with poorly developed infrastructure act to prevent large-scale investment. The often-mentioned risk of a return to conflict during the first years after a peace agreement (Collier and Hoeffler 2004) may also contribute to the prevalence of a 'wait and see' attitude among potential investors, including members of the diaspora. Rumours of an imminent coup d'état are rife among the diaspora (Turner 2008), and are influencing the willingness to invest and to return. Continued perceptions of instability in Burundi also stem from the government's inability to manage expectations of a quick recovery.

The legacy of the colonial period and consecutive decades of 'catastrophic governance' (Nkurunziza and Ngaruko 2008: 54) further contribute to the economic situation of today's Burundi. Historically, the formal private sector was owned by the government, controlled by Belgian owners, or run by former politicians without managerial experience or expertise (ibid.). The civil war, along with the UN-imposed trade embargo, weakened the economic monopoly of the political elite and created opportunities for a greater range of actors, although it has been claimed that some sectors of the war economy remained under the control of the government (ICG 2012).

Despite the limited size of the formal private sector, the encouragement of individual initiative and celebration of personal success have long traditions in Burundi (Uvin 2009). Individual gains were considered personal property, but it was expected that successful individuals would contribute towards a redistribution of wealth, and failure to live up to such expectations met with sanctions from the community. The 'capitalist ethos' is thus not considered a recent phenomenon, although Burundi's civil war has increased the level of individualism within Burundian society (Turner and Brønden 2011). Despite the widespread view that it was the war that undermined values of hard work and honesty and fed corruption, Uvin (2009) holds that systematic corruption existed long before the war, and was in fact one of the causes of the war, rather than a consequence.

Burundi's peace agreement – the Arusha Accords – significantly altered the country's power structure, and is seen as an ethnic turning point in the political field (Turner 2008). Whereas the political and economic elite were previously Tutsi-dominated, Burundi's Hutus have now secured political representation as well as the majority of leadership positions within the judiciary, the police, the army and various parastatal enterprises (Uvin and Bayer 2013). Uvin (2009), however, argues that the ethnic discrimination of the past, whereby Tutsis had better access to education and other resources, continues to have an effect on the economic field in Burundi, and that Tutsis are generally better off and have greater opportunities for upwards social mobility. A report from the International Crisis Group (ICG 2012) suggests that this pattern may be changing. According to this report, opportunities in the labour market are increasingly controlled by the Hutu-led government. The majority of the directors of state-owned companies are members of the Hutu-dominated party in the government, with directorships granted as a reward for earlier military and political engagement, or offered to the highest bidder within the Conseil National pour le Défense de la Démocratie (CNDD) network. Even private companies have claimed to be under pressure to increase the numbers of Hutus on their staff.

The economic field in Burundi is also increasingly international. In addition to the country's membership of formalised regional economic agreements such as the Eastern African Community, remittances and direct economic engagement by members of the diaspora contribute to the (re)production of the economic field. This chapter will therefore incorporate the voices of both returnees and members of the diaspora when discussing opportunities and challenges in this area. Understanding the economic field as being created in the process of its being contested (Bourdieu 1990; Bourdieu and Wacquant 1992) allows for a more dynamic understanding of reintegration and of changes in individuals' ability to contribute to the development of the country of origin. Let us now see how returnees argue for engagement in the economic field.

## Returnees as actors in the economic field

The absence of a welfare state in Burundi means that individuals are responsible for securing the basic needs of their families. The country's protracted economic crisis, however, has created a more individualised society, and the family support system is not as strong as it once was (Uvin 2009; Vervisch 2011). Most returnees are therefore unable or unwilling to depend on their family networks to secure an income. As other research has shown (see, for example, Solimano 2010; Piracha and Vadean 2010), the probability of becoming self-employed is higher among returnees than among non-migrants. In Burundi, building an enterprise is considered the best option for gaining necessary income, maintaining one's independence and applying imported skills or principles.

Regarding the last point, we should note that not all returnees had the opportunity to work or study while abroad. For instance, failed asylum seekers without work permits often return with minimal skills acquired abroad, although some failed asylum seekers had work permits for several years. Therefore, a clear-cut distinction between forced and voluntary returnees does not seem particularly useful for analysing the developmental impact of returning migrants. Returnees with work experience from the private sector often comment that it is not necessarily the specific tasks that they carried out that are seen as an added advantage upon return, but their exposure to different work ethics and principles of business management. Principles of equality, respect, time-keeping, perseverance and work morale are often mentioned as values upon which they would like to build their businesses in Burundi. In addition to providing jobs and income for people, introducing these values is seen as a key aim of their businesses, and as an important contribution to Burundian society.

As actors in the economic field, returnees differ as to whether they present their activities in the field as a goal in themselves or as a means to achieve other aims. Some returnees see activities in the economic field as a stepping stone for building enough financial capital to develop humanitarian projects for the poor. Building orphanages, schools and resource centres are common plans. Joseph[4] is in the process of developing a business in Bujumbura, but says he dreams of building an educational centre. He emphasises the importance of being independent in order to achieve his goals:

---

4 All names are pseudonyms.

I am planning to make a lot of money. I am not planning to go and ask for money from organisations and stuff, because they bring their own rules. They bring their own limitations. As a 'rebel', I know I have to make it on my own, or find someone who thinks like me ... but it is not going to be an institution that tells me what to do.

Others say that the redistribution of wealth through job creation or donations to family members is their main goal. Yan explains that job creation is the most important way of helping the poor in Burundi. He is encouraged by the opportunities in the country:

You know, the good thing about coming back is that you see so many opportunities that you would never have dreamed of seeing. Because Africa is like a virgin land. There is nothing. If you go to Europe, USA or Australia, everything has been done. You know, you just have to repeat it.

However, this optimistic view of current opportunities in Burundi was not shared by all. Raoul, for instance, used to work in a pizza restaurant before returning. He expresses a more sober analysis of the structural challenges, arguing that many things are simply not possible in Burundi. He had initially thought of starting a pizza restaurant in Burundi, but gave up because of the instability and the high prices of electricity, as well as because he realised that pizza was not as popular in Bujumbura as it was abroad. In other words, the 'virgin' characteristic of the country does not always translate into opportunities for everything and everyone. The role of the relevance and acceptance of new ideas, in addition to infrastructure challenges in the country of origin, as Ghosh (2000a) and others have emphasised, is also crucial for business development in Burundi.

Lack of alternative employment opportunities is cited as the second most important reason for engaging in the economic field. Jobs in the non-governmental organisation (NGO) sector are scarce, and returnees do not always see working in the public sector as desirable, even if they have relevant education and work experience. The public sector offers low salaries and is seen as too conservative and resistant to change. Some researchers argue that work in the public sector is the most efficient way for an individual to increase his or her development impact in the country of origin (Nyberg-Sørensen et al. 2002). Some returnees shared this view, and took up jobs in the government upon return. Many of these returnees also engaged in private business on the side, to be able to raise sufficient income. These returnees had all had strong bonding and bridging networks with people in the government before returning. Many returnees working in the government were of the opinion that it was easier to get a job in the years immediately after 2005 than today.

The Burundi case shows that working in the public sector is not an option for many returnees. High levels of vertical mistrust between individuals and the state discourage returnees from seeking or accepting employment in the public sector. In general, the government is associated with corruption and impunity. As Kamana explains:

> I don't trust those people in Burundi. You know, those people in power, they have done something bad. Those who are coming [into power], they are coming with hate towards others. People are divided, regional, ethnic … Everyone who takes power, they don't unite the people. That's why it is difficult to trust. You know, in Africa, when people take power they only think about themselves and their own people.

Because of this poor reputation, job offers from the government are sometimes viewed with suspicion. Gaston, for example, claims that the job offer he received from the government was motivated by a wish to neutralise his political activism abroad, and he opted to decline it. Moreover, getting a job in the public sector is seen as practically impossible without the right connections. As Deni says:

> If you know somebody you might be able to get a job, but if you don't know anybody … Those who are running the country, who knows them? Before, everybody knew somebody. But now, people who have been living abroad for God knows how many years … who we don't know. Who has returned to take over the country … how many know them? Nobody … you are looking at the news and you ask who are you? You don't recognise a single minister. You don't have a chance to get a job.

Let me now move on to the main rule of the game in the economic field in Burundi, as described by the returnees: namely, staying well connected. I start with a brief history of the role of social capital in Burundi.

### Social capital in the Burundian economic field

The role of social capital is not a new topic of discussion in the literature on Burundi. Before the terminology of social capital was introduced, Trouwborst (1973) was conducting fieldwork on what he called 'partial networks' in the rural Burundi of the 1950s and 1960s. Trouwborst identified two types of networks. The first – what he called 'beer friends' – were networks made up of neighbours, friends and relatives. This type of bonding network (Putnam 2000) was located in the individual's immediate vicinity and was based on principles of equality, trust and reciprocity. According to Trouwborst (1973: 112), the aim of the network was the 'establishment and confirmation of pleasant social relations', rather than furthering one's own interests to the detriment of others.

Trouwborst's second network was the patron–client network. Here, the patron in the relationship was expected to extend his help and protect the client, while the client would provide assistance in the form of labour, offerings in kind and loyalty (Lemarchand 1994). This type of network was found to be asymmetric in nature, with elements of competition, mutual distrust and conflicting interests inherent in the dyadic relationship (Trouwborst 1973). Based as they are on differences in status, income and power (Selboe 2008), asymmetric relationships tie individuals and groups from different social strata together in a field; this type of network can therefore be considered a form of bridging social network (Putnam 2000).

The city of Bujumbura today is a more complex society than the rural communities of the Burundi of the 1950s and 1960s. The economic field in particular encompasses many more actors involved in far more varied types of activity. Internationalisation of the economy, along with international aid, is also a recent phenomenon. Despite the evolution of the economic field, the two types of network described above remain essential components of people's social capital, and have perhaps become even more important due to the greater level of complexity of the information and opportunities available. Finding information about where to rent a house, how to buy land, where to hire good workers, how to get a job, where to find a loan and so on can be achieved only with the help of networks. In other words, the networks act as conveyor belts for flows of information (Harpviken 2006). However, while networks have become increasingly important, their dynamics have changed over time. Burundi's protracted crisis has resulted in weakened bonding networks and broken bridges with patrons, reducing the possibilities for converting social capital into economic capital (Vervisch et al. 2013). In this protracted crisis, returnees are generally considered to be worse off than locals because 'they have been out and they have to learn everything'.[5] This quote indicates how capital is context-dependent and is valued within the field, and also that the rules and positions in a field evolve over time. People who have spent considerable time outside the field have to learn the new rules of the game.

*Assessing the market* Developing a business idea and assessing the market require a good overview of current and probable future economic and political conditions. Since very limited information is publicly available, reliance on networks is high. Burundi is often described as a country where rumours and conspiracy theories flourish and form part of the political ontology (Turner 2005; 2008). Lemarchand (1970: 9) writes of Burundi as 'a cultural environment in which concealing or distorting the truth are traditionally regarded as both a virtue and an art'. When trying to sift out groundless rumours and conspiracy theories from the wealth of information available, a common strategy is to

---

5 Quote from a focus group discussion with local people.

maintain as many social relations as possible (Uvin 2009). As Trouwborst (1973: 116) argues, 'a person with many beer friends has more influence, possesses more information and has greater access to places than someone who has relatively few beer friends'. This still holds true in Burundi today. Having few social relationships or networks in only one ethnic group, social group or political faction reduces the possibilities for triangulating the wealth of information that is available and increases vulnerability.

Having a rich, well-connected network also makes it easier to find out who the important patrons are and to develop a strategy for approaching them. Patrons can give valuable advice as well as direct assistance, and may even be able to find shortcuts in the bureaucracy involved in the process of establishing a business. Some returnees have never lived in Bujumbura before returning to Burundi, and find themselves in a particularly precarious position, with few – if any – family or friends living there. Nick, for example, had never lived in Bujumbura before deciding to return to Burundi. He wanted to buy land and equipment for business purposes, but ended up losing several thousand dollars because he trusted the wrong people. The land did not exist, and the equipment never arrived. Nick explains that his 'mistake' was that he did not know how to distinguish between honest entrepreneurs and criminals. He believes that the criminal actors have an advantage, as they have connections in the government, police and judicial system and know how to play the system. Returnees, on the other hand, are described as easy targets because they do not have an overview of the various actors in the field, and they are easy to distinguish from the locals owing to differences in language, clothes and behaviour.

Bonding networks are supposed to be based on the exchange of honest and altruistic advice (ibid.). However, in rural Burundi, Vervisch, Vlassenroot and Braeckman (2013: 277) found that, during the country's protracted crisis, 'bonding social capital degenerated into an unproductive asset'. They even established that 'brothers stole from each other, which created an atmosphere of mistrust among community members' (ibid.: 277). In addition to war and protracted economic crisis, migration – especially to the global North – can change the nature of bonding networks. The local expectation of the migrant's social mobility, as well as the practice of sending remittances, alters the bonding networks in a way that results in the principles of equality, mutual solidarity and proximity fading into the background. The result may be greater inequalities of power. Few returnees express expectations of receiving economic capital from their networks in Burundi upon return; however, when the expected benefit of receiving encouragement and advice from their bonding network fails to materialise, they experience feelings of alienation. Gordien recalls how everyone wanted to 'hang out' with him in the beginning, but when the money dried up he was abandoned. Joseph complains that far too many people ask him for money, or expect him to pay for the beer, simply because they know that he has returned from Europe. When he refuses to pay, he tells me, his friends react by saying: 'How can we believe that you don't have money? No, you are a liar. You have money.' While reciprocity produces a sense of belonging, the two experiences described above reflect reduced feelings of belonging in a network defined by strong bonds. These experiences also illustrate how trust tends to diminish when the density of a network decreases, and it becomes a challenge to discover where to turn to for advice when trying to implement a business idea. Many returnees said that it was difficult to know whether the advice offered is unbiased or not. Ildephonse, for example, returned with an innovative business concept. His local network dismissed the idea because it was considered 'too Western' and not suitable for the local context in Bujumbura. He decided to disregard the advice from his local network in Burundi, and listen instead to other returnees and his friends in the diaspora. This proved to be a wise decision, and he now runs a very successful business.

*Identifying employees* The success of the returnees' investment often depends on the skills and commitment of their employees. Informants emphasised that finding workers with sufficient knowledge, capacity and reliability requires physical presence and interactions with people over time. An additional challenge when hiring people is the obligation to hire family members. Moreover, a lack of trust in society is mentioned as the reason for hiring from one's own network, normally the bonding network. However, informants explained that hiring from within one's network of family and friends does not automatically lead to success: one reason for a possible lack of success that was often mentioned concerned differing temporal perspectives on profit. According to returnees, members of the local population focus on meeting short-term needs, so they want to be involved in businesses that can provide immediate gains. Better-off returnees, in contrast, can afford the luxury of thinking with a more long-term horizon. This conflict of interest has resulted in many unsuccessful joint ventures, and stories about such failures flourished among returnees. Failed attempts have also created disappointment within bonding networks. Bertin recounts:

> Many years ago I owned a car business. I bought cheap cars from Brussels and sent them to Dar es Salaam, where they were supposed to be received and then sold to NGOs. But people steal from you. Not only because they are criminals, but because they don't have a choice. You lose faith in people, even cousins, and it takes time to rebuild that trust. Should I invest in something I have to be there and make sure that things happen.

These stories about their own and others' unsuccessful experiences of business collaboration with local people are often given as explanations for why running a business requires close supervision, which in turn places limitations on the possibility of running a business from abroad.

*Attracting customers* As already noted, independence was expressed as one of the reasons for establishing a business. However, many informants discovered that a good business idea is often not enough. Instead, the size and composition of social networks become the means for securing a sustainable livelihood, thus limiting the possibility of achieving independence. Agathon comments: 'Your success and failure is not always entirely up to you. It is up to all these people behind you, or not behind you.' Economic opportunities could be won or lost due to the composition of one's networks. The size of these networks also determines how far the news of a new business can be disseminated. Yan explains:

> In Burundi you need to know people, you need to talk to people. You need to know how to talk to people and they need to trust you ... Everywhere you go, you have to sell yourself.

A large bonding network might not attract the most prosperous customers needed to sustain a business. If the desired customers belong to a higher social stratum than the business owner, it is necessary to establish bridging networks. This can pose a challenge in Burundi, owing to two factors. The first involves ethical considerations. Yan, who is struggling to gain customers, says that 'probably the smartest thing to do is to be associated with somebody in the government, but I know myself. I am not that kind of guy.' Yan's comments point to the porous border between the economic and the political field in Burundi (Nkurunziza and Ngaruko 2008; ICG 2012). People in the political field have direct and indirect influence on the economic field, and thus have an impact on the individual freedom of actors in the economic field. Bernard confirms the reality of this challenge:

> You are under control. Life and success will be conditioned by the political environment. Mixing with the political class is not a good idea, but you have to join the right political party to do businesses.

The second challenge relates to access. Research from rural Burundi has confirmed that the patron–client network is central for accessing resources, and that developing such access has become more and more difficult owing to increased poverty. The result is a greater division between the rich and the poor (Vervisch et al. 2013). The challenge of building bridges to patrons is also confirmed in my own research. As Louis explains:

> We care a lot about social classes, you know. People don't involve people from

different classes. Rich people collaborate with rich people. Poor collaborate with poor. So the rich will be richer and the poor will be poorer. You know, there is kind of a wall dividing the classes.

In the competition for the attention of patrons, returnees argue that migration-related resources such as foreign citizenship, language skills, diplomas and consumer goods may offer an advantage, because they can contribute to social mobility. However, a migrant returning without economic or cultural capital will lose out in such a competition, and will also face challenges in building up bonding social capital.

## Activating, building and maintaining social capital

The fact that activating, substituting, expanding or building new networks are time-consuming processes was clearly expressed in the interviews. Building relations between locals and returnees is often described as particularly challenging, owing to the existence of mutual mistrust. From the viewpoint of the local population, this mistrust may stem from the returnee's original act of leaving and living in a part of the world that is not known or understood. It should also be seen in light of the fact that migration, in a historical perspective, has been considered an abnormal social practice, linked to negative associations such as death, illness and moral degradation (Uvin 2009). Even though the war created massive population movement, most people have returned to a relatively immobile lifestyle since it ended. A survey in rural Burundi showed that 80 per cent of the population had not travelled outside their own villages within the last year (ibid.), so mobility is still the exception rather than the rule. Returnees say that people who move back to Burundi empty-handed, without having made any pre-return visits, are met with particular suspicion. Egide explains:

> Some do not trust us because they do not know us. They don't know exactly where you were, why you came back and in which [political] party you belong. Sometimes when you come back they think you failed and they cannot trust you because you have failed.

Returnees, for their part, often say that the local population has changed in a negative way. Low morale and a culture of silence are often mentioned as obstacles for developing close relationships with them. According to Uvin (ibid.: 160), 'after years of anarchy and a weak state, people developed instinctive protective mechanisms for not speaking up or revealing the truth when it may lead to personal danger or conflict'. Bertin, for one, struggles with these protective mechanisms, which he feels are destroying any possibility of him assisting people in Burundi: 'In Burundi everything is secret. Nobody tells you the truth. You can't know how to help, if they don't tell you the truth.'

Similarly, Leonce wants to trust people, but feels unable to do so. He believes that people are trying to cheat him all the time and that they never tell the truth. Jean, who has also been disappointed, describes the changes in Burundi in the following manner:

Because of the war and everything, you have nobody to trust. You can't trust anybody. Impossible! So, because of the war, there is that kind of individualism which has come to the people. Before, I am telling you, people used to like each other. You could go to somebody at night and say 'I am hungry' and then he would give you food. Before, you could go to somebody at night and say 'I am going very far and I need a place to sleep', because they didn't have hotels. I used to live in the rural area. People would travel, they went very far. They used to come to my father's house and say 'We are travelling very far and we cannot continue at night. Can you give us a place to sleep?' And then I remember in my grandfather's house they gave them a place to sleep. They didn't know them, but they gave them a place to sleep. They gave the strangers food and in the morning they continued on their journey. But now, things are not like that.

The war is given as the reason why the relationship between individualism and redistribution has changed. Many returnees describe individual gain as the only thing that matters in Burundi now – collective responsibilities have been forgotten. Gervais argues that, in the new Burundi, cheating family and friends is considered acceptable. He tells me a story about a person who cheated his own father-in-law. In the end, he comments:

The greed is unbelievable. Actually it really, really scares me a lot because you come to one point where you ask 'Who are you going to trust?' It is shocking. If you can't trust your people, then who do you trust?

Adam links trust with security. He thinks that 'their [the locals'] minds have become very dangerous. People can be killed, even by their friends.' His strategy is to stay away from local people and to socialise instead with other returnees from Europe. 'I trust them more, and they can give me good advice,' he says. Whether these descriptions are more linked to individual changes in perspective and preferences as a result of living abroad and not actual change in Burundi is not important in this context. What matter here are returnee experiences and perceptions of the mismatch between themselves and the local population. The joy of being back home, together with family and friends, is therefore often mixed with feelings of frustration, alienation and mistrust. Gervais was particularly frustrated by the lack of support from his father's network in his efforts to find a job:

The funny thing is, when they first saw me they were nice. They told me stories about how my father was a nice man and how he helped them. But as soon as I mentioned the reason for why I am there [to ask for a job], they changed. From being humble and welcoming when I first walk through the door and then it gets totally different when we get to the middle of the conversation. I can tell when I look into their faces, I can see. They give me their phone numbers, but nobody picks up the receiver.

In this case, the acquaintances of Gervais' father were not willing to reciprocate the services received from the father in the past. He says that he found more help and support among other returnees. Cafés inspired by Western design and menus act as hubs for some returnees. Here, they can drink cappuccinos, surf the internet, and find support among like-minded people. Common challenges and frustrations are shared, and advice and encouragement given. Bonding among returnees is highly rewarded and seen as a lifeline and the key to survival in Bujumbura. Ildephonse comments on the networks among returnees:

Yeah, when you find yourself in this kind of culture, which is a strong one, you truly like to live with people who are close ... it is different, so different. Like the fact that you cannot buy what you want. For example, the fact that you are telling something to somebody and he's not getting what you are saying. It's not a matter of the language but communication. After a while you feel like you want to go ... So most ... they get tired. Some, they just can't take it.

Another strategy for returnees is to mobilise their transnational social capital to access financial capital, as well as to obtain feedback on business ideas.

Importantly, my research shows that pre-war networks may no longer be in a position to offer any assistance, and in the worst case may be a liability, as many of Burundi's political changes are recent. Leonce, for example, found that his family background – his father was a political leader before the war – has limited his mobility, owing to concerns about physical insecurity. He has also experienced difficulties in building social networks, as people tend to distance themselves from a fallen political star. Returnees view the value of social networks as being linked to the political system, fluctuating in accordance with its changes.

Pre-return preparations are crucial for establishing oneself in the economic field. Making a return visit is a vital tool for assessing possibilities of the market, preparing a business plan and procuring the necessary equipment – particularly since access to quality equipment is a challenge in Burundi, and most items need to be imported. However, the most important role of the return visit is to build or reactivate networks. In order to establish contact with patrons (to 'bridge'), it is essential to show off existing economic capital and the potential to increase that capital further. Renting an expensive house or a car, carrying an expensive phone, and having a fancy hairstyle and clothes that distinguish a returnee from the local population were seen as important strategies. Making generous donations and mixing the local Kirundi with elements of French and English was cited as another way of displaying social mobility. In addition, citizenship in a European country was described as an added advantage. According to returnees, the second-best position is to have a track record of obtaining tourist visas in Europe. Gaining a tourist visa is considered proof of a truly voluntary return, since deportees will not be considered trustworthy travellers by the embassies. Moreover, showing off social capital was noted as one important aspect of bridging. Getting married, for example, performs an important function in terms of displaying and strengthening social networks; investing in large wedding celebrations is thus seen as a good investment in social capital. Gift-giving and social interactions are also important strategies for strengthening bonding networks. After returning, it is essential to 'hang out' in order to stay in the loop. Establishing a public profile by greeting people on the street, making frequent phone calls, spending time in cafés, offering a beer to an acquaintance, and so on – these are all necessary for maintaining and expanding one's networks.

Investing in symbolic assets such as phones, cars and clothes, in addition to participating in social events, has an influence on one's position in the economic field. That calls into question the assumption that spending financial capital on seemingly unproductive investments is one of the characteristics of 'the return of failure'. Rather, as Gmelch (1987) argues, 'what is considered unproductive investment is often a prerequisite for return and could have [a] positive economic and social impact [in] the long run'.

Gifts, remittances and investment in symbolic assets can bring about a shift in power dynamics, and the effect may be a verticalisation of the horizontal bonding network. In other words, these gifts and investments are regarded as symbols of a successful stay abroad, and lead to increased social status among the local population, with the result that the migrant may be upgraded to the status of a patron – a status linked to certain expectations regarding redistribution. Such a responsibility is often viewed with ambivalence. Becoming a patron is a dream for many, as one is then in a position to help and influence other people and thus bring about social change. Gabriel, for example, says that 'if you work in private business it might be easier to make them think like you do', and mentions being more structured and efficient as values he would like to see in others. On the other hand, premature status as a patron can have a negative effect on one's business development, as financial capital is redistributed instead of invested in the business. Failure to adhere to the expectations of redistribution can generate questions regarding the migrant's activities abroad, and may lead to the devaluation of the person's social status and influence his or her position in the field. Renegotiating one's position within the bonding network is therefore often required before one can ask for services and advice.

## Conclusion

I have argued against focusing narrowly on cultural capital such as education and work experience brought back to the country of origin when evaluating or predicting the developmental impact of returning migrants, as it gives an incomplete picture. The rules that govern how various forms of capital can be converted shape the possibilities available to returnees for applying their skills as they have planned. In order to succeed in translating savings and skills into a prosperous business, it is necessary to spend time and money on building social capital. In societies where oral communication plays an important role, especially post-conflict countries, information is always relational and must be triangulated before it can be acted upon. Bonding and bridging networks – both essential elements of social capital – are needed to obtain enough reliable information to succeed in the economic field in Burundi. Building or reactivating bonding and bridging networks, however, can be a cumbersome process. As we have seen, trust is a scarce commodity that complicates this process. A sustained physical presence is often required to establish the trust, reciprocity and generosity needed for bonding networks to function. For this reason, frequent visits are an essential first step in establishing a presence in the economic field and getting a feel for the game, as Bourdieu described the success factor (see, for example, Bourdieu and Wacquant 1992). Returnees who are unable to make these visits struggle to develop a sufficient overview of the field to plan effectively for the future. That disadvantage can be overcome if the returnee can obtain the same overview through existing social networks.

Social capital is therefore the central factor for enabling or restricting the application of skills brought back to the country of origin, and is a catalyst for creating the 'feel for the game' that is necessary for making sound decisions. Building social capital requires time, symbolic assets and persistence. The potential of a business will therefore evolve in parallel with the process of accumulating social capital. Categorising return as a 'success' or 'failure' based on a one-off exploration may not always hit the nail on the head: return is a dynamic process.

## References

Bakewell, O. and A. Bonfiglio (2013) *Moving Beyond Conflict: Re-framing mobility in the African Great Lakes region*. Oxford: International Migration Institute, University of Oxford.

Bourdieu, P. (1986) 'The forms of capital'. In J. Richardson (ed.) *Handbook of Theory and Research for the Sociology of Education*. New York NY: Greenwood, pp. 241–58.

— (1990) *The Logic of Practice*. Cambridge: Polity Press.

— and J. B. Thompson (1991) *Language and Symbolic Power*. Cambridge: Polity Press.

— and L. J. Wacquant (1992) *An Invitation to Reflexive Sociology*. London: University of Chicago Press.

Cassarino, J.-P. (2004) 'Theorising return migration: the conceptual approach to return migrants revisited'. *International Journal on Multicultural Studies* 6(2): 162–88.

Cerase, F. P. (1974) 'Expectations and reality: a case study of return migration from the United States to southern Italy'. *International Migration Review* 8(2): 245–62.

Collier, P. and A. Hoeffler (2004) 'Conflicts'. In B. Lomberg (ed.) *Global Crisis, Global Solutions*. Cambridge: Cambridge University Press.

Fransen, S. and A. O. Ong'ayo (2010) *Migration in Burundi: History, current trends and future prospects*. Maastricht: Maastricht Graduate School of Governance.

Fukuyama, F. (1995) *Trust: The social virtues and the creation of prosperity*. New York NY: Free Press.

Ghosh, B. (2000a) 'Introduction'. In B. Ghosh (ed.) *Return Migration: Journey of hope or despair?* Geneva: International Organization for Migration (IOM), pp. 1–5.

— (2000b) 'Return migration: reshaping policy approaches'. In B. Ghosh (ed.) *Return Migration: Journey of hope or despair?* Geneva: International Organization for Migration (IOM), pp. 181–226.

Gmelch, G. (1987) 'Work, innovation, and investment: the impact of return migrants in Barbados'. *Human Organization* 46(2): 131–40.

Hammond, L. (2004) 'The making of a good citizen in an Ethiopian returnee settlement'. In L. D. Long and E. Oxfeld (eds) *Coming Home? Refugees, migrants, and those who stayed behind*. Philadelphia PA: University of Pennsylvania Press, pp. 187–205.

Harpviken, K. B. (2006) 'Networks in transition: wartime migration in Afghanistan'. PhD thesis, Department of Sociology and Human Geography, University of Oslo.

Hillier, J. and E. Rooksby (2005) 'Introduction'. In J. Hillier and E. Rooksby (eds) *Habitus: A sense of place*. Burlington VT: Ashgate Publishing, pp. 19–42.

ICG (2012) 'Burundi: a deepening corruption crisis'. In ICG, *Africa Report*. Brussels: International Crisis Group (ICG).

Lemarchand, R. (1970) *Rwanda and Burundi*. Pall Mall Library of African Affairs. London: Pall Mall Press.

— (1994) *Burundi: Ethnic conflict and genocide*. Cambridge: Woodrow Wilson Center Press.

— (2009) *The Dynamics of Violence in Central Africa: National and ethnic conflict in the twenty-first-century*. Philadelphia PA: University of Philadelphia Press.

Long, L. D. and E. Oxfeld (eds) (2004) *Coming Home? Refugees, migrants, and those who stayed behind*. Philadelphia PA: University of Pennsylvania Press.

Ngaruko, F. and J. D. Nkurunziza (2005) 'Civil war and its duration in Burundi'. In P. Collier and N. Sambanis (eds) *Understanding Civil War*. Washington DC: World Bank, pp. 35–62.

Nkurunziza, J. D. and F. Ngaruko (2008) 'Why has Burundi grown so slowly? The political economy of redistribution'. In B. J. Ndulu, S. A. O'Connell, J.-P. Azam, R. H. Bates, A. K. Fosu, J. W. Gunning and D. Njinkeu (eds) *The Political Economy of Economic Growth in Africa 1960–2000*. Cambridge: Cambridge University Press, pp. 51–85.

Nyberg-Sørensen, N., N. van Hear and P. Engberg-Pedersen (2002) 'The migration–development nexus: evidence and policy options. State-of-the-art overview'. *International Migration* 40(5): 49–73.

Piracha, M. and F. Vadean (2010) 'Return migration and occupational choice: evidence from Albania.' *World Development* 38(8): 1141–55. doi: 10.1016/j.worlddev.2009.12.015.

Putnam, R. D. (2000) *Bowling Alone: The collapse and revival of American community*. New York NY: Simon & Schuster.

Reyntjens, F. (1995) *Burundi: Breaking the cycle of violence*. London: Minority Rights Group.

Selboe, E. (2008) 'Changing continuities: multi-activity in the network politics of Colobane, Dakar'. PhD thesis,

Department of Sociology and Human Geography, University of Oslo.

Siisiainen, M. (2003) 'Two concepts of social capital: Bourdieu vs. Putnam'. *International Journal of Contemporary Sociology* 40(2): 183–204.

Solimano, A. (2010) *International Migration in the Age of Crisis and Globalization: Historical and recent experiences.* Cambridge: Cambridge University Press.

Transparency International (2012) *Annual Report 2012.* Berlin: Transparency International. Available at http://issuu.com/transparencyinternational/docs/annual_report_2012?e=2496456/4244871.

Trouwborst, A. (1973) 'Two types of partial networks in Burundi'. In J. Boissevain and C. J. Mitchell (eds) *Network Analysis: Studies in human interaction.* Paris: Mouton & Co.

Turner, S. (2005) '"The Tutsi are afraid we will discover their secrets" – on secrecy and Sovereign Power in Burundi'. *Social Identities* 11(1): 37–54.

— (2008) 'The waxing and waning of the political field in Burundi and its diaspora'. *Ethnic and Racial Studies* 31(4): 742–65. doi: 10.1080/01419870701784505.

— and B. M. Brønden (2011) *From Watch-Dogs to Nation-Builders: The dilemmas of diaspora engagement in post-conflict Burundi.* DIIS Working Paper. Copen-hagen: Danish Institute for Interna-tional Studies (DIIS).

UNHCR (2009) *Money Matters: An evalua-tion of the use of cash grants in UNHCR's voluntary repatriation and reintegration programme in Burundi.* Geneva: United Nations High Commissioner for Refu-gees (UNHCR). Available at www.unhcr.org/4a5f436d9.html.

Uvin, P. (2009) *Life after Violence: A people's story of Burundi.* London: Zed Books.

Uvin, P. and L. Bayer (2013) 'The political economy of statebuilding in Burundi'. In M. Berdal and D. Zaum (eds) *Poli-tical Economy of Statebuilding: Power after peace.* New York NY: Routledge, pp. 230–45.

Vervisch, T. (2011) 'The solidarity chain: post-conflict reconstruction and social capital building on three Burundian hillsides'. *Journal of Eastern African Studies* 5(1): 24–41. doi: 10.1080/17531055.2011.544541.

— K. Vlassenroot and J. Braeckman (2013) 'Livelihoods, power, and food insecurity: adaptation of social capital portfolios in protracted crises. Case study Burundi'. *Disasters* 37(2): 267–92. doi: 10.1111/j.1467-7717.2012.01301.x.

World Bank (2012) *World Development Report.* Washington DC: World Bank. Available at https://openknowledge.worldbank.org/handle/10986/4391.

# 7 | Threatening miniskirts: returnee South Sudanese adolescent girls and social change

Katarzyna Grabska

In September 2008[1] some 30 women and girls, recently returned from displacement caused by the 22-year-long civil war in Sudan, were rounded up and beaten by police in the southern Sudanese capital, Juba. Officials castigated them for their 'indecent clothing': tight trousers, miniskirts and fitted T-shirts. It was seen as evidence of a 'Nigger illicit culture' that was banned.[2]

The ensuing cultural debate that erupted was not an isolated event. Across southern Sudan there has been controversy over the new cultures brought back by returnees from Khartoum, East Africa and elsewhere. In 2008, the *Sudan Tribune* called on politicians to speak out about social issues such as dress codes, abortion and racism, warning that hip-hop is 'cultural pollution', luring children from their studies:

> unregulated culture norms will destroy our social fabric. I believe special measures like Juba city ordinance[3] are needed to safe guard [*sic*] our social way of life and democracy ... We are all for change (positive one) but spreading hazardous behaviors like seen in Juba should be treated as a crime, because if not brought into an end ultimately it will infest the entire nation.

Return migration, in the aftermath of conflict or following a search for better livelihood options, is often depicted in policy discourses as being beneficial to the migrants as well as to their communities of origin (Chapter 1; UNDP 2009). These assumptions are based on the idea that capital accumulated by migrants translates into useful resources for the development of their 'home'. As this chapter and other contributions in this volume show, this assumption

---

1 In 2008, South Sudan was still part of the Republic of Sudan, with a regional government of southern Sudan headquartered in Juba. I use the term 'South Sudan' to refer to the independent South Sudanese state (as of July 2011) and 'southern Sudan' to pre-independence South Sudan.

2 Several articles appeared in the local Sudanese press following the arrests (for example, on 9 and 15 October 2008 in the *Sudan Tribune*) and on the website of the Sudan People's Liberation Movement (SPLM). The Juba Commissioner's Local Order No. 4/2008 referred to a section of the Social and Cultural Affairs of Local Government Act 2003 that criminalised 'all bad behaviors, activities and imported illicit cultures'. The order specifically mentioned 'Niggers' in Juba County without explaining who they are.

3 Juba Commissioner's Local Order No. 4/2008.

overlooks the complex links between individual migrants, the type of capital accumulated, and the structural and institutional context of the place of migration and the context of return.

In this chapter, I focus on the experiences of forced displacement and return among South Sudanese Nuer[4] adolescent girls and young women in the aftermath of the war that took place from 1983 to 2005. While most of the return migration literature examines the economic dimension of development instigated by returnees, I conceptualise wartime displacement as a catalyst for social change more generally. In this perspective, development is understood as part and parcel of social change. I draw particular attention to the processes and experiences of 'settling in' of adolescent girls, who so far have received rather limited attention in policy and academic discourses. This often overlooked dimension sheds light on the gendered and generational characteristics of return experiences and the type of social change associated with post-war (re)construction.

Due to its abrupt nature and often traumatic gendered experiences, conflict-induced displacement produces changes in gender and generational relations resulting in new configurations of social relations (see Indra 1999; Schrijvers 1999; De Alwis 2004; Essed et al. 2005; Kaiser 2010; Grabska 2014). I therefore argue that displacement might not only result in a loss but also create opportunities to construct new social norms in the context of interactions between returnees and those who have stayed behind. Such an approach places the returnee adolescent girls and young women at the centre of these transformations. I demonstrate that Bourdieu's (1986) concept of social capital as accumulated by migrants and refugees during displacement needs to be deconstructed in its gendered and generational dimensions and in its place- and context-specific meaning. As I show, access to new resources and the conversion of such resources into personal and community capital are redistributed unequally, and often determined by gender and age. An examination of diverse returnee and stayee girls' conflicting and contradictory positioning with regards to social change in general, and development more specifically, benefits from a critical evaluation of the diverse effects of social capital acquired in displacement and its 'usefulness' (see Chapter 1) for instigating social change in the context of return. It also emphasises the need to understand the broader processes of social transformations rather than focusing only on the economic dimension of development associated with migration.

In this chapter, I ask how the returning girls are affected by the process of settling in within the ever changing post-war environment of South Sudan.

---

4 The Nuer people, the second largest ethnic group in South Sudan, reside mainly in the Western and Eastern Upper Nile regions, bordering North Sudan and Ethiopia. Until recently, their lives centred on agro-pastoralism (Evans-Pritchard 1940; Hutchinson 1996).

What are the diverse effects that the differently positioned returnee girls inflict on their communities of origin? How do we account for social change in an environment where not only people but social norms are in motion? By analysing the experiences of a diverse group of returnee girls, and by focusing on the resulting moral panics, I highlight the central importance of power and the positionality of the girls in the context of evolving and transforming social orders, norms and identities. The analysis brings to light connections between agency, individual and community capital, social forces and change. This, I argue, allows us to discern the links between moving people and moving terrains in situations of volatility and social change.

In the following section, I set out the context of the research and discuss the methods used. I then consider the local meanings of settling in and social change as articulated by Nuer stayees and returnees, before discussing the diverse experiences of returnee girls and emphasising their varied positions. Finally, I consider the perceived and actual contributions to social change made by returnee adolescent girls.

## The evolving post-war environment in South Sudan and research methods

War and displacement have characterised life in Sudan and South Sudan for a number of decades. The political and civil turmoil that erupted in southern Sudan as a result of the conflict that began in 1983 claimed over 2 million lives and resulted in one of the largest displacements in the world. The January 2005 Comprehensive Peace Agreement (CPA) between Khartoum and the Sudan People's Liberation Army/Movement (SPLA/M) made population repatriation possible. The dynamics of this repatriation changed on 5 July 2011, when South Sudan became an independent state. According to International Organization for Migration (IOM) estimates, 2.5 million South Sudanese had returned by 2012, settling across all ten states that make up the Republic of South Sudan. This mass influx of returnees had a significant impact on the new country and the host communities' ability to share limited basic services, livelihood opportunities and economic resources.

For the Nuer population, as for other pastoralist groups, the process of displacement has to be seen in the context of their wider migratory livelihoods (Horst 2006; Monsutti 2005). As agro-pastoralists, they have always been highly mobile, with seasonal migrations from villages to cattle camps. In the past 60 years, this has been coupled with migration for work and trade (see Hutchinson 1996). Physical mobility is highly gendered and generational. Historically, seasonal cattle migrations were male-dominated. For young men, movement was and continues to be linked to their transformation from childhood to adulthood. Added to this seasonal migratory pattern is the long-term legacy of conflict in Unity State (formerly Western Upper Nile). Due to its abundance of oil, the area was a major battlefield in the South–North conflict as well as hosting inter- and intra-ethnic fighting between different Nuer and Dinka groups throughout the 1990s.

Since 2002, I have been carrying out multi-sited ethnographic research among the displaced southern Sudanese in Cairo and in Kakuma refugee camp in Kenya. Throughout most of 2007, I followed the lives of the South Sudanese Nuer returnees and stayees in the small market town of Ler, a county headquarters in Unity State located on the border with the Republic of Sudan. The research data from this period is of particular interest as it was gathered during a time of post-war hopefulness and real prospects for durable peace in South Sudan.[5] It brings to light the experiences, hopes and aspirations of adolescent girls and young women.

In 2006–07, Ler was a melting pot of returnees from different parts of Sudan and across its borders. Every day I witnessed people coming from Khartoum and other parts of Sudan, Kenya, Uganda, Ethiopia, and even from the USA, Australia and Canada. Ler County was heavily impacted during the conflict: almost all its inhabitants were displaced. Many had been displaced several times before eventually coming 'home'. During my ten-month stay in Ler, I observed its transformation. New *duëel* (traditional grass and mud houses) and *luaak* (barns) were being constructed, market enterprises were opened as traders arrived from all over Sudan and East Africa, and transport links improved due to Chinese and Malaysian oil companies. Ler was booming. The influx of returnees and the construction of homes and local administration offices were signs of peace. Prolonged conflict had resulted in general impoverishment, burned houses, dispersed households, stolen or killed cattle and lost livelihoods. The social and cultural context of settling in of returning and stayee populations was dominated by the legacy of militarisation of Nuer life, which saw widespread violence in inter- and intra-community conflicts (Jok and Hutchinson 1999).

An analysis of the various wartime experiences (differentiated by gender, age, place of origin, social class and length and trajectories of displacement) reveals intricacies of social change. Wartime militarisation of the Nuer communities had led most young men to enlist in the SPLA, either voluntarily or forcibly. Younger men, due to their social mobility, enjoyed better access to migration across borders. Being less mobile, because of their position within the household, most women and girls either stayed behind or were displaced internally, often settling on the outskirts of Khartoum. Those women who were part of privileged social networks of male relatives linked with the SPLA, churches or international humanitarian organisations were able to access refugee camps in Ethiopia, Kenya or Uganda or resettled further afield in the USA, Canada or Australia. As in other conflicts, women and children were the primary targets

---

5 Sadly, war broke out yet again in December 2013.

of ethnicised and gendered violence (Jok and Hutchinson 1999; Yuval-Davis 1997). Women and children were raped, kidnapped and killed by both northerners and southerners (Jok and Hutchinson 1999; Jok 2007). South Sudanese anthropologist Jok Madut Jok argues that 'war in Sudan has affected women in more and different ways than men, but beyond the usual ways in which such state-sponsored violence affects women and children – through rape, abduction, sexual slavery, and labor exploitation' (Jok 2007: 206). Yet the roles of Nuer girls in the civil conflict also expanded, as they became combatants, rebel and army support personnel and heads of households (Grabska 2014). Thus, differentiated positionings due to gender, class and social status resulted in diverse wartime experiences and access to resources such as flight options, and hence diverse levels of accumulation of social and cultural capital.

The autonomous southern Sudanese administration and its emerging structures were also changing the socio-political landscape. This was coupled with emerging discourses on women's rights and gender equality in law, often influenced by donors and the Sudanese women's movement. New provisions guaranteeing equal rights for women and men in terms of access to land, resources, education and political representation were included in the CPA and the South Sudanese interim constitution. Provisions included a guarantee of women's right to consent to marriage, and the introduction of the Child Act 2008, which assures equal rights for girls and boys in terms of access to education, health, life, survival, development and freedom of expression.

The analysis presented in this chapter is based on long-term ethnographic research with a group of 25 adolescent girls and young women in Kakuma, following ten of them to Ler. In addition, I interviewed and participated in the lives of another 15 returnee girls from Kakuma and Khartoum in Ler, and some 20 girls who had stayed in Ler or nearby during the civil war. The term 'adolescent' does not exist in the Nuer language; girls (*nyaal*) pass from childhood to full adulthood on marriage and the birth of their first child. Thus, in this research, I use the term 'adolescent girls' to describe those girls who were unmarried, and the term 'young women' for those who were married but with no children.

I also collected family life stories from members of the girls' households in Kakuma and Ler, and I interviewed their peers, representatives of local and international organisations, local administrators and government officials. By presenting the different wartime experiences of these girls and young women, I show their diverse positioning with regards to processes of social change. The stories that I collected give us an insight into historical social change as perceived by different generations.

### Settling in and social change

Over the last ten years, international organisations such as the World Bank, regional development banks, the European Union and various United Nations

(UN) agencies have begun to see migrants as 'vital agents of international development' (Glick Schiller and Faist 2009: 1; UNDP 2009: Introduction). Policy discourses have tended to focus on the financial qualities of remittances and their developmental effectiveness, often ignoring more complex insights and migrant perspectives (Levitt and Nyberg-Sørensen 2004; Faist 2010; Van Hear 2010) as well as the broader global contexts within which migration is embedded (Glick Schiller and Faist 2009). This chapter draws on research findings that detail the potential economic, social, political and cultural contributions mobility may bring to both migrants and their communities of origin (see, for example, Nyberg-Sørensen et al. 2002; Ratha 2003; Glick Schiller and Faist 2009). It points to social change as a more overarching and multidimensional process, rather than focusing exclusively on the economic side of development. In particular, it complements more critical studies that warn of the diverse experiences of migration and the potential social inequalities that migration inflicts on both migrants and those who stay behind (INSTRAW 2006; Hansen 2008; Lutz 2010; Nyberg-Sørensen 2010). Building upon critical child migration research (Whitehead et al. 2007; Hashim and Thorsen 2011), I emphasise the agency of adolescent girl migrants who have been invisible so far in policy and research debates. I will now develop my analysis around two central concepts: settling in and social change.

*Settling in* In Ler, returnees referred to the process of settling in as *nyuuri piny* (sitting on the ground or earth). In their description of the process, they emphasised a myriad of activities needed to be performed, including accessing land, building a house, farming, finding work, cooking, reconnecting with and visiting friends and relatives and taking part in community events. These strategies were experienced and employed differently by women and men, young and old, depending on their access to social networks, their experiences during displacement and their accumulated social capital. In addition, settling in was linked to the practice, negotiation and (re)production of gender relations, and to processes of identity formation. Adolescent girls, for example, referred to *nyuuri piny* as a process of becoming a good Nuer girl (*nyal nuara ma goa*), a congruent identity that linked the personal experiences of place and *cieng* (community or home) to wider gendered social and communal obligations, rights and networks of mutual support. In this way, settling in involved both material and moral aspects of place making (Migdal 1988; Hammond 2004; Turton 2005). This was often a dialectic between gendered practices, aspirations and representations of returnees and stayees, that in turn set social change in motion.

Such a dynamic conceptualisation of settling in relates to notions of place making developed in studies that have situated forced migration and displacement in the wider context of migration as part of people's livelihood strategies

(Hammond 2004; Turton 2005). Turton (ibid.) argues that place making is closely intertwined with a person's social and individual identity and not only constitutes a stage for social activity but is a 'product' of it. This definition closely reflects the Nuer concept of *nyuuri piny* and the inherent dynamism and interaction between people (returnees and stayees), physical spaces, social relations, norms and identities.

*Social change* There has been much discussion in social sciences of what constitutes change and how to account for it (see Portes 2010 for an overview as well as Bakewell 2010; Bourdieu 1986; Castles 2010). However, the analysis often gets stuck in the structure–agency debate (see Bakewell 2010) and fails to provide wider insights into the link between moving people, evolving post-war environments and changing social institutions. Moreover, as Portes notes:

> Examining the multiple ways in which migration relates to social change is
> a daunting task. It requires, first of all, defining what social change is and,
> secondarily, delimiting the scope of analysis to certain types of migration and
> not others. The greatest dangers that I envision in this enterprise are, first, get-
> ting lost in generalities of the 'social change is ubiquitous' kind and, second,
> attempting to cover so much terrain as to lose sight of analytic priorities and of
> major, as opposed to secondary, causal linkages (Portes 2010: 1537).

In order to understand social change from an emic perspective, I refer to the metaphors used by my respondents. In the Nuer language, *gɛɛr ro* means 'to change', while the transitive verb *gɛɛrɛ ro* indicates 'to separate' or 'to split apart'. Hence, the Nuer metaphor for change relates to 'splitting apart' or 'separating oneself from the past' (Hutchinson 1996: 39). Thus, some of the moral panics were provoked by the dress and behaviour of returning young women and men, who were seen as 'splitting apart' and 'separating' from the norms of the 'old days', which are referred to by many as *cieng nuära* (Nuer culture, community or home). Nyakuol, a widow in her forties who had been displaced for 15 years in Ethiopia and then in Kakuma, described changes in the refugee camp in Kakuma and on her later return to Sudan:

> In Kakuma, there are schools, UN, churches, women rights. Our children go
> forward/progress [*wa nhiam*]. Now Nuer girls and boys are knowledgeable and
> educated. In Kakuma, a new Nuer custom/mode of value has arrived [*cieng mi
> pai ben*]. Things are done differently from the past. In Sudan, the Nuer are still
> [behind].

As in other refugee camp settings, Nuer girls, boys, women and men who settled in Kakuma experienced dramatic shifts in gender and generational relations (see Essed et al. 2005; Indra 1999; Turner 2000; 2010; De Alwis 2004). Younger generations increased their social status through education, gender equality, human rights sensitisation programmes and the multicultural environment. Educated young men versed in the language of humanitarianism and gender equality generally gained status at the expense of their seniors. Adolescent girls and younger women also benefited from enhanced social status vis-à-vis their male peers and older women. Their ability to enjoy greater freedoms was also linked to the set-up of the camp, with international organisations promoting gender equality and protecting women and girls at risk.

Education and knowledge acquired through, for instance, UN awareness raising and churches were understood as a certain form of cultural capital that refugees had accumulated in exile (see Grabska 2011, 2013). In Ler, this capital set the returnee girls from Kakuma apart from their peers who had not experienced similar displacement. For example, those displaced to Khartoum were exposed to Islamic codes that generally relegated women to a lower social position (see Abusharaf 2009). I often heard statements along the lines: 'I am Nuer, but somehow I am different. War and life in Kakuma has changed me and now I feel part but also apart from the Nuer here in Ler.' As Nyakuol's narrative indicates, change was often associated with a move forward (*wa nhiam*). Men and women often voiced uncertainty about their identities as well as their belonging.

Nuer women and men often understood a new custom as the arrival of modernity, development and civilisation into their lives (see Grabska 2011). There were two diverse interpretations of change, which was often equated with development. One linked to structural development – with the arrival of services, infrastructure, and government laws and gender equality. The other interpretation was linked to personal identities. The English words 'developed' and 'civilised' were often used by returnees to distinguish their new identities and modes of behaviour from the new identities of those who had stayed behind in Nuerland. The Nuer metaphor used by my respondents to describe these new identities was *nei ti cike ker*. This signifies people who have awoken and have seen the light, and many of my Nuer respondents associated this with literacy, Christianity, awareness of human rights and gender equality. For others, gender equality discourses represented a threat to the established order – a type of development that was bringing destruction to the local community. Some returnee Nuer adolescent girls referred to being 'in flux' between cultures of 'modernity' and 'progress' and 'their parents'. The experiences and practices of their gender identities reveal fluidity in the reworking and reshaping of social norms, orders and identities.

The varied displacement experiences sparked debate about changing social norms, the future of South Sudan and what it meant to be a Nuer. Social change is an ongoing process and a range of other processes affects it in a variety of ways: for instance, displacement brings about more rapid and abrupt social change. These processes are negotiated by differently positioned actors

– those who stay and those who move – whose power and social status are at stake in the (re)construction of gender and generational order. To understand social change, one needs to employ a historical perspective, yet this is never an easy or non-political endeavour. It is difficult to talk about what used to be 'before' and how things are 'after', as the points of reference are constantly in motion (Abusharaf 2009; Vigh 2009). Thus, I propose to look at social, and in particular gender and generational, relationships between displaced and stayee communities as being continuously reshaped, with displacement just one of the factors of ongoing social change. We need to see the social, political and economic environment in post-war South Sudan as constantly evolving rather than as a fixed point in time (Vigh 2009).

## Diverse experiences of girls' settling in: threatening miniskirts and transforming gender and generational order

*Gendered* cieng *and settling in* Returnees to Ler often used the phrase *beben cieng*, which literally means 'going or coming home'. To understand the experiences of settling in Ler, we have to consider the meaning of 'home' for Nuer women and men. For Nuer women and men, *cieng*, signifying lineage, segment, home, community or village (Evans-Pritchard 1940), is a gendered space that is both shaped by and affects gender relations (Whitehead 1981). The underlying gender ideology embedded in the creation of *cieng* through marriage influences the different social positioning of women and men and of girls and boys within the home and household space (Hutchinson 1996). The visual and lived representation of this difference is practised in separate spheres of life within the household, whereby men and boys traditionally sleep with the animals in a barn whereas women, girls and smaller children live in the house (Evans-Pritchard 1940; Hutchinson 1990). Their different spatial and social positions determine their responsibilities and status in the household and society at large, decision making, and access to resources and entitlements. Formation of their own household through marriage and procreation relates to their passage to full adulthood. Through shared division of responsibilities and procreation, the identities of men and women are socially intertwined and, similarly, their identities are interwoven with *cieng*.

Girls and women referred to two ideas of *cieng*, each representing different stages in their passage to adulthood. Nyayena, a young returnee woman, explained: '*Cieng* is a place where I was born. This is when I was a girl in my father's home. Now, I am married, I have a child, I am a woman and I am in my own home, in my husband's *cieng*.' Through marriage, transfer to their husband's house and subsequent procreation, a girl becomes a woman and gains rights to property in the house and the ability to control domestic work and resources through her own cultivation.

*Multiplicity of positions and experiences of returnee girls* Gladys, the 17-year-old daughter of a local SPLA commander, spent 15 years in Kenya before returning to Ler in 2006. When I ran into her at a water pump in January 2007, she explained:

> When I arrived in Ler, I thought I would not survive here. Most of my life, I spent in Kenya and didn't know the life in *cieng nuära*. I didn't know how people were behaving and what I was supposed to do as a girl. I spent all my life in schools and had no idea about the responsibilities of a Nuer girl [in a village]. At the beginning I refused to do anything, but then I realised that I could only survive if I learned the life of the village. I slowly learned how to carry water on my head, look at me, I am a professional now! I learned how to make traditional foods such as *walwal, kisra, akop*; how to grind sorghum on a stone and how to serve people. At first, I didn't even enjoy the local food, I didn't like the taste. I missed *chapatti* [Indian corn flatbread also popular in Kenya]. After a while I adjusted and now my life has become much better. The one problem that I had was lack of a job. I had nothing to do apart from the work at home, because despite being an educated girl it is difficult to find work here. People don't want you to work outside the house. There is no freedom for girls here, and girls are valued only when they are married and bring bridewealth.

For some long-displaced girls, coming home was a fundamental challenge. They had to learn to (re)negotiate the greater space and freedoms gained in displacement, and their education and gender equality awareness acquired in Kakuma were not always appreciated by those who stayed behind or who were displaced to Khartoum. Thus, the process of settling in involved learning to be a Nuer girl and becoming acquainted with local customs, obligations and responsibilities that were considered to be 'female'. The type of social and cultural capital acquired by the girls in exile was not easily translated into access to resources and improved social status in the return context. Rather, it required them to learn 'anew', and at times involved losing their migration capital.

Yet, there was also a variety of scenarios in the returnee girls' experiences. Some, who had been displaced for shorter periods of time and who had not benefited from access to education and ideas of gender equality popularised in the refugee camps, saw their process of settling in as less burdensome. As one girl displaced to Khartoum commented, in Ler she finally felt at home. She was not harassed as much as she and other Nuer girls had been in Khartoum. She also felt that she could enjoy more freedom in Ler as her parents were not afraid for her safety. 'We can be free here in our homes,' she added. The context of displacement often determined the settling-in experiences of the returnee girls.

The settling-in process took place within the framework of family reunification. The coming together of dispersed family members reveals other dilemmas of households fragmented by war. NyaSunday, a teenager who had been in Kakuma and had finished seven grades of primary school, found it difficult to communicate with her father, who for 15 years had been in Khartoum without any contact with his daughter. When they started living together in a village near Ler in 2007, NyaSunday was often frustrated:

> These people do not understand that we, the ones who were in Kakuma, are different. My father insists that I get married because he is in need of cattle. But I want to continue with my education, I am not a cattle-camp *nyal nuära* [Nuer girl]. I have changed, I am a modern town girl and I want to finish my school before I get married. Our lives were too different during these years. We do not understand each other.

The statements about 'difference' and 'feeling different' could be read as an account of a different type of socio-cultural capital accumulated by the displaced girls. Being 'modern' – as girls often referred to themselves – (in other words, educated and with worldly experience outside the village or the country) sets them apart in their own eyes and in the eyes of their peers and their families who underwent different experiences during the war. These experiences and narratives show that displacement and return are highly complex processes. The social context of exile affects the types of capital that the displaced accumulate as well as the type of changes that they go through. The complexity and irreversibility of displacement and its consequences for social relations, and for gender relations in particular, were discussed by young and old and by women and men seeking to reconcile 'old' modes of life with 'new' ways learned in the places of displacement. For those who grew up in refugee camps, moving to South Sudan was part of their ongoing migratory trajectory. They experienced and adapted to life in different places, which often resulted in changes in gender identities and ideologies. Moving to Nuerland was filled with anxiety. Although they were supposedly coming 'home', South Sudan was a place they barely remembered. In addition, 'home' was not static and Ler had undergone dramatic changes during the war. For some returnees, they needed to get to know a new place, where their skills and ways of being were poorly understood or appreciated by stayees.

Many returnee adolescent girls and young women aged between 14 and 20 were educated, single and more open in their behaviour and attitudes than their stayee peers, who were mostly illiterate, married and more constrained in terms of social mobility. Within Nuer gender ideology, girls were subjugated within the household to their male relatives and senior women. My conversations with elders confirmed that early socialisation was a vital component in the creation of the ideal girl and wife. The values of respect for and obedience to their fathers – and later their husbands – were instilled in girls from an early age. Women's social power and limited freedoms are linked to their reproductive capacity. In Kakuma, some of these rules had been relaxed due to the human rights discourse and gender equality programming, access to education for girls, and distance from the 'real' Nuer culture of 'home'. For displaced girls, coming 'home' meant confronting stricter views on the obedient and respectable behaviour required of them.

*Resilience and coping with settling in* To survive and ease the stigmatisation that they often felt as 'bad girls' in Ler, the 'Kakuma girls', as they were known, kept together. The network of friendships that had sprung up in the classrooms, workshops, and meetings at water points and food distribution centres in Kakuma were perceived by the girls as their source of resistance. This social network was also seen as a type of social capital, and allowed them to share stories, concerns and secrets; cook 'Kenyan food' together and undertake small acts of resistance.

Some returnee girls' contestations of social status were reflected in their speech, dress and social interactions, and particularly in their mobility. Returnee girls, especially those from East Africa, stood out on the dirt roads of Ler. Wearing tight trousers and miniskirts and colourful hair extensions, they played sport with young men, conversed freely with their male friends, moved around the village and often travelled far by themselves. They had little idea about such Nuer girls' duties as milking and grinding sorghum, having received pre-ground flour from the UN in Kakuma. Most returnee girls also stood out as being the only female students in higher primary education, with most local girls never having enrolled or dropping out to marry.

Male relatives and other returnee men observed the constraints faced by the returnee girls. Amaring, a brother of NyaSunday, shared his concerns:

Girls here have no rights and no freedom. They are punished for wearing trousers and miniskirts, not allowed to play sports and don't go to school. Their only right here is to get married and do domestic work. They are very tired as they are overworked. It is hard for my sister and others like her who were in Kenya. They are not used to this.

Some of the stayee girls and women also emphasised the difficulties for younger generations to adjust to life in Ler. As a woman chief in Ler stressed: 'These girls from Kakuma suffer the most. In Kenya they had more opportunities and they were more respected. Here, they do the most work at home and have no voice.' Despite the South Sudanese authorities' professed dedication to gender equality and equal legal rights, girls could not speak for themselves in court. During a court session in Ler, I witnessed a returnee girl being blocked from expressing her views in a divorce case by a male chief: 'You are a girl, you have no right to talk here. It is your father who will decide. Girls have no brains.' This was one of the many salutary reminders for 'Kakuma girls' that in Nuerland their social status was different. Their education and awareness of gender equality and their rights as women did not necessarily result in access to resources upon their return. Caught up between different gender ideologies yet aware of their legal rights, their readjustment to an inferior gender status was painful. Nyakuol, a returnee widow, complained about the situation in Nuerland:

Here in Ler, life for women is different [than in Kakuma]; there are no human rights [for women]. When you disagree with your husband, he will just beat you and even if you complain to the court or the police, they will laugh at you. Your neighbour, Nyakuma, complained about her cousin beating her, and the police wanted to put her in jail. These people here are still [backward]. They have no idea how to treat women. They say they give us 25 per cent [representation in government offices according to CPA], but in fact, they are the ones who always talk in meetings. There are no women in the Ler administration, and the ones that are there are wives of commanders and big people. When they give a woman a job, they just want you to do domestic work, like serving food, cooking, washing and sweeping the compound. The life for us women here is more difficult, because we learned in Kakuma that as humans we have rights and we are equal but here, the women are still behind. For the girls it is hard, because they were free in Kakuma to attend school, to participate in the community, but here, they are just expected to cook and do domestic chores.

This narrative shows that women displaced to Kakuma were acutely aware of their subordination, experiencing return and settling in as a loss of freedom and rights, a loss of the capital they had acquired in exile. They often reminisced about their lives in Kakuma, their schooling, their freedom to move around and interact with other girls and boys and the reduced domestic obligations they had shared with their brothers and other male relatives. 'In Kakuma, our brothers used to cook and help us with domestic work. But here, they say that they are men, and they cannot go to the kitchen,' commented Gladys. Adolescent girls and young women had also enjoyed greater freedoms in choosing boyfriends and husbands. Returning to Nuerland meant entering stricter community and family obligations, undermining privileges and freedoms acquired in Kakuma. In order to settle in, these returnee girls had to navigate the ever changing terrains of their new/old 'homes'. This demonstrates the fact that social change is not a linear process, but rather is fluid, contradictory, complex and time- and space-dependent. It often involves a redefinition of the value of socio-cultural capital that individuals and communities accumulate over time.

These processes of transformation are negotiated between differently positioned actors whose agendas do not always ally with gender or age. Gendered settling in for displaced Nuer adolescent girls involved several challenges to their gender identities and rights, which had been altered during wars and displacement. The characteristics of girlhood acquired in Kakuma – education, freer inter-gender socialisation, movement, freedom of dress, decision making, leadership – were (re)negotiated during contact with those who had stayed behind or had been displaced to Khartoum. Gendered settling in and place making upon return implied (re)negotiation, adaptation and contestation of gender norms, identities and self in the context of the diverse gender identities produced through varied war and displacement experiences. The social, economic and political context of these negotiations was crucial in determining the durability of social change.

### Returnee girls and their ambiguous positions in relation to change

Comments about the inappropriate behaviour of Kakuma girls were commonplace in daily conversations. Returnee girls were often ostracised and looked down upon with disdain by stayees. These girls were introducing a threatening foreign culture and, as 'loose' girls, they brought shame on their families. Some of the socio-cultural capital acquired in exile did not translate into a higher social status in the place of return. A mother of four children who had stayed in Ler during the war commented:

> Look at Nyariek [a returnee girl from Kakuma], she thinks she is a man. She is not behaving like a good girl. She roams loose, wears bad clothes and talks with men. My daughter, Nyamuc, she is a good girl. She stays at home, does the [domestic] work, does not go out unless to fetch water or charcoal and does not socialise with boys. She shows *pöc* [respect/shyness]. These Kakuma girls are *jiäke* [bad]!

In her study of northern Sudanese communities in Cairo, Anita Fábos (2008) used the concept of propriety, *adab*, to describe the moral stances and attitudes of Sudanese migrants. For them, being a real Sudanese meant subscribing to certain moral, ethical and aesthetic values, to have *adab*. In Ler, *adab* for adolescent girls meant the acquisition of a good reputation by being shy, showing respect and not straying far from the domestic space. It implied losing some of the social capital gained in Kakuma.

The concerns and moral panic prompted by the alleged 'bad' behaviour of some returnee girls led to the police commissioner outlawing the wearing of miniskirts and trousers. Sermons in both Catholic and Presbyterian churches were punctuated by references to 'bad behaviour'. Some of my Kakuma friends were beaten up and arrested for wearing shorter skirts. It was common to see local men and women disparagingly flicking returnee women's clothing. The Kakuma girls with their short skirts and tight tops were in striking opposition to those women who had been displaced to Khartoum, whose clothing was influenced by Arabisation and cultural adaptation (Abusharaf 2009).

Arrests of young women and girls in 'dangerous' trousers and 'threatening' miniskirts represent a contestation of the emerging social order in post-war Ler and elsewhere in South Sudan. For returnee adolescent girls and young men from Kenya (and from other East African countries), the wearing of fitted clothes, miniskirts and baggy trousers represented a new lifestyle; however, for those who were exiled in Khartoum or who had stayed behind, such clothes were evidence of 'cultural pollution'. My neighbours and friends in Ler were preoccupied with transforming social relations, especially changes in youth behaviour and contestations around what made for a 'good' girl or a 'respect-able' woman or man.

Hodgson and McCurdy show how women and girls are labelled 'bad' or 'loose' because 'they disrupt the web of social relations that define and depend on them as daughters, sisters, wives, mothers, and lovers' (2001: 6). As with Tutsi and Ha women studied by Lovett in Western Tanzania, Nuer girls and women 'learned that their subordination was a life-long condition' (2001: 53). The fact that stayee girls who conform to the authority of their male rela-tives and who do not challenge the prevailing gender norms are labelled as 'good' served to maintain existing gender hierarchies but also creates new inequalities. The 'knowledge' that stayee girls demonstrated through carrying out their domestic duties, not speaking back to men, agreeing to marriages arranged by their fathers (and mothers) and not roaming around was more appreciated in Ler. Returnee girls such as Nyariek went against the hegemonic configuration of gender, 'the norms of "appropriate" gender roles, relations, responsibilities, and behaviour' (Hodgson and McCurdy 2001: 6). Passed on through internalisation and socialisation, bestowed through references to *cieng nuära* and tradition, these gendered norms become sources and thresholds of local moral and social orders. As in other communities, women and girls were seen as bearers of national or community culture (Yuval-Davis 1997; Schrijvers 1999). When Nuer adolescent girls overstep these gendered boundaries, they threaten the community's moral foundations, a keen threat to those men and (mostly stayee) women with much to lose from changing norms.

The position of returnee adolescent girls and young women was, however, highly ambiguous. Their socio-cultural capital was mostly seen as 'threatening', but occasionally enabled them to be seen as 'agents of positive change' by bringing new concepts of femininity and challenging the local and militarised forms of womanhood. The subtle and more visible actions in the daily practice of 'gendered self' were forms of often hidden resistance to the existing gender inequalities within their own communities, without openly challenging the existing power inequalities (Cowan 1990; Ortner 1995). Educated, outspoken, seen as good cooks, perceived as being able to take better care of children and contributing to the community through their ability to find paid work, some returnee girls and young women were expanding the realm of possibilities and freedoms for women. Notwithstanding their reputation as 'loose', they were often seen as desirable marriage partners due to their education and ability to contribute to household income. With an enabling environment, some were able to turn their exile-acquired capital into a resource for change and for increasing their own status and position within the Ler community.

There were, however, differences between the returnee girls. Those girls whose parents and brothers were in Kakuma and were themselves exposed to different gender ideologies and social relations in the camp were supported in their quest for greater freedoms in their lives. Those whose parents or brothers stayed in Sudan faced greater opposition at home and often felt more isolated in their ability to take advantage of their Kakuma social capital. Thus, social environment and support were important elements in returnee girls' ability to take advantage of their exile-gained capital.

Despite being shamed by stayees and returnee women and men from Khartoum, some returnee girls from Kakuma continued to challenge their limited status, playing volleyball, socialising with men, going to market, speaking at public meetings and expressing their views in court. A few managed to continue their education despite pressure from their extended family members to marry. Others managed love marriages instead of being pressured into relationships negotiated by their relatives.

Local adolescent girls and younger women envied and emulated their returnee peers' fashion choices and mobility. Jeans became 'must-have' garments. At the wedding of a young returnee man, both the bride and her bridesmaid (who had never left Ler) wore denim and red hair extensions. Although returnee girls had to conform to some extent to local expectations, they were also contributing to social transformations. During my time in Ler, there were increasing numbers of girls riding bicycles, playing sports, attending school, going to discos and moving around unconstrained.

Cosmetics became desirable items for locals, a demand met by Kakuma women selling soaps, body lotions and hair extensions brought from Kenya. On my trips to Nairobi, they often asked me to bring new supplies. Fashion and body styles were seen as contributions to *wa nhiam* (progress), introducing the local stayee population to East African and Western ideas experienced in displacement. These everyday forms of resistance were manifestations of girls' agency and the power that they were willing and able to exercise, albeit within limits (see Ortner 1995).

Returnee young women were working as teachers, nurses and community organisers. Returnee adolescent girls were promoting schooling among the local girls. Nyakuma and other women who had stayed in Sudan often commented on the benefit of education for girls:

When they know something, they will be able to be more respected by the husband and manage independently even if the husband does not support them.

I wish I could have had this chance before. These Kakuma girls are better off this way.

Under the influence of other returnee girls (and perhaps me), Nyakuma decided to join an adult education programme run by the Catholic church. She insisted that her 13-year-old daughter Nyamuc continue primary education. They often asked me to help them with homework and quiz them in mathematics and English. Despite her numerous domestic tasks, Nyamuc was diligent in her homework. 'I want to be like your friend from Kakuma, who knows how to read and write, speaks English and has a job,' she explained.

The local (male) authorities were slowly recognising education as a resource for girls. On a visit to the Ler commissioner, Nyayena, a returnee woman, directly asked for land, a job and financial support. She was outspoken. Spotting a mattress in the commissioner's compound she asked for it: 'I am a returnee and need a bed for my daughter and myself. Can you assist me? Once I get a job, I will pay you back.' The commissioner smiled and told me:

> Returnee women are very different from those who stayed behind. They have been educated and they are not afraid to ask for their rights. They have no fear, are able to represent the community and support their families. They are bringing development for women here.

Although this attestation may have been influenced by my presence, other senior men and women were also acknowledging the difference in the social and cultural capital of returnee women.

As with similar 'wayward', 'dangerous', 'wicked' and 'vagabond' African women (Cornwall 2001; Lovett 2001; Hodgson and McCurdy 2001), the 'transgressive' behaviour of adolescent Nuer girls was proving pivotal in transforming gender relations and other domains of social life. This was not only through fashion, but also through their desire for schooling. 'Somehow educated', as they referred to themselves, returnee girls and young women enjoyed greater access to paid jobs and communication with outsiders, could raise issues with the authorities, and were able to expand their marital choice and (re)negotiate unequal power relations within the household (Kandiyoti 1998; Kabeer 1994). Of the few women formally employed in the school, church, hospital and commissioner's office in Ler, all were returnees from Kakuma. Their mothers, and often fathers, who had also spent a substantial amount of time in displacement supported their quest for further education. Several returnee women sent their daughters to schools in Bentiu and often talked about the importance of female education.

Some 'loose' girls were thus able to translate their socio-cultural capital into a resource and contribute to the transformation of social norms in Ler. Whether change was seen positively depended on the position of the different actors whose social power was at stake in the (re)negotiation of the gender order. By moving freely, young women and girls were contesting and stretching gender space and boundaries. Through solidarity and support from some women (and men), girls and younger women were able to exercise their limited agency (Ortner 1995) and subvert some of the strict constraints to their status enshrined in the hegemonic structures of the 'our culture' discourse. These actions became 'sites for debate over, and occasionally transformations in, gender relations, social practices, cultural norms, and political-economic institutions' (Hodgson and McCurdy 2001: 2). Sherry Ortner's comments on the nature of agency and resistance are insightful here.

> The question of adequate representation of subjects in the attempt to understand resistance is not purely a matter of providing better portraits of subjects in and of themselves. The importance of subjects (whether individual actors or social entities) lies not so much in who they are and how they are put together as in the *projects* that they construct and enact. For it is in the formulation and enactment of those projects that they both become and transform who they are, and that they sustain or transform their social and cultural universe (Ortner 1995: 187).

The settling-in experiences and aspirations of adolescent girls were part of a transformative project that was affecting the returnee girls themselves as well as those who had stayed behind. The everyday practices that returnee girls and young women had to negotiate carefully contributed to the transformation of themselves and their communities. What it meant to be an adolescent girl was being questioned, contested and (re)negotiated in post-war Nuerland. While some were able to use capital gained in exile as a resource for transformation, others suffered marginalisation due to their 'difference'. While the role of individuals and their agency in bringing about change is pivotal, for the change to become a fully fledged transformation there needs to be change at the institutional level to support such an overall transformation of gender relations.

## Return as a gendered and generational patchwork

In this chapter, I have examined the gender and generational dynamics of return in the context of displacement, an often overlooked dimension of return migration in the existing literature. Settling in after return entails particular challenges for the gender and generational relations of both those who were displaced and those who stayed behind. The Nuer girls' experiences of settling in show that social change was central during their different stages of displacement. The analysis demonstrates how returnees and stayees are part of ongoing social change rather than exclusively locating them in relation to economic development. It shows that change is not a linear process, but rather one negotiated between different actors and their different capitals. The context-specific experiences of different actors, their gender, age and social position shape their identities, aspirations and social privilege (Kaiser 2010). This finding confirms the view of Glick Schiller and Faist (2009), Van Hear (2010) and Castles (2010) that social change is a key category for examining processes of migration and displacement. Such analyses, as Castles argues, attempt to 'facilitate understanding of the complexity, interconnectedness, variability, contextuality and multi-level mediations of migratory processes in the context of rapid global change' (ibid.: 1565).

This chapter challenges several assumptions in the return migration literature. First, I show that return is not only – or predominantly – a male activity, and, as a gendered and generational process, settling in poses several important challenges for the female returnee youth. Second, the gendered and generational nature of exile-accumulated capital reveals that social and cultural capital is not always easily transferable in the context of return. While social and cultural capital is differently and unevenly distributed (Bourdieu 1986), the gender and generational dimension of such hierarchies has important implications for the experiences of settling in within the context of return.

Third, settling in within an evolving post-war environment becomes a transformative process for those who are returning and for those who stayed behind, as well as for the social structures and institutions in the place of return. Displacement not only results in a loss but also creates an opportunity to construct new social norms in the context of interactions between returnees and those who stayed behind. While returnee girls are coping with the change of their environment as linked to a specific place, through the use of their differently accumulated social and cultural capital from exile, they are also participating and contributing to larger transformative processes at the individual and community level. In order to minimise the marginalisation and the hardship related to return, social navigation becomes a way in which returnee girls can cope with the evolving social and physical environment, but also as a way of responding to and instigating change. In a context where 'home' has changed or ceased to exist, gendered and generational settling in involves not merely learning *cieng nuära* but also (re)negotiating gender order, gender identities, aspirations and norms.

Displaced populations have brought different cultural habits, including education, dress, religion and manners, and, because of war and displacement, these have now collided with gender ideology and identities among stayees. Returnee women and girls are visibly challenging gender inequality and the vested authority of elders and men in post-war Ler. Discourses about returnee adolescent girls position them at times as positive agents of change and at times as being dangerous to the established gender hierarchies. These discourses are used strategically and indicate dilemmas about the type of gender relations that will underpin post-war South Sudan. Returnees' social and cultural capital is double-edged: it can be both a resource for transformation and a source of marginalisation. For those who spent most of their lives in exile, their social and cultural capital is incompatible with the local context of return. This chapter highlights the limits of returnee adolescent girls' contributions to social change as they are mediated through the institutional context in which they take place.

## Bibliography

Abusharaf, R. M. (2009) *Transforming Displaced Women in Sudan: Politics and the body in a squatter settlement*. Chicago IL: University of Chicago Press.

Bakewell, O. (2010) 'Some reflections on structure and agency in migration theory'. *Journal of Ethnic and Migration Studies* 36(10): 1689–708.

Bourdieu, P. (1986) 'The forms of capital'. In J. Richardson (ed.) *Handbook of Theory and Research for the Sociology of Education*. Westport CT: Greenwood Press.

Castles, S. (2010) 'Understanding global migration: a social transformation perspective'. *Journal of Ethnic and Migration Studies* 36(10): 1565–86.

Cornwall, A. (2001) 'Wayward women and useless men: contest and change in gender relations in Ado-Odo, S.W. Nigeria'. In D. L. Hodgson and S. McCurdy (eds) *'Wicked' Women and the Reconfiguration of Gender in Africa*. Portsmouth NH, Oxford and Cape Town: Heinemann, James Currey and David Phillip.

Cowan, J. (1990) *Dance and the Body Politic in Northern Greece*. Princeton NJ: Princeton University Press.

De Alwis, M. (2004) 'The "purity" of displacement and the reterritorialization of longing: Muslim IDPs in north-western Sri Lanka'. In W. Giles and J. Hyndman (eds) *Sites of Violence: Gender and conflict zones*. Berkeley CA: University of California Press.

Essed, P., G. Frerks and J. Schrijvers (2005) *Refugees and the Transformation of Societies: Agency, policies, ethics and politics*. New York NY: Berghahn Books.

Evans-Pritchard, E. E. (1940) *The Nuer: A description of the modes of livelihood and political institutions of a Nilotic people*. Oxford: Clarendon Press.

Fábos, A. (2008) *'Brothers' or Other? Propriety and gender for Muslim Arab Sudanese in Egypt*. Oxford and New York NY: Berghahn Books.

Faist, T. (2010) 'Towards transnational studies: world theories, transnationalization and changing institutions'. *Journal of Ethnic and Migration Studies* 36(1): 1665–87.

Glick Schiller, N. and T. Faist (2009) 'Introduction: migration, development and social transformation'. *Social Analysis* 53(3): 1–13.

Grabska, K. (2013) 'The return of displaced Nuer in Southern Sudan: women becoming men?'. *Development and Change* 44(5): 1135–57.

— (2011) 'Constructing "modern gendered civilised" women and men: gender mainstreaming in refugee camps'. *Gender and Development* 19(1), 81–93.

— (2014) *Gender, Identity and Home: Nuer repatriation to Southern Sudan*. Martlesham: James Currey.

Hammond, L. (2004) *This Place will Become Home: Refugee repatriation to Ethiopia*. Ithaca NY: Cornell University Press.

Hansen, P. (2008) 'Circumcising migration: gendering return migration among Somalilanders'. *Journal of Ethnic and Migration Studies* 34(7): 1109–25.

Hashim, I. and D. Thorsen (2011) *Child Migration in Africa*. London: Zed Books.

Hodgson, D. L. and S. McCurdy (eds) (2001) *'Wicked' Women and the Reconfiguration of Gender in Africa*. Portsmouth NH, Oxford and Cape Town: Heinemann, James Currey and David Phillip.

Horst, C. (2006) 'Buufis amongst Somalis in Dadaab: the transnational and historical logics behind resettlement dreams'. *Journal of Refugee Studies* 19(2): 143–57.

Hutchinson, S. (1990) 'Rising divorce among the Nuer, 1936–1983'. *Man* 25: 393–411.

— (1996) *Nuer Dilemmas: Coping with money, war and the state*. Berkeley CA: University of California Press.

Indra, D. (ed.) (1999) *Engendering Forced Migration: Theory and practice*. New York NY and Oxford: Berghahn Books.

INSTRAW (2006) 'Gender, migration, development and remittances'. Working paper. Washington DC: UN International Research and Training Institute for the Advancement of Women (INSTRAW).

Jok, J. M. (2007) *Sudan: Race, religion, and violence*. London: Oneworld.

— and S. Hutchinson (1999) 'Sudan's prolonged second civil war and the militarization of Nuer and Dinka ethnic identities'. *African Studies Review* 42(2): 125–45.

Kabeer, N. (1994) *Reversed Realities: Gender hierarchies in development thought*. London: Verso.

Kaiser, T. (2010) 'Dispersal, division and diversification: durable solutions and Sudanese refugees in Uganda'. *Journal of Eastern African Studies* 4(1): 44–60.

Kandiyoti, D. (1998) 'Gender, power and contestation: rethinking bargaining with patriarchy'. In C. Jackson and R. Pearson (eds) *Feminist Visions of Development: Gender analysis and policy*. London: Routledge.

Levitt, P. and N. Nyberg-Sørensen (2004) *The Transnational Turn in Migration Studies*. Geneva: Global Commission on International Migration.

Lovett, M. (2001) '"She thinks she's like a man": marriage and (de)constructing gender identity in colonial Buha, Western Tanzania, 1943–1960'. In

D. L. Hodgson and S. McCurdy (eds) *'Wicked' Women and the Reconfiguration of Gender in Africa*. Portsmouth NH, Oxford and Cape Town: Heinemann, James Currey and David Phillip.

Lutz, H. (2010) 'Gender in the migratory process'. *Journal of Ethnic and Migration Studies* 36(10): 1647–63.

Migdal, J. (1988) *Strong Societies and Weak States: State-society relations and state capabilities in the third world*. Princeton NJ: Princeton University Press.

Monsutti, A. (2005) 'La migration comme rite de passage: la construction de la masculinité parmi les jeunes Afghans en Iran'. In C. Verschuur and F. Reysoo (eds) *Genre, Nouvelle Division Internationale du Travail et Migrations*. Cahiers Genre et Développement 5. Paris: L'Harmattan, pp. 79–186.

Nyberg-Sørensen, N. (2010) 'The rise and fall of the "migrant superhero" and the new "deportee trash": contemporary strain on mobile livelihoods in the Central American region'. Working Paper 22. Copenhagen: Danish Institute for International Studies (DIIS).

— N. Van Hear and P. Engberg-Pedersen (2002) 'The migration–development nexus: evidence and policy options. State-of-the-art overview'. *International Migration* 40(5): 49–73.

Ortner, S. (1995) 'Resistance and the problem of ethnographic refusal'. *Comparative Studies in Society and History* 37(1): 173–93.

Portes, A. (2010) 'Migration and social change: some conceptual reflections'. *Journal of Ethnic and Migration Studies* 36(10): 1537–63.

Ratha, D. (2003) 'Worker remittances: an important and stable source of external development finance'. In Word Bank, *Global Development Finance: Striving for stability in development finance*. Washington DC: Word Bank.

Schrijvers, J. (1999) 'Fighters, victims and survivors: constructions of ethnicity, gender and refugeeness among Tamils in Sri Lanka'. *Journal of Refugee Studies* 12(3): 307–33.

Turner, S. (2000) 'Vindicating masculinity: the fate of promoting gender equality'. *Forced Migration Review* 9: 8–12.

— (2010) *Politics of Innocence: Hutu identity, conflict and camp life*. New York NY: Berghahn Books.

Turton, D. (2005) 'The meaning of place in a world of movement: lessons from long-term field research in southern Ethiopia'. *Journal of Refugee Studies* 18: 258–80.

UNDP (2009) *Overcoming Barriers: Human mobility and development*. New York NY: United Nations Development Programme (UNDP).

Van Hear, N. (2010) 'Theories of migration and social change'. *Journal of Ethnic and Migration Studies* 36(10): 1531–6.

Vigh, H. (2009) 'Motion squared: a second look at the concept of social navigation'. *Anthropological Theory* 9(4): 419–38.

Whitehead, A. (1981) 'I'm hungry, mum: the politics of domestic budgeting'. In K. Young, C. Wolkowitz and R. McCullagh (eds) *Of Marriage and the Market: Women's insubordination internationally and its lessons*. London: CSE Books.

— I. Hashim and V. Iversen (2007) 'Child migration, child agency and intergenerational relations in Africa and South Asia'. Working paper. Falmer: Sussex Centre for Migration Research.

Yuval-Davis, N. (1997) *Gender and Nation*. London: Sage.

# 8 | Obstacles and openings: returnees and small-scale businesses in Cape Verde

Lisa Åkesson

'To run a business in Cape Verde is an art of dying poor but happy.' – Ronaldo, returnee

In recent years, the Cape Verdean government has come to see migrants as key actors in national development (Ministério das Comunidades 2014). Programmes have been set up to attract migrants' savings and investments, and to stimulate entrepreneurial activities among returnees. These efforts form part of the government's more general promotion of small- and medium-sized businesses as a primary solution to both the high national rates of unemployment and economic dependence on the outside world. At the same time, the impetus to return to Cape Verde has increased. During the last decade there has been substantial macro-economic growth in Cape Verde, averaging at more than 6 per cent,[1] while at the same time the Eurozone crisis has severely hit some of the most important countries of destination for Cape Verdeans, such as Portugal, Spain and Italy. This means that an increasing number of Cape Verdeans in southern Europe envision return to Cape Verde as an alternative to unemployment and exploitative wages in their countries of immigration. The sheer number of potential returnees in relation to the population in the archipelago is also important. Extensive out-migration has been going on since the late nineteenth century and national authorities sometimes maintain that the majority of Cape Verdeans live outside the homeland. There is a substantial community of Cape Verdeans in more than 20 countries in Africa, South and North America and Europe. Thus, return migration plays – potentially – an important role for development in Cape Verde.

The overall aim of this chapter is to provide an ethnographic overview of the opportunities and constraints Cape Verdean returnees encounter when trying to set up a business. My approach is twofold, and it builds closely on the narratives of the returnees who have participated in the study. Their stories made it clear that specific economic conditions in the island state of Cape Verde play an absolutely crucial role in determining their room for manoeuvre when starting up a business. The chapter therefore explores the

---

1 See http://data.worldbank.org/country/cape-verde (accessed 30 January 2014).

everyday conditions of returnees' businesses in Cape Verde, and especially the multi-layered economic challenges that returnees have to confront. In addition, I analyse the importance of 'bridging' (Putnam 2000) or 'weak' (Granovetter 1973) social ties, which the returnees describe as key to their success. Bridging/ weak ties are connections to social networks outside the intimate sphere of family and friends. Most Cape Verdean returnees have been living abroad for between 20 and 40 years, and upon return they often lack the ties necessary to navigate a stratified social and political system that is partly foreign to them. In particular, I look into ties to politicians and analyse these ties as part of a system of political clientelism that permeates society. In addition, I look into ties to customs officials. This line of enquiry may appear somewhat peculiar, but for the returnee entrepreneurs, the customs service plays a key role as gatekeeper to the inflow of goods from the outside world.

As this chapter will show, the returnees' contribution to economic development in Cape Verde is quite limited, even though there are some individuals who have been moderately successful. Thus, the chapter primarily explores why it is difficult for returnees to set up a viable business, but it also highlights some of the openings that returnees with an entrepreneurial spirit may identify. I first discuss some tendencies in research on returnees' business activities in Africa, and then present my material and the different categories of returnees in Cape Verde, with a special emphasis on small-scale business owners. Subsequently, I consider Cape Verde's liminal position in a globalising world economy, and discuss how this position affects returnees' businesses. The following sections address the problem of access to bridging ties, and I conclude by summarising the constraints and opportunities that interplay with returnees' efforts to create viable small-scale enterprises. As a final point, I highlight some positive examples and discuss why these returnees have been successful.

### Returnees and small-scale businesses in Africa

In ethnographic studies of return migration, returnees' ways of making a living have played a surprisingly small role. When return migration became a topic on the research agenda, scholarly interest was largely directed towards questions of symbolic belonging and identity (Anwar 1979; Brettell 1979). Later on, return came to be seen as part of transnational circuits (Al-Ali and Koser 2002; Levitt 2001) and as diasporic imagination and root-seeking (Hirsch and Miller 2011). These themes have often overshadowed the more practical and material issues of homecoming (Stefansson 2004). It is telling that a volume such as *Coming Home: Refugees, migrants and those who stayed behind* (Long and Oxfeld 2004), which is dedicated to a broad overview of return migration, only in passing brings up the question of returnees' livelihoods. In contrast, pragmatic economic considerations are absolutely fundamental to many migrants' return projects. Probably this discrepancy reflects a bias in the research interests of migration scholars, which in turn is associated with a more general trend in anthropology and related disciplines where economy has become a rather peripheral topic on the academic agenda (Gregory 2009).

Also, returnees' entrepreneurship – and by extension migration in general – has attracted little attention in development studies. This is quite surprising given the prevailing optimism about migration and development in policy circles (de Haas 2010). Explorations of the migration–development nexus have instead mainly been carried out by migration scholars. These scholars have primarily been concerned with the impact of remittances, migrant diasporas' engagement in transnational practices and migrants' transfer of new identities, norms and ideas, whereas in-depth studies of returnees' economic activities are rare. In economics, some studies have been undertaken on this topic, but, in accordance with the disciplinary tradition, these studies tend to focus on sharply delimited questions: for example, in comparison with those who have stayed behind, is it more common that returnees are business owners (Kilic et al. 2009)? Which variables determine returnees' decisions to become self-employed (Lianos and Pseiridis 2009)?

In one of the few studies focusing on African returnees starting up businesses, Ammassari (2004) argues that it is important to distinguish between unskilled and highly skilled returnees, as the latter exert more influence on development in the country of return because they have more power and authority. Also, Tiemoko (2003) has looked into differences between skilled and unskilled returnees, and he maintains that unskilled return migrants tend to be less innovative in their business ventures. This is a finding that resonates with the Cape Verdean case. As I will demonstrate, the majority of the less skilled returnees have started up an 'imitative business' (Stewart 1991), while some of the skilled returnees have tried to develop new ideas. A view of highly skilled migrants as ideal returnees is also evident in the recent Cape Verdean national strategy on migration and development (Ministério das Comunidades 2014), in which the government sets out especially to support the return of highly qualified nationals.

In another study on return migration, entrepreneurship and development in Africa, Black and Castaldo (2009) argue that returnees' small- and medium-sized enterprises play a positive role in economic growth and poverty alleviation in Ghana and Côte d'Ivoire. Such a role, however, is dependent on the accumulation of economic capital abroad. Returnees who have not accumulated savings in the country of immigration are generally unable to support development through business activities. Thus, discrimination in countries of immigration thwarts migrants' efforts to accumulate savings, in turn limiting their ability to support development upon their return. Black and Castaldo also note the importance of social capital and argue that such capital – 'especially when defined in terms of "strong" rather than "weak" ties – remains a double-edged sword' (ibid.: 45). 'Strong' (Granovetter 1973) or 'bonding' (Putnam 2000) ties refer to ties to family members and close friends, and a consistent finding in studies of return migration is that such ties often place high demands on sharing the returnees' economic resources (Meintel 1984; Salih 2000; White-house 2011). Yet Black and Castaldo demonstrate that it is still of critical importance to maintain and develop social networks while away. Migrants who, during their sojourn abroad, have been in regular contact with people in their country of origin tend to have a more realistic and nuanced picture of the economic and social conditions they will encounter upon return.

As this chapter will show, social networking plays an important role for Cape Verdean returnee entrepreneurs. In the literature on small-scale businesses, it is well established that, particularly during the start-up stage, social capital can be critical for exploiting business opportunities (Field 2008: 59). Many of my interlocutors emphasised the importance of 'bridging' (Putnam 2000) or 'weak' (Granovetter 1973) ties in order to succeed as business owners. Such ties make it possible to access different resources, and, according to Putnam, are crucial for 'getting ahead'. This means that the creation of weak or bridging ties is key to succeeding as an entrepreneur. According to Pierre Bourdieu (1986), both the number and the quality of an individual's social ties may play a role. Bourdieu was interested in social capital as a basis of inequality, and he saw the cultural, social and economic capital possessed by each connection as important for an individual's success. Of special importance are heterogeneous relationships that link together people with different socio-economic positions (Field 2008: 73). In the present case, returnees who have multiple connections with different sectors of Cape Verdean society are more likely to succeed, but it is also true that their access to some forms of social capital is more important than others. In the following section, I show that the creation of ties to politicians, and also to custom officials, plays a special role in this case.

**Method and material**

The ethnography presented in this chapter was primarily collected during three visits to Cape Verde between 2010 and 2012, when I carried out open-ended interviews with 44 returnees. Out of these, 22 owned a small-scale business, and I interviewed nearly all of these business owners more than once. I have known a couple of the business owners since the end of the 1990s when I started carrying out anthropological fieldwork in Cape Verde. My long-term experience of the rapidly changing economic and political conditions in Cape Verde, and of how they affect people from different socio-economic strata, has been crucial for contextualising the interviews. Cape Verde is a small and tight-knit country with only 500,000 inhabitants. This is excellent for anthropological fieldwork as it provides an opportunity to get to know people from different strata of society.

My long-term acquaintance with people in Cape Verde meant that it was comparatively easy to locate returnees who were willing to talk to me. I asked a number of friends and acquaintances to help me locate returnees of different ages, genders, educational background, country of immigration and type of business. This means that my interlocutors represent a wide range, which, in turn, implies that, although this is an ethnographic study based on a small sample, I intend to paint a broader picture. The only difficulty with regard to variation lay in finding return migrants who were prepared to share stories of business activities that had totally failed, which is a common outcome. In Cape Verde, losing money on a failed business is often viewed as a shameful sign of bad judgement, and it is therefore understandable that people who have lost all their money try to avoid talking about it. In the end, however, I managed to locate and talk to a few of those who had been unsuccessful in their business activities.

All my interlocutors were living in Cape Verde at the time of the interviews, except two who were staying in Portugal and Sweden. This means that I have not included people who, because of their failed businesses, have re-migrated to the country of immigration. My research shows that it is common for migrants to come back to Cape Verde for a year or two, set up a business, lose money, and then return to Europe or the US and try to recover their losses. If these re-migrants had been included in the study, my picture of returnees' chances of setting up a viable business would probably have been even bleaker.

One factor that distinguishes the Cape Verdean returnees from return migrants in many other African countries is the relatively high proportion of females, which is reflected in my sample: out of the 44 interviewees, 20 were women. The background to this situation is the feminisation of Cape Verdean migration, which has taken place since the 1970s when young girls started to migrate to southern Europe as domestic workers. The instability of conjugal relations, the large proportion of female-headed households and the fact that a mother's first and fundamental duty is to provide her children with material necessities all explain the relatively high frequency of female migration (Åkesson 2004). During the last decades, both women and men have tended to migrate individually, rather than as families, and also to return individually. About two-thirds of those I interviewed returned individually: that is, they were neither accompanied by a partner who had lived in the country of immigration nor did they return to a partner living in Cape Verde.

The study focuses on people who have returned to the islands of São Vicente and Santo Antão. São Vicente is dominated by Cape Verde's second city, Mindelo. The island of Santo Antão functions as the rural agricultural hinterland of Mindelo. On both of these islands, people regret their increasing economic and political marginalisation in relation to the capital of Praia, where 45 per cent of Cape Verdean formal enterprises are located. São Vicente pays host to 19 per cent of enterprises, which means that this island has the second highest number of businesses, while Santo Antão, with 7 per cent, ranks fifth among the nine islands (Instituto Nacional de Estatística 2013). Over the years, I have visited nearly all the Cape Verdean islands, and my observations indicate that conditions for returnee businesses in São Vicente and Santo Antão are quite representative of those in the whole of the country, except for Praia. Below, I discuss the different categories of returnees, and especially the types of migrants who have started up a business.

### Returnees' involvement in business activities

Like many other migrants, Cape Verdeans living abroad often harbour the idea of returning one day. Whether they actually realise this dream depends on a mixture of family and economic reasons, but concerns about securing a reliable livelihood are often paramount. Many consider it too hazardous to return without being able to rely on a pension from an overseas employer. There are no statistics on return migrants and their sources of revenue, but my impression is that the majority have a retirement pension, which means that both their age and their relatively privileged economic situation make them less interested in setting up a business. If, however, they do, their ambition is usually to establish a kind of 'hobby' or pastime. Young, highly skilled persons constitute another category of returnee. Generally, their ambition is to secure public or private employment after completing university studies abroad. Young people with a university degree are less likely to become entrepreneurs, as ideals of upward mobility are still largely connected to public employment. A third category consists of returnees whose migration trajectory is described in Cape Verdean Creole as migration *mal sucedid* ('unsuccessful'). The 'unsuccessful' returnees may have been deported from the country of immigration, or they may have returned because of personal problems or illness. These returnees tend to become an economic burden on their family, rather than an asset for the local economy.

A relatively limited number return with the objective of setting up a business. In comparison to the retirement returnees, people in this category are younger and some of them (but far from all) are better educated. Some of these returnees see their business as an experiment – a test of whether it could be viable for them to stay permanently in Cape Verde. To be able to live in Cape Verde is often their main interest rather than the entrepreneurial activity in itself. The returnee quoted in the introduction who sees business in Cape Verde as the art of dying happy but poor is one of those who values life in Cape Verde higher than the material benefits that can be gained abroad, and is therefore willing to try his luck as a business owner. Returning migrants normally have little chance of finding employment in Cape Verde, and thus the creation of a small-scale firm is their only option. Many of these return migrants are caught between their desire to live in Cape Verde and the economic security they have experienced abroad. As a result, they try to keep doors open in both directions. Calú, who has opened a grocery shop but is making very little money, is one of them:

> My business here is only an experiment. Yes, an experiment. It's an activity. I'm not sitting idle at home. My intention is to spend the rest of my life here. It has always been my hope. Kap Verde is *sab* [tasteful, but also enjoyable], but in Luxembourg I had a total security. I had decided to close down my grocery store here, but now I will wait and see a few more months. You can't think of returning to Europe and earn more money all the time. But I don't want to run into debts because then I become sleepless.

However, in this category there are some returnees who are determined to become entrepreneurs in Cape Verde. The majority of these people move to the capital of Praia, where business conditions are better than elsewhere in Cape Verde. Yet sentiments of island belonging are still strong, which means that some of the determined returnee entrepreneurs also settle on islands such as São Vicente and Santo Antão. Although economic conditions on these islands are less favourable, even here a few actually manage to establish successful businesses. However, 'successful' in this context has quite modest connotations. Returnee business owners who are described as 'successful' have a viable business venture that generates a profit that guarantees the owner and their dependent family members a middle-class standard of living. In the rest of this chapter, I will use this local definition when discussing 'successful' businesses.

I have chosen to categorise my interviewees as small-scale business owners rather than entrepreneurs. In a classic essay on the anthropology of entrepreneurship, Fredrik Barth (1963) defines entrepreneurs as brokers in situations of contact between cultures – a definition that applies to returnees. However, I hesitate to collectively classify the people I have talked with as entrepreneurs, if we define entrepreneurs as being characterised by innovative behaviour (Dana 1995: 62) and a propensity to take advantage of opportunities with an orientation towards expansion (Stewart 1991: 74). Instead, some of my interlocutors run 'imitative businesses' (ibid.: 75) and copy what other returnees have done before them. This imitative pattern is particularly evident with regard to the multitude of small grocery stores set up by return migrants. An elderly male returnee described how this pattern goes back to Portuguese colonial rule and the high status conferred to the owners of grocery stores:

> Cape Verdeans are not so innovative, and that is a heritage from the Portuguese. Since I was a child those having some money have opened a grocery

store. To have money has been the same thing as opening a store. Today those who return with a little money continue to open a grocery store, despite the fact that there already are too many.

The connection that he and other Cape Verdeans make between the lack of innovative behaviour, or 'entrepreneurial spirit', and the Portuguese postcolonial heritage can be linked to the recent debate in Portugal that points to the low number of new businesses as one of the causes of the present economic crisis in that country. According to the 2005 report from the Global Entrepreneurship Monitor, Portugal has one of the lowest rates of entrepreneurial activity in the European Union (Acs et al. 2005). In both Portugal and Cape Verde, young people often hope to find a job as a public employee. To be a risk-taking, hard-working and profit-seeking entrepreneur is normally not part of their vision for the future.

Despite the lack of an entrepreneurial tradition in Cape Verde, returnees have increasingly started to realise that it is not feasible to open yet another grocery store. Most imitative businesses are either closed down shortly after they have opened, or have a very low turnover. My material shows that a major factor in entrepreneurial success in Cape Verde is coming up with something that is both new to the local market and attractive to customers with limited buying power. Between them, the 22 returnee entrepreneurs I interviewed run 32 businesses, which means that many of them run more than one business. Their businesses are of various kinds: restaurants, bars and guesthouses (nine businesses); agriculture and fisheries (five); small-scale shops (five); import businesses (four); and various services such as manicure parlours, car rental companies and internet cafés (nine). These enterprises represent a mixture of imitative and innovative tendencies. There are some typical imitative returnee businesses such as traditional restaurants and bars, grocery stores and boutiques, and on rural Santo Antão there are returnees who practise traditional agriculture. The more innovative enterprises are of two kinds. First, there are those returnees who introduce something new to the local market; in my material, this group is exemplified by, among others, a car rental company, a massage studio and a music school. Second, there are enterprises that do not market a new product or service, but offer an improved version of something that already exists on the local market. Among these are a restaurant offering a much more varied menu than other restaurants and a farmer introducing new agricultural techniques and new crops.

The more innovative business owners in my sample generally have a higher standard of education than those who have established an imitative business; this finding is in line with previous research (cf. Tiemoko 2003). The majority of Cape Verdean migrants, however, are low skilled, have monotonous and unqualified jobs and live in segregated neighbourhoods, conditions that are hardly conducive to accumulating social and cultural capital or becoming an innovative entrepreneur. Despite this, among the innovative returnees there are a few with little formal schooling and no experience of qualified jobs abroad. Rather, their entrepreneurial spirit seems to be rooted in personal attributes, for example a capacity to create social ties with all kinds of people, including important gatekeepers such as politicians and customs officials, and an immediate perception of local business opportunities.

Thus, the majority of the Cape Verdeans who return hardly correspond to the 'entrepreneurial returnee' envisioned in policy documents. Yet those who start a business fulfil policy expectations on one point: they create jobs. Most business owners in my study have between two and four employees, except those who run imitative businesses with a very low turnover. Returnees in this category tend to rely on one or two family members who offer a helping hand for a symbolic salary. The most innovative and successful of my interviewees have around ten employees. Running an enterprise in Cape Verde is normally synonymous with being an employer, and a primary reason for this is the fact that labour is cheap. The official minimum wage is only €100 per month, and those who are employed by the returnees I have met seldom receive more than that. This means that, although some returnees generate employment, the salaries they pay hardly guarantee a livelihood. The uncertain viability of the returnees' businesses also means that their employees run a high risk of losing their jobs. The volatility of business in Cape Verde, in turn, is inherently linked to the structural problems of the national economy, to which I now turn.

### A globalising island economy

All the returnees I interviewed talked about the weak local island economy as a fundamental obstacle for the development of their business ideas. Most of them described this problem as resulting from bad governance, and from a centralisation of economic investments in the capital of Praia. Some even argued that the national government followed a secret strategy that was aimed at redirecting all investments to Praia, while some of those supporting the government maintained that the economic problems were grounded in the liminal position of Cape Verdean interests in a globalised economy.

A very common complaint among business owners in Santo Antão and São Vicente relates to the reduced buying power of potential customers. '*Falta d'moviment*' (there is no movement) was an oft-repeated comment when people talked about their businesses, and often it was uttered in a resigned voice. A couple of my interlocutors pointed out that there are returnees with good business ideas, but nobody has any money to buy their products or services. When I visited returnees' businesses, there were often many people around but generally they turned out to be visitors rather than customers. One of my interviewees had opened a boutique for quality clothes, and she had a steady stream of visitors who kept themselves updated on every new article she put out for sale, but nobody bought anything.

The 'lack of movement' basically depends on two factors. The first is the widespread poverty and the low national income per capita, which in 2014 the World Bank estimated to be about €2,500 per year.[2] The second factor relates to geography. The Cape Verdean population of only half a million people is distributed on nine different islands, which means that the local market on each island is very small. This is a situation that entrepreneurs can hardly be expected to change. Alejandro is a highly skilled migrant who returned from Europe after having accumulated substantial economic and social capital, but despite this he has never been able to create what he calls 'a strong business'. He describes his economic situation as 'equilibrated' thanks to various small businesses, which he opens and closes at short intervals, in combination with small-scale agriculture and income from housing rents. He maintains that this is what you can normally expect to achieve in Cape Verde, especially if you choose to live outside the capital of Praia.

Besides the 'lack of movement', those who start up a business in Cape Verde also have to struggle with the lack of credit. Interest rates are high, periods of repayment are short, and demands on collateral securities are excessive. There are some credit programmes for new entrepreneurs, but none of my interlocutors had participated in them, basically because they were unaware of them. The few who had approached the credit programmes had found that the amounts of credit available were too small for their needs, generally only up to €1,500. This lack of credit in combination with low buying power and the fragmented market means both that migrants cannot return before they have accumulated substantial start-up capital abroad (which everyone says takes at least 20 years) and that they run a high risk of losing the money they invest.

The lack of credit is one of the disadvantages Cape Verdean investors have in relation to foreign investors, who in recent decades have come to dominate some important economic sectors in the country. Returnees starting up a business are increasingly competing in a globalised economic market. One example is the small-scale retail market. Since the late 1990s, Chinese migrants have established shops selling cheap consumer goods, such as clothes, shoes, kitchenware and consumer electronics. By providing cheap goods adapted to local tastes, the Chinese shops have managed to capture most of the local market (Haugen and Carling 2005) and have made it harder for returnees to set up successful import businesses. As regards large-scale investments, both the construction and tourism sectors are dominated by foreign investors. In construction there are mainly Portuguese companies, whereas British, Italian and French enterprises control much of the tourism sector.

---

2 See http://data.worldbank.org/country/cape-verde (accessed 30 January 2014).

For returnees' entrepreneurship, competition with foreign investors is strongest in the tourism sector, as many migrants return with the idea of opening a small hotel, a restaurant or a bar. The islands of Sal and Boa Vista are the main destinations for charter tourism, while there is no mass tourism on the islands on which this study focuses, São Vicente and Santo Antão. Yet tourism plays an increasingly important economic role on these islands as well, although the tourism is small-scale and described as 'cultural' in São Vicente and 'ecological' in Santo Antão. Cape Verdeans trying to establish themselves in the tourism sector often regret the fact that foreign investors are exempt from paying taxes for the first five years, while national investors do not benefit from this exemption. They also criticise foreign investors for being involved in money laundering and other illicit activities. These rumours are hard to corroborate, but it seems clear that some of the foreign business owners fail to register their tourist companies. One of my interlocutors who had a hard time establishing an ambitious tourist agency complained about the illegal status of her foreign competitors:

> All foreign tourist agencies here are illegal. The small agencies here in São Vicente organising excursions to Santo Antão are all illegal except one. And those who receive people disembarking from the cruise liners in São Vicente are also illegal.

Other people working in the tourism sector supported this statement, and said that small-scale foreign tourist agencies generally avoid registering their companies as they find it too expensive and cumbersome. Historically, the Cape Verdean government has been criticised for receiving all types of investment with open arms. There has been a dependency on different forms of transfers from abroad, such as migrant remittances and development aid, and the government's position has always been to welcome any kind of monetary inflow. Today, the same uncritical stance seems to continue in relation to growing foreign investment. This brings about increased, and sometimes distorted, competition for the returnee entrepreneurs. In the following section I raise another fundamental problem for the returnees, namely their lack of bridging ties to politicians and custom officials.

### Access to bridging ties

A prominent theme in many of the returnees' narratives was a feeling of being excluded from rights and opportunities that others have. 'Others' could be foreign investors, but also those who had stayed behind. In particular, returnees complained about being excluded from access to politicians and the power games played out in political parties. In addition, many of returnees spoke about their lack of beneficial access to a key authority: customs. The majority of the returnees do not come from influential families, which means that they cannot use bonding ties (Putnam 2000), or ties to family and friends, to access politicians and customs officials. Instead, they have to try to create new bridging ties to these actors. Bridging ties enable individuals to connect to individuals outside their immediate social sphere, and while returnees generally have to forge new bridging ties, those who have stayed behind have had a chance to continuously develop such ties to people in their social surroundings. On the small Cape Verdean islands, people tend to have quite diversified and heterogeneous social networks, but that is not true for recently arrived returnees.

*Politicians* In the 2012 global Democracy Index (Economic Intelligence Unit 2012), Cape Verde was ranked as the second most democratic African country, surpassed only by another small island state, Mauritius. The Democracy Index measures not only electoral processes and pluralism, but also categories such as the functioning of government and the level of democratic political culture. The relatively high ranking of Cape Verde in the Democracy Index seems to indicate that the political climate for business is good. My interviewees' narratives, however, point in another direction. One common statement is that the 'politicisation' of Cape Verde seriously hampers their efforts to establish a viable business. Leonilda, who is trying to establish herself as an entrepreneur in the tourism sector, is an outspoken critic of 'politicisation':

> Before one could find a job because of one's merits, but nowadays only contacts count. It is enough to have an uncle ... It is complicated, revolting, impossible. I refused to candidate for MpD [Movimento para a Democracia] in the local elections, and then I became a 'persona non grata'. They [the politicians] are destroying our land. It was better under the one-party rule. Nowadays you have to belong to a party, otherwise you're excluded.

Leonilda has a good education and many years of work experience in tourism in Europe, and she believed that it would be easy for her to find a job when she returned to Cape Verde. Yet at the time of our conversation she had been back for nearly two years without finding a job; she blamed this on the influence of MpD, one of the two dominant political parties, which governs the municipality where she lives. As a last resort, Leonilda had decided to start her own business, but she regarded this as highly risky. The same criticisms that Leonilda directs at MpD are directed by others at PAICV (Partido Africano da Independência de Cabo Verde), the other dominant party. PAICV has been in government since 2001 but currently rules only a minority of the 22 municipalities.[3] An individual's ability to get a bank loan on decent terms

---

3 The political regime in Cape Verde has gone through fundamental changes since the country gained independence in 1975. Immediately after independence, the liberation movement PAIGC (Partido Africano da Independência da Guiné e Cabo Verde,

or find cheap premises for a business is often described as depending on political contacts within the party currently governing the municipality and/or the country.

Leonilda's disillusionment when she says that it was better under the one-party system is reflected in other returnees' narratives, and there is a strong sense of disappointment with the results of 20 years of multi-party rule. The transition to a multi-party system in 1991 was widely supported in Cape Verdean diaspora communities in both Europe and the US, and many migrants who were politically excluded during PAICV's one-party rule hoped that they would gain more beneficial contacts with ruling politicians. Yet political clientelism, or *padrinhagem* ('godfatherhood'), did not disappear after the multi-party elections, but took on new forms that were often opaque to the migrants living far away from Cape Verde. Upon their return, highly skilled returnees believed that they would easily gain beneficial contacts in political circles, and when such contacts did not materialise they became bitterly disappointed. Some are disappointed because they have not been accepted as members of the ruling political elite, whereas others are more critical of the whole system of *padrinhagem*.

Many of these critiques maintain that there are strong similarities between PAICV and MpD, which go beyond the lack of clear ideological differences between the two parties. 'The system is the same' is a common phrase, and hints at politicians' practice of supporting those who show loyalty to their party. The payment of bribes is often referred to, but I have no evidence of money actually being paid to individual politicians.[4] Rather, the practice of political power reveals a general lack of impartiality, and thereby a lack of 'good governance' as defined by the political scientists Rothstein and Teorell (2008). I have, for instance, seen concrete cases where business people acquire the right to certain favours through financially supporting one of the parties, especially during election campaigns. For those who cannot afford to give money to a political party, an alternative is to prove one's commitment by providing outspoken support for a party, and thereby perhaps gaining the right to some favour. However, as in all kinds of clientelism, it is never

---

later renamed PAICV) established a one-party system and ruled Cape Verde until the first multi-party elections in 1991. The main opposition party, MpD, won these elections and stayed in power for ten years. Legislative elections in January 2001 returned power to PAICV, which has been governing the country since then. However, PAICV's dominance has been curtailed since the last elections in 2011, both because the country's president is a former MpD member and because the majority of the 22 municipalities are dominated by MpD.

4 It is hard to draw a line between the widespread discourse on politicised clientelism and its actual practice: first, because people who are favoured by politicians avoid talking about it; and second, because hinting at illicit political contacts is sometimes a way of vilifying those who are successful.

certain to what extent different kinds of economic or social investment will be reciprocated.

The influence of the system of political clientelism is aggravated by the fact that the competition between the two parties is tough and their practices of including and excluding people are pervasive. When there is a change of government, state bureaucrats even at intermediary levels lose their jobs and are substituted by others who are loyal to the new governing party. Thus, there is a politicisation of the state that constitutes an obstacle to progressive governance, especially because the country is small and human resources limited. Many returnees see this form of competitive politics as the very source of the injustice and corruption they believe is becoming more widespread in their country. Politicians are seen as the masters of the game, who can use the state to achieve what they want and to support those who are loyal.

The politicisation of the state is all the more important as little difference is made between the society and the state. The state is seen as both vertical and all-encompassing (Ferguson and Gupta 2005). It is above everyday life, but at the same time 'everywhere', and it is understood to influence and restrict people's ability to improve their lives. As the nation is often seen as being synonymous with the state and the state as synonymous with the political party in power, people's relationship with the nation is coloured by their relationship to the governing political party. This means, for instance, that migrants may be reluctant to return and invest in Cape Verde when the 'wrong' party rules the country. One of the returnees I interviewed exemplified this by saying that 'a migrant who supports MpD doesn't want to contribute to the country when PAICV is in power'. The smallness of the country, both in terms of population and geographical space, implies that the state is not only all-encompassing but also 'close' in a personalised sense. The state has an informal nature and people present their everyday concerns high up in the hierarchy. I have witnessed poor farmers asking the municipality president for a sack of cement and urban business people calling a secretary of state in order to get a container through customs. This means that, at all levels of the state bureaucracy, there are personalised circuits of distribution reciprocated by clients' loyalty.

What, then, does all this imply for returnees' businesses and for their ability to contribute to social and economic development? Here it is necessary to distinguish between those who run a small 'imitative business' (Stewart 1991: 75) and those who try to set up something larger and more innovative. In most cases the small-scale imitative businesses are not dependent upon political support. You can easily turn a former garage into a bar without the helping hand of a politician. For those who try to set up a more innovative and larger enterprise, however, support from politicians is important. I have seen political connections opening up access to better bank credit, lower rents for business premises, favourable business contracts, the free use of machinery and equipment belonging to the state and more clients. I have also witnessed the opposite: ambitious returnees who have seen their businesses dwindle because of the lack of a *padrinj* ('godfather') in the state hierarchy. This was the case for Soraya, who had started evening art classes for children and who tried to establish cooperation with local schools:

> We have no *padrinj*, which among other things implies that it is hard for us to establish contacts with schools. They always ask whether I've been in contact with the Ministry of Education, so I arranged a meeting with the Ministry's representative on this island. He gave me five minutes and then he put my ideas in his drawer. That happened because I lacked a *padrinj*.

Thus, the politicisation of the state and the state's pervasive influence on social and economic life hamper new and innovative ideas. Few returnees have beneficial relations with politicians high up in the hierarchy, which means that there is an invisible 'glass ceiling' for their businesses. Some of them may succeed in earning a living and employing a handful of people, but business development beyond that is seemingly dependent on being on good terms with highly placed politicians. Naturally, these 'offstage' politics are all informal in character.

*Customs officials* My interlocutors complained more about their (lack of) informal contacts with politicians than about the formal bureaucracy. For example, they described the registration of a business and payment of taxes as quite unproblematic. Yet when the returnees talked about their dealings with state authorities, there was one agency they dwelled on – customs. The customs service in Cape Verde plays a very visible and important role. The country's lack of natural resources and manufacturing industries means that nearly everything is imported. Moreover, a steady inflow of gifts from migrants to non-migrant family members passes through customs. Each island has its own customs office and most families can tell stories about complicated dealings with customs officials when they have tried to clear something through customs as rapidly and cheaply as possible. Many Cape Verdean business owners are dependent on the workings of the customs service, not least the returnee entrepreneurs who send for goods from abroad. Brenda Chalfin's depiction of customs in Ghana as 'territorially expansive in its reach, centralized in authority and penetrating the social fabric of the nation overall' (2010: 23) is also valid in the Cape Verdean case.

As in many other African countries (ibid.), the customs authority in Cape Verde has historically had considerable autonomy in relation to the government. With its roots in the colonial order and its central importance for national revenues, customs is a sector of the state that has developed an independent form of organisation and functioning that the political parties are unable to confront. This was corroborated in my interview with a government official working with Reforma do Estado – a comprehensive programme aimed at modernising the whole state apparatus. According to him, public control of customs is impossible because of the corporatism within the authority, which, moreover, leads to 'inefficiency and a rentier policy'.

Frustration about customs was more pronounced among those of my interlocutors who had recently returned and had no previous experience of dealing with the agency. Sonya is one of these recent returnees, and she said:

> I have paid so much money to customs. I tried to contact people at two different ministries to get things in cheaper, but as I have no *padrinj* it did not work. Customs bureaucracy is horrible; it delayed the start of my enterprise by a month.

Bribes in the form of direct payments to officials seem not to be very common, although rumours about such incidences abound. It is rather a lack of impartiality (Rothstein and Teorell 2008) that influences the speed of customs clearances and the fees to be paid. Regarding the speed, my interviewees agreed that a rapid clearance depends on contacts at the customs. One of them said: 'It is much easier if you know a clearance agent. Some returnees do not understand that it works this way.' The importance people attribute to a smooth process should be understood within the context in which goods are sometimes stuck in customs for months, or even years. One returnee described how he sent a container to Cape Verde in 2008 and was only able to get it out of customs three years later.

My interlocutors also maintained that custom officials sometimes let commodities pass through without demanding any fees. Some described this as an act of conscience aimed at supporting poor people. Carlos, who belongs to an evangelist church and supports justice for the poor, said: 'Sometimes they do not ask for a fee from people without means. I do not know if that is corruption or morally upright.' Besides this benevolent treatment of people with a limited ability to pay, which is definitely not extended to all poor people in a consistent manner, customs officials are sometimes also willing to lower the fees for people they know. This takes place in a quite arbitrary way. One returnee said that the fees he pays at customs are dependent on the 'conscience' of the officer. Others said that they always paid the full fees, whereas by contrast one person described in detail how he managed to import all kinds of goods for very low fees thanks to his various contacts in the customs office. This arbitrariness in itself causes resentment and jealousy among those who believe that 'others' are treated better than they are by customs officials. In particular, this is true for people who have recently returned and who feel insecure about the workings of 'the system'. It is common for returnees to express feelings of insecurity and distrustfulness, and the arbitrariness of procedures at the customs office feeds into returnees' fears of being cheated by a 'system' they do not fully comprehend.

## The questionable advantage of being a returnee

In conclusion, it is uncertain whether returnee business owners in general are more resourceful than those who have stayed behind. The greatest advantage of returnee entrepreneurs compared with business owners who have never migrated is that they have access to economic capital accumulated during their stay abroad. As mentioned earlier, research has clearly shown that the accumulation of savings abroad is fundamental to returnees' ability to support development through business activities (Åkesson forthcoming; Black and Castaldo 2009). When it comes to cultural capital, due to discrimination and segregation in the countries of immigration, most Cape Verdean migrants do not accumulate skills or knowledge that are useful for establishing a business. In addition, compared with those who have stayed, many returnees have less insight into the workings of local markets. Some return after decades abroad with quite a naïve and antiquated understanding of supply and demand. Thus, although some returnees may have acquired new insights abroad, they have much to learn when they return. This transition is naturally easier for those who have regularly visited the country during their years as a migrant, and thereby have been able to follow its economic and social development.

The economic constraints described above are the same for returnees and stayers. The smallness and isolation of the market and the uneven competition with resourceful non-national investors are felt equally by both groups. The returnees tend to be more critical than the stayers of what they see as the government's favouring of foreign investors. Many returnees believe that they should have the same rights as non-national investors, as they too have brought in capital from abroad.

When it comes to social capital, the returnees' lack of bridging ties is sometimes detrimental to their success. On a psychological level, returnees' exclusion from political networks and the distribution of favours causes much frustration. This is especially common among ambitious males who return with some money and feel that they should be in a position to gain acceptance among highly placed politicians. The country is small and many of the 'successful' male returnees believe that they have an automatic place in the political landscape. Yet many of them do not have the right contacts or the skills to manoeuvre in the cut-throat competition of the political game. Others are outspoken about what they see as bad governance and injustices, and are therefore not let in. Antonio is one of the returnees who have tried to influence politics:

If you are from the wrong party nobody listens to you, but neither do they listen if you are from the right party. They will never change. It is impossible to influence them.

Antonio's feeling of never being let in can be seen as an empirical reflection of Bourdieu's understanding of 'social capitalism', which he sees as an 'ideology of inclusion and exclusion' (Arneil 2006: 8). Social relationships can sometimes serve to exclude and deny as well as to include and enable, and the returnees understand their exclusion from influential positions as being determined by the amount and weight of their social capital, and especially by their bridging ties to politicians. Sometimes the limitation of the returnees' social networks is detrimental not only to their businesses but also to their state of well-being. Having returned to something they imagined to be a tight-knit home island society, they are instead confronted with unknown people behaving in new and unforeseen ways. New generations have grown up, the rules of the political game have changed, and power is played out in new ways. Some returnees are afraid of being cheated and at the same time ashamed of not knowing the rules of a game they had imagined would be easy to play. The feeling of alienation at home is disturbing to some returnees, and it turns some of them into distrustful individuals constantly complaining about the changes they believe have destroyed their old/new home.

### Openings: exploiting a small and competitive market

Yet despite this rather bleak picture, it is possible to identify some positive social and economic contributions made by returnees. Stayers in Cape Verde often mention that returnees' construction of houses has facilitated the introduction of new building techniques and materials and has created employment in the construction sector. Moreover, returnees' exclusion from the system of political clientelism has resulted in some of them taking an independent stance in relation to both of the dominant political parties, and contributing with critical opinions from a position outside the entrenched political 'system'. In addition, there are a few returnees who have been able to recognise commercial openings in the small market and have therefore succeeded with their businesses.

From a sociological point of view, it is hard to predict who is going to be a successful business owner. The successful returnee entrepreneurs who appear in my material have strikingly little in common in terms of socio-economic background and migration experience. This can be exemplified in the following four cases: the first concerns a returnee who is a former shift worker at the Heineken brewery in the Netherlands and who has returned to his rural origins and introduced new crops and sustainable agricultural methods. A second returnee worked as a night guard before he was deported by Portuguese immigration authorities. Upon his unwanted return, he managed to set up a thriving internet café, where he offers lower prices and a broader range of services than his competitors. A third person is a former waitress, who, after her return from Sweden, started a restaurant that offers a much more varied menu than other restaurants. A fourth returnee has a university degree in social work from the US and has started a music school for children. All of them have accumulated the skills needed for their new businesses through social networks both abroad and in Cape Verde (Åkesson forthcoming), but only the restaurant owner has a direct use for the skills and knowledge she gained in her working life as a migrant.

Beyond their different social and migratory backgrounds, however, these people have something in common that might be called 'entrepreneurial spirit'. They have an immediate perception of the local market, which makes them good at recognising and exploiting opportunities (Zahra et al. 2005). They know what people want to pay for, but also how to make potential customers interested in what they are offering. They are all devoted to developing their businesses, and not only for the sake of profits. All four of them take a strong interest in improving the particular product or services their business is offering. These are individual attributes that are hard to link in a simple way to their respective history as migrants. In none of these four cases did the work experience abroad seem to have been instrumental in the development of an entrepreneurial spirit. Thus, there is no clear-cut answer to why these four individuals have been able to foster an entrepreneurial spirit, while other returnees have not.

Finally, in relation to the broader question of whether migrants acquire any capital abroad that may be useful upon return, it is noteworthy that these four returnees had all been able to save some money abroad, which they subsequently invested in their businesses in Cape Verde. In addition, it is possible that these returnees' experiences of other ways of life abroad have inspired them to think in a less conformist and more creative manner, which implicitly may have been important to their efforts to introduce novelties in a small and competitive market. A more innovative way of acting distinguishes these four entrepreneurs from many of the business owners who have stayed behind, but it is also clear that their entrepreneurial approach is shared by only a minority of returnees. Accordingly, the Eurocentric policy celebration of returnees as 'new developers' has proven to be overly simplistic and naïve in this case – as in many other cases. The lack of attention to structural constraints in combination with a lingering colonial imaginary of migrants' sojourns in Europe as inherently useful has produced a policy discourse that poorly reflects the experiences of Africa's return migrants.

# Bibliography

Acs, Z., P. Arenius, M. Hay and M. Minniti (2005) *Global Entrepreneurship Monitor: 2004 executive report*. London: London Business School.

Åkesson, L. (2004) 'Making a life: meanings of migration in Cape Verde'. PhD thesis, University of Gothenburg.

— (forthcoming) 'Multi-sited accumulation of capital: Cape Verdean returnees and small-scale business'. *Global Networks*.

Al-Ali, N. and K. Koser (eds) (2002) *New Approaches to Migration? Transnational communities and the transformation of home*. London and New York NY: Routledge.

Ammassari, S. (2004) 'From nation-building to entrepreneurship: the impact of élite return migrants on Côte d'Ivoire and Ghana'. *Population, Space and Place* 10: 133–54.

Anwar, M. (1979) *The Myth of Return: Pakistanis in Britain*. London: Heinemann.

Arneil, B. (2006) *Diverse Communities: The problem with social capital*. Cambridge: Cambridge University Press.

Barth, F. (1963) 'Introduction'. In F. Barth (ed.) *The Role of the Entrepreneur in Social Change in Northern Norway*. Oslo: Norwegian Universities Press, pp. 5–18.

Black, R. and A. Castaldo (2009) 'Return migration and entrepreneurship in Ghana and Côte d'Ivoire: the role of capital transfers'. *Tijdschrift voor Economische en Sociale Geografie* 100(1): 44–58.

Bourdieu, P. (1986) 'The forms of capital'. In J. Richardson (ed.) *Handbook of Theory and Research for the Sociology of Education*. Westport CT: Greenwood Press, pp. 15–29.

Brettell, C. (1979) '*Emigrar para voltar*: a Portuguese ideology of return migration'. *Papers in Anthropology* 20(1): 1–20.

Chalfin, B. (2010) *Neoliberal Frontiers: An ethnography of sovereignty in West Africa*. Chicago IL: University of Chicago Press.

Dana, L. P. (1995) 'Entrepreneurship in a remote sub-Arctic community'.

*Entrepreneurship, Theory and Practice* 20: 57–72.

de Haas, H. (2010) 'Migration and development: a theoretical perspective'. *International Migration Review* 44(1): 227–64.

Economic Intelligence Unit (2012) *Democracy Index 2012: Democracy at standstill*. London: Economic Intelligence Unit. Available at https://portoncv.gov.cv/dhub/porton.por_global.open_file?p_doc_id=1034.

Ferguson, J. and A. Gupta (2005) 'Spatializing states: toward an ethnography of neoliberal governmentality'. In J. X. Inda (ed.) *Anthropologies of Modernity: Foucault, governmentality and life politics*. Malden and Oxford: Blackwell Publishing.

Field, J. (2008) *Social Capital*. London and New York NY: Routledge.

Granovetter, M. (1973) 'The strength of weak ties'. *American Journal of Sociology* 78(6): 1360–80.

Gregory, C. (2009) 'Whatever happened to economic anthropology?' *Australian Journal of Anthropology* 20: 285–300.

Haugen Østbø, H. and J. Carling (2005) 'On the edge of the Chinese diaspora: the surge of *baihuo* business in an African city'. *Ethnic and Racial Studies* 28: 639–62.

Hirsch, M. and N. K. Miller (eds) (2011) *Rites of Return: Diaspora poetics and the politics of memory*. New York NY: Colombia University Press.

Instituto Nacional de Estatística (2013) *Inquérito Anual às Empresas: Folha de informação rápida*. Praia: Instituto Nacional de Estatística. Available at www.ine.cv/actualise/publicacao/files/6561336121262013IAE%202011.pdf.

Kilic, T., C. Carletto, B. David and A. Zezza (2009) 'Investing back home: return migration and business ownership in Albania'. *Economics of Transition* 17: 587–623.

Levitt, P. (2001) *The Transnational Villagers*. Berkeley and Los Angeles CA: University of California Press.

Lianos, T. and A. Pseiridis (2009) 'On

the occupational choices of return migrants'. *Entrepreneurship and Regional Development* 21(2): 155–81.

Long, E. and L. Oxfeld (2004) *Coming Home: Refugees, migrants and those who stayed behind*. Philadelphia PA: University of Pennsylvania Press.

Meintel, D. (1984) 'Emigração em Cabo Verde: solução ou problema?' *Revista Internacional de Estudos Africanos* 2: 93–120.

Ministério das Comunidades (2014) *Estratégia Nacional de Emigração e Desenvolvimento*. Praia: Ministério das Comunidades.

Putnam, R. (2000) *Bowling Alone: The collapse and revival of American community*. New York NY: Simon & Schuster.

Rothstein, B. and J. Teorell (2008) 'What is quality of government? A theory of impartial government institutions'. *Governance* 21(2): 165–90.

Salih, R. (2000) 'Moroccan migrant women: transnationalism, plurinationalism and gender'. In R. Grillo, B. Riccio and R. Salih (eds) *Here or There? Contrasting experiences of transnationalism. Moroccan and Senegalese in Italy*. Falmer: Centre for the Comparative Study of Culture, Development and the Environment, University of Sussex.

Stefansson, A. (2004) 'Homecomings to the future: from diasporic mythographies to social projects of return'. In F. Markowitz and A. Stefansson (eds) *Homecomings: Unsettling paths of return*. London: Lexington Books.

Stewart, A. (1991) 'A prospectus on the anthropology of entrepreneurship'. *Entrepreneurship, Theory and Practice* 16: 71–91.

Tiemoko, R. (2003) 'Unveiling local opportunities and challenges in return migration and development nexus: the case of Côte d'Ivoire and Ghana'. Working paper. Falmer: Sussex Centre for Migration Research, University of Sussex.

Whitehouse, B. (2011) 'Enterprising strangers: social capital and social liability among African migrant traders'. *International Journal of Social Inquiry* 4(1): 93–111.

Zahra, A. Z., J. S. Korri and J. F. Yu (2005) 'Cognition and international entrepreneurship: implications for research on international opportunity recognition and exploitation'. *International Business Review* 14: 129–46.

# About the contributors

*Lisa Åkesson* is Associate Professor in Social Anthropology at the School of Global Studies, the University of Gothenburg, and Senior Researcher at the Nordic Africa Institute. She has primarily carried out research in Cape Verde and the Cape Verdean diaspora, focusing on transnational families, remittances and relationships, migration and development and cultural meanings of migration. Her recent research focuses on the new Portuguese labour migration to the former colony of Angola. She has published in various journals, including *Ethnos*, *Journal of Ethnic and Migration Studies*, *Global Networks*, *International Migration* and *Africa Spectrum*. In addition, she has co-edited two books (in Swedish) on transnational migration.

*Maria Eriksson Baaz* is Associate Professor at the School of Global Studies, the University of Gothenburg and Senior Researcher at the Nordic Africa Institute. Recently, her research has focused on the Congo (DRC), involving research projects on civil–military relations and conflict-related gender-based violence, but also on circular and return migration. She is the co-author (with Maria Stern) of *Sexual Violence as a Weapon of War? Perceptions, Prescriptions, Problems in the Congo and Beyond* (Zed Books, 2013) and the author of *The Paternalism of Partnership: A Postcolonial Reading of Identity in Development Aid* (Zed Books, 2005). Additionally, her articles have appeared in several journals, including *International Studies Quarterly*, *Third World Quarterly*, *African Affairs*, *Journal of International Relations and Development*, *Journal of Modern African Studies* and *African Security*.

*Katarzyna Grabska* is an anthropologist and currently a Research Fellow at the Department of Anthropology and Sociology of Development and the Global Migration Centre at the Graduate Institute of International and Development Studies in Geneva. She has been carrying out research among South Sudanese refugees and returnees, and more recently among Ethiopian and Eritrean adolescent girl migrants, focusing on experiences and transformations related to conflict, forced displacement, gender and generational relations. She has published widely on these issues as well as produced documentary films. She is the author of *Gender, Home and Identity: Nuer repatriation to Southern Sudan* (James Currey, 2014) and a co-editor (with Lyla Mehta) of *Forced Displacement: Why rights matter?* (Palgrave, 2008).

*Laura Hammond* is Reader and Head of the Development Studies Department at SOAS, University of London. An anthropologist by training and a former humanitarian aid worker, her research focuses on migration, displacement and return as well as diaspora/homeland dynamics. She has been working in and on the Horn of Africa region since the early 1990s, including the Somali territories and Ethiopia. Hammond is the author of *This Place Will Become Home: Refugee repatriation to Ethiopia* (Cornell University Press, 2004) and editor with Christopher Cramer and Johan Pottier of *Researching Violence in Africa: Methodological and ethical challenges* (Brill, 2011). Over the past several years she has been working on the social, economic and political interactions between the Somali diaspora and their areas of origin, and has written several journal articles, book chapters and reports on this subject.

*Nauja Kleist* is Senior Researcher in the Global Transformations Unit at the Danish Institute for International Studies. Her research focuses on various kinds of return migration, diaspora mobilisation, migration and development, gender relations and identity. She has especially worked on Ghanaian migration and Somali diaspora groups. Kleist is currently coordinating a research programme on the social effects of migration management for West African migrants. She has published in several journals, including *African Affairs*, *Journal of Ethnic and Migration Studies*, *Diaspora* and *African Studies*, has contributed chapters to edited volumes and is co-editing a book on hope and uncertainty in African migration (Routledge).

*Tove Heggli Sagmo* is a Doctoral Researcher at the Peace Research Institute Oslo (PRIO). Her doctoral thesis explores return migration to Burundi. This study is part of an international research project called 'Possibilities and Realities of Return Migration', which is premised on the idea that the *possibility* of return – not just actual return – is an important phenomenon. She has previously worked for the United Nations High Commissioner for Refugees (UNHCR) and the Norwegian Ministry of Foreign Affairs.

*Giulia Sinatti* is a Lecturer in the Department of Anthropology, Vrije Universiteit Amsterdam, and Research Fellow at the International Institute of Social Studies, Erasmus University, the Netherlands. Her research is concerned with ethnicity and nationalism; transnational mobility and return migration; diaspora mobilisation; and development effects of migration in critical areas, including urban transformation, gender and family relations. She has many years of ethnographic research experience among Senegalese migrants. Her most recent research focuses on the governance of migration between Africa and Europe from a (human) security perspective. Her work has appeared in various academic journals, including *Ethnicities*, *Ethnic and Racial Studies*, *Population Space and Place* and *Studies in Ethnicity and Nationalism* and she has contributed chapters to several edited volumes.

# INDEX

civil society: organisations of, 52–7; returnees' involvement in, 55
civil war, 18, 47, 69, 111, 130–1; transformative effects of, 114–15
clan system, 60–1
class, questions of, 28, 38–40, 122–3
colonial legacy, 114–5
commerce, imported goods, 93
communal violence *see* violence, ethnic
Comprehensive Peace Agreement (CPA) (Sudan), 132, 134
conceptual and analytical framework of book, 9–15
conflict, risk of, 114 *see also* violence
Congolese people: as diaspora, 32; as investors, 96; negative portrayals of, 30, 35
Conseil National pour le Défense de la Démocratie (CNDD) (Burundi), 115
conservative behaviour, increase of, 52
conspiracy theories, 119
corruption, 4, 34–6, 115, 118, 165–6; management of, 41
cosmopolitanism, 62
Côte d'Ivoire, 94, 97, 154
country of origin: portrayed as underdeveloped, 15, 89; structural context of, 101
credit, lack of, 105, 161
credit schemes, 90–1; suspicion towards, 99
criminal actors, ties to government, 120
cross-fertilisation, 82
cultural norms, transformation of, 51
cultural pollution, 130, 144
customers, attracting of, 122–3
customs officials, 36, 166–8; ties to, 19, 37, 153, 155, 160, 162

Davies, B., 68
*dayuusboro*, 51
De Hass, H., 7
deficit, relational, 39
democracy, 55, 69
Democracy Index, 163
Democratic Republic of Congo (DRC), 2, 23–43; violence in, 15
deportees, 69, 126, 157, 169
developing countries, unfinished nature of, 73
development: definitions of, 112; goals

of, economic, 103; international organisations in, 54; migrants' contribution to, 11–12, 17, 23–43, 77–8; potential, 79; structural, 137
development and return *see* return and development
developmental impact, of self-employment, 93
*dhaqan ceelis*, 51, 61
diasporas: Congolese, 32; contributions of, to development, 11; developmentalist discourse regarding, 92; economic engagement of, 115; highly skilled, 91; impact of (on development, 44; on NGOs and SSPs 45); interactions with stayees *see* returnees, interactions with stayees; involved in politics, 44, 61; organisations supported by, 53; 'part-time' *see* migration, circular; policy interest in, 58–9, 64, 87–8, 90, 104; politicisation of, 23; problematic nature of, 60–2; return of, 51; Somali, 48; volunteers, 55
diaspora involvement, objections to, 44
diasporic imagination, 153
difference, statements of, 140
discrimination: exploitative wages as, 152; housing segregation as, 7; in country of immigration, 7, 19, 23, 30, 74, 154, 168; in country of origin, 147–8, 156–7; in the labour market, 7
displacement, 138–4; and return, 140; forced, 18; social change, 137–8; 147–9
Dual Citizenship Act (2002) (Ghana), 69–70

economic advancement, expectations of, 90–2
economy: crisis of, 26–7, 120; globalisation of, 160–2; informal sector in, 95; internationalisation of, 119; post-war, 111; social capital in, 118–23
Edna Adan University Hospital (Somaliland), 52–3
education, 2, 30, 75, 145–6; benefits of, 145; English-language, 54; importance of, 146
elite returnees, 66–7, 74, 82; Ghanaian, 8; in business, 105
elites, 50–1; emigration of, 68
emigration, of accumulation, 91
employees: identification of, 121–2;

**176**